LA FAMILIA

La Familia

Chicano Families in the Urban Southwest,
1848 to the Present

RICHARD GRISWOLD DEL CASTILLO

University of Notre Dame Press
Notre Dame, Indiana 46556

Library of Congress Cataloging in Publication Data

Griswold del Castillo, Richard.
    La familia: Chicano families in the urban Southwest, 1848
to the present.

    Bibliography: p.
    Includes index.
    1. Mexican American families—Southwest, New—History.
2. Southwest, New—Social conditions. I. Title.
II. Title: Chicano families in the urban Southwest, 1848 to the
present.
F790.M5G75   1984   306.8'50896872073   84-40356
ISBN 0-268-01272-5
ISBN 0-268-01273-3 (pbk.)

Manufactured in the United States of America

To Maryann

wife, mother, and friend

Contents

Tables

Preface

IN RECENT YEARS there has been a growing interest in the study of the contemporary Chicano family. Yet in all the research that has been done so far we still do not know whether the present-day manifestations of family behavior are entirely new or whether they are part of a longer historical process. The purpose of this book is to investigate the social and economic history of families of Mexican heritage in the urban Southwest since 1848, the year that marked the end of the war against Mexico and the American incorporation of almost half of that nation's territories. My intention is to link the past with the present.

The thesis I propose is that in the past 150 years there has been a conflict between the beliefs and values held by Mexican Americans regarding the proper and desirable way to live within families and the economic pressures of the American capitalist system. The Mexican-American culture, itself a dynamic hybrid, and United States economic development in all its ramifications have been historically opposed. This is because in the middle of the nineteenth century the Mexicano culture and economy of the borderlands region, today the American Southwest, were divorced by war and conquest. During a long period of colonization the Americans sought to subordinate those aspects of Mexicano culture that were incompatible with their economic and political order.

Because the beginnings of this schism between culture and the economy developed in the previous century, the primary research emphasis of this book is the nineteenth-century urban experience of families in four towns: Los Angeles, Tucson, Santa Fe, and San Antonio. There were, of course, other cities and towns in the American Southwest during the last part of the nineteenth century. I thought it appropriate to select those urban areas which were the most significant regional centers. Albuquerque and El Paso also became inportant regional centers in the twentieth century. The decision to study the cities and not the rural areas or small towns was one dictated by economy of purpose and by a realization of our need to understand varieties of family experience that have the most relevance to our present time.

This book is far from a definitive treatment of the subject, even as limited as I have defined it. Nevertheless, I anticipate that its shortcomings will be remedied by others who choose to enter this field. My hope is that as a result of this book, and others like it which are bound to surface, social scientists and historians will reconsider the historical dimensions of the Mexican-American familial experience in their writings. Certainly the time is long overdue for the Chicano family to be included in debates and discussions about the American family.

Those who write about the history of the Mexican heritage populations in the United States always have to wrestle with problems of terminology, what to call the groups they are describing and analyzing. When discussing the historical family I have consistently used the term "Mexican American" to describe a heterogeneous population that included both Mexican immigrants and long-term residents in the United States. When discussing the contemporary family, I use the term "Chicano," because this seems to bring the subject closer to our present-day reality. A full discussion of the problem of terminology may be found in the appendices.

There are many individuals and institutions who made the completion of this book possible. The National Endowment for the Humanities gave me a generous summer research stipend in 1981 that enabled me to begin serious research on this topic. In 1982 San Diego State University gave me a sabbatical leave which freed me from my teaching responsibilities and gave me time to rethink and write key portions of the manuscript. The university also contributed a number of small grants and a great deal of computer time and paper to help me gather the quantitative portions of the study and do the typing. Susan Archer and Rick Crawford of the University Computer Center were more than generous with their time, helping me to disentangle seemingly endless problems in computer applications. During the summer of 1982 the Huntington Library gave me a stipend to enable me to use their outstanding library for research and writing. I am especially in debt to Martin Ridge, senior research associate at the library for his encouragement, advice, and most of all for his careful reading of the manuscript. Like all researchers I owe a great debt to many research librarians in the various archives I have consulted: the Huntington Library; the Arizona Historical Society; the State Archives and the Museum of New Mexico in Santa Fe; and the Benson and Barker libraries in Austin, Texas, Helpful suggestions for the revision of the manuscript in various stages of its preparation were made by Ramón Gutiérrez, professor of history at the University of California, San Diego; William Vega, chair of the Mexican American Studies Department at San Diego State University; Carlos E. Cortés, chair of the Department of History, University of California, Riverside; Mark Poster, professor of history at the University of California, Irvine; Howard Shorr, instructor of social science at Roosevelt High School, Los Angeles; and by students in my Chicano social history classes at San Diego State University, the University of California, Irvine;

and California State University, Los Angeles. Carol Pederson helped eliminate many errors in my typing of the manuscript through her careful proofreading. Of course I take full credit for the errors that remain. Finally, I want to thank John Ehmann, associate director of the University of Notre Dame Press, for his encouragement and advice.

.

CHAPTER 1

Myth, History, and Theory

> *The explanation for changes in family structure must await the fuller comprehension of family history. One must know what it is that is changing before one explains the change.*
> –Mark Poster, *A Critical Theory of the Family*, p. 164.

MYTHS HAVE AN IMPORTANT relationship to our understanding of everyday reality. Widely shared myths such as those of Santa Claus, George Washington and the cherry tree, and the free-market economy serve to promote hope, exemplary behavior, and social unity. Many historical myths exist to promote patriotism. Thus American history is a required subject in the schools, and not too surprisingly the schoolbook version of the American past is saturated with nationalistic mythology. By the time they graduate from high school young Americans learn that the Puritans were harsh and repressive individuals, that the American Revolution was fought to gain freedom from Britain, that Lincoln freed the slaves, that the stockmarket crash of 1929 caused the Great Depression, and that the New Deal ended this disaster. All of these "truths," however, turn out to be false myths, distortions of the actual events or gross oversimplifications of the historical record.[1]

Having their origin in the distant past and passed on in the popular culture, myths may or may not be true. It is somewhat easier to check the myths that deal with events of the recent American past than to verify those that have their origin in prehistoric periods. False historical beliefs in American history that deal with relatively recent events have often been molded by the political and cultural milieu of the age in which they arose. For example, in the 1860s and 70s the reformers who fought to control runaway monopolies developed a mythology about the Robber Barons. Supposedly, as a group, American business leaders were corrupt, greedy, scheming individuals who robbed working-class poor as the feudal lords had exploited the peasants during the Middle Ages. The future historical study of

1

nineteenth-century businessmen and corporate practices has been influenced by this myth of the Robber Barons.[2] Other historical myths have influenced international relations and national policy. The still controversial myth of a monolithic Communist conspiracy to take over the world was born in the Cold War years immediately after World War II when Marshall Stalin faced President Truman over the explosive issues of Poland and the atomic bomb. To this day our nation's debate over foreign policy has been framed in terms of a mythic conception of the Soviet Union's intentions.

It is said that myths endure because they express essential truths. In the case of American history, however, it may well be that myths condition how we perceive the world and as a result how we interpret "truth" itself. One of the more useful purposes to which a historian can devote his or her energies is the correction of false historical beliefs and the elimination of simplified stereotypes. This book has as its object both these purposes in regard to its subject: an analysis of the historical experience of Mexican American families in the American Southwest.

Mexicans in the United States have labored under a number of stereotypes and prejudices. Recently Chicano historians have researched and written histories to challenge some of these misconceptions.[3] In the area of the family life of Mexican Americans there are still a number of popular myths that need to be examined historically, and there are those doing sociological research who are trying to correct these distortions and stereotypes. A later chapter discusses in some detail this recent research literature as well as the misunderstandings of Mexican American family life that continue to plague even academic studies. I am concerned here with a popular, not an academic, mythology, one that is shared by a large number of people, including many Mexican Americans themselves.

In the popular imagination Mexican Americans, including the most recent immigrants from Mexico, are assumed to be and always to have been family oriented. Mexicans are seen as being emotionally bound to a large extended family and as having lots of children. Within the family Mexican Americans are supposed to be unusually warm, caring, and protective. Another belief is that Mexican Americans have a great respect for the elder family members and a great respect for parental discipline and familial authority. At the same time these positive stereotypes are often also interpreted by some as being detrimental to the economic achievement of Mexican Americans. The tightly knit family is frequently blamed for the lack of educational and occupational advancement of Mexican Americans. The protective and nurturing family is also sometimes blamed for promoting a low degree of assimilation into American society. The respect for male authority in the home is sometimes viewed as evidence of *machismo*, almost always interpreted as a selfish male subordination of women and a sexual irresponsibility. Mexican-

American women are seen as virtual slaves of the family, lacking the will or initiative to stand up for their rights. Mexican-American women are supposed to be quiet homebodies, self-sacrificing, and virtuous. In the popular mind the Mexican family in the United States is a constellation of paradoxes: it is warm, supportive, and well ordered while also being authoritarian, dysfunctional, and essentially un-American.

THE HISTORICAL STUDY OF THE MEXICAN-AMERICAN FAMILY

The popular mythology surrounding the Mexican-American family conditions how the administrators and policy makers in American society perceive the social life and condition of those of Mexican heritage in the United States. Although social scientists have produced scores of monographs and essays on the contemporary Mexican-American family, there has been very little research on its historical antecedents.

Perhaps the only work thus far that treats the historical dimensions of Mexican-American family life is Alfredo Mirandé and Evangelina Enríquez, *La Chicana: The Mexican American Woman.*[3] They argue that the contemporary Chicano family has been heavily influenced by pre-Columbian, non-Western traditions. In their view Chicano families have played a historic role in resisting assimilation and oppression. Present-day Chicano families, while having a wide diversity of values and characteristics, share certain common ideals which derive from their heritage. Mirandé and Enríquez believe that these ideals have remained relatively unchanged over time, even given the dramatic transformations that have occurred in the social and economic environment. The most prominent features of this system of ideals are the belief that there should be a strict separation of male and female roles, a respect for elders, a positive value given to male superiority (*machismo*), a priority on maternal devotion to the home and children, and the importance of the family as an emotional and physical support system.

To what degree have these ideals been held by Mexican Americans through history? What has been the relation of these beliefs to everyday reality? What has been the role of culture and the economy in creating diversity in family life? Does history offer any clues as to the origin of values and beliefs and the ways in which they were realized within the family? These are questions that can be debated but not without empirical evidence concerning family life from the past. Contemporary sociological studies seem to point to the fact that the Chicano family has undergone a good deal of change in recent decades. Diversity and not uniformity of practices and values seems to be the most salient characteristic mentioned in the contemporary literature. For the social historian the question becomes how has the Chicano family changed, in what directions, and for what reasons?

This book is an introduction to these complex questions. The approach I have taken is to examine the families of Mexican heritage beginning in the nineteenth century and specifically those living in four towns: Los Angeles, Tucson, Santa Fe, and San Antonio. Currently more than 90 percent of all Spanish speaking of Mexican descent live in urban areas. By studying the urban history of nineteenth-century families we can begin to trace patterns of continuity and give a historical dimension to debates over the dynamics of Mexican-American family life.

The late nineteenth century was a period of rapid industrial change, and for this reason the study of this period is important for our understanding of modern social processes. It was in the period 1848-1910 that Mexican Americans first felt the effects of industrialization and urbanization. In that era they also had to begin to deal with problems associated with being an ethnic group. Issues of immigration, assimilation, and identity first surfaced in these decades.

Noticeably absent from all the published American family histories is a comparative study of Hispanics. Most histories of the American family stop short of the Mississippi River and assume that samples of family life drawn from colonial New England, metropolitan regions of the Midwest and the Northeast, and the rural South are representative of patterns in America as a whole. While there have been numerous historical studies of black families, there have been only a few serious investigations of the history of Spanish-Mexican families in the American Southwest.[4] This region, with the American West for that matter, is largely unexplored territory as far as historians of the family are concerned.

The Spanish-Mexican borderlands region and the American Southwest offer unique opportunities for us to test, in a comparative way, generalizations that have been arrived at through an analysis of non-Hispanic groups in American society. Since the nineteenth century this region has been a social laboratory which has brought together peoples of radically different cultures: the Mexican, the Anglo-American, a great variety of European and Asian immigrants, native Indians, and blacks. By the turn of the century the peoples of the Southwest were mostly living in villages, towns, and cities located near strategic water sources. The history of families in this region has especially been influenced by the economic growth of the twentieth century. Railroads and later superhighways linked its regional economy—mining, ranching, and agriculture—to a rapidly developing national financial and industrial system. In the process patterns of American economic development displaced or submerged native populations and constructed a sprawling economic network that depended on cheap European, Mexican, and Oriental labor for its prosperity.

THEORETICAL APPROACHES TO FAMILY HISTORY

The historical study of Mexican-heritage families in the Southwest is a new field that has yet to be defined with precision. As history is not an exact science, we should not expect that a theory of family history will be able to explain everything. Most often historical understanding is characterized by a humanistic perspective that is argued with logic and clarity. A theoretical approach to family history serves as a guide to give form and direction to our historical research. A satisfactory theory of family history should have several attributes. First, it should be general enough to enable us to organize a rich diversity of historical expression, ranging from census enumerations to poetry. Second, any theory of family history should be economical in its statement, being clear and concise, easily understandable by the layperson. Third, it should be capable of "explaining" the dynamic relationships among larger social, cultural, economic, and political forces. In this sense it should be provocative through leading toward critical thinking and toward further elaboration and research.

There are, of course, many possibilities for articulating a theoretical approach to family history and Chicano family history in particular. The 1970s witnessed a rapid growth in sociological theory dealing with the family, and there are increasing efforts to incorporate this body of material into historical analysis.[5] At least three sociological-based theories may be relevant for a beginning conceptualization of the field: modernization theory, Barbara Laslett's reproduction and production paradigm, and Mark Poster's critical theory of the family.

Modernization theories have been developed by social scientists to explain social and economic changes in large geopolitical areas. Generally they hypothesize two historical eras: (1) a traditional or premodern stage, which is characterized by a subsistence rural economy, the lack of developed economic infrastructures, widespread poverty, and nondemocratic forms of government; and (2) a modern stage, characterized by a developing urban industrial base, the emergence of a sizable middle class, generally a higher standard of living, and increased egalitarianism at all levels of society. Modernization theorists attempt to analyze the social, political, and economic dynamics involved in the transition between these stages.[6]

Many criticisms have been leveled at the proponents of modernization. Some scholars believe that the modernization approach is yet another attempt by Western and American imperialists to justify the hegemony of the capitalist economic and social system. Modernizationists, they charge, overgeneralize and stereotype "traditional" nonindustrial societies, tending to discount the value of the latter. Modernization theory lacks precision, especially when dealing with societies at the micro level. Modernization concepts fail to explain satisfactorily why fundamental changes have taken place, often relying more on descriptive statements of low explanatory value. The social historian Tamara Hareven has charged that modernization approaches advance overly simplistic views of the complex processes involved in social and economic change. The theorists, she notes, often do not distinguish between men's and women's roles during the process of modernization. Nor do they recognize that so-called traditional patterns often coexist alongside modern ones.[7]

Maxine Baca Zinn has pointed out that for Mexican-American families modernization does not result in "a simple substitution of modern patterns for traditional ones."[8] She found that while employed wives in Chicano families demonstrated more egalitarian behavior in conjugal decision-making, they still retained many family values labeled as "traditional." Zinn argues that more research must be done on the variation of Chicano family life and that historians as well as sociologists should abandon the simplistic modern-traditional dichotomy.

A critical view of the ethnocentric stereotypes often found in the modernization approach is necessary if we are to use it to explain change in the Chicano family. Modern forms of family life are not inherently better than traditional ones, as is usually implied by proponents of modernization. Changes associated with industrialization and urbanization have not always been uniformly progressive or positive vis-à-vis the family. The complexity and variability of the "traditional" rural Mexican and Chicano family should be recognized. So-called "static" rural societies are always the result of a dynamic and long-term historical process. Enough criticism of the social science stereotypes of the "changeless" traditional Mexican family has been leveled to make us suspect idealized and overly romantic notions of family life prior to the American conquest.[9]

For all its limitations, modernization may still prove to be useful for the study of the Mexican-American family. Few would deny that industrialization and urbanization have had an impact on the structure, function, and composition of the Chicano family. A systematic study of the modernization pressures experienced by the Mexican rural and urban family during the nineteenth century could reveal patterns and processes clarifying later changes undergone by Mexican-immigrant families in the twentieth century.[10] The problems of assimilation and acculturation, both culturally and economically, may most usefully be studied in light of the modernization approach. Further research on the impact of industrial Western societies on non-Western rural peoples may, in the future, produce more sophisticated concepts and theories which will have a greater explanatory value for our understanding of Mexican-American family history.

A central issue Chicano historians must confront is the relation of economic development to family change. Modernization theory for reasons already mentioned is not easily adapted to a study of the social history of the family. Most recently Barbara Laslett has proposed a theory of family history in relation to the economy, which may prove to be useful to social historians.[11]

Basically Laslett's approach is to analyze how the historical needs of the capitalist economic system have been in conflict with the needs of families. Since reproduction and production are vital for the continuation of society, a dialectical conflict often exists. This conflict is at the heart of what should be studied by family historians. Capitalists seek cheap factors of production and profits, while heads of families seek higher wages, surplus time, and earnings to enable them to raise children and provide sustenance for nonemployed household members. The theory revolves around an analysis of "those actions which families take in order to secure material resources necessary for reproduction of their members."[12] Using this approach, she suggests that historians concentrate on the ways in which families have responded to uncertainty created by the economic system. A vital part of any historical analysis of family history should be how class conflict affects family change and how social and political institutions affect the well-being of the family.[13]

A problem with Laslett's theory, at least as it is stated in its preliminary form, is that it cannot account for different responses to the same economic exigencies. Nevertheless, Laslett's theory offers a dynamic view for explaining very important social processes within the family. Collective family actions, such as the formation of *mutualistas*, family-based businesses, and the organization of trade unions and political movements along family lines, have been important phenomena in Chicano history. When fully developed and applied to a specific historical setting, Laslett's theory will be an important one, complementing and adding a new dimension to Mario Barrera's synthesis of internal-colonialism and class-segmentation theory.[14] Barrera has developed a systematic analysis of the socioeconomic processes affecting Mexican Americans since 1848, but his theoretical approach deemphasizes the social and economic realities of family life.

A weakness of Marxian-based theories in general is their tendency to discount the importance of psychological or emotional aspects of family life. In perhaps the most sophisticated and challenging theory of family history developed thus far, Mark Poster has constructed a theoretical system which treats both the economic and psychological issues of family history.[15] Poster's theoretical formulations emerge out of a critical reading of Freudian psychology, Marxian interpretations of Freud developed by Wilhelm Reich, Max Horkheimer, and the Frankfurt School, and a wide range of European and American theorists including Eric Erickson and Talcott Parsons.

From a sweeping and critical review of these formative theoretical formulations, Poster hypothesizes that family history must be conceptualized
from three perspectives: the psychological, the reality of everyday life, and
the interrelations between the family and society. The family on the psychological level is conceived of as being constituted of hierarchies of age and sex,
each of which having its own psychological or emotional issues.[16] Relations
between children and parents along patterns of identification and authority are
the focus of historical analysis. The psychological consequences of child-
rearing practices are seen as central for understanding the emotional reality
of family life.

Prior to an understanding of the family on the psychological level, however, it must be described as a mundane reality from the point of view of
everyday life. Categories of family life, derived from a detailed ethnographic
study, are used to reconstruct the daily functioning of family participants,
their physical environment and interactions. The study of the family on this
level includes an analysis of household composition, sexual relations, life
cycles, residential patterns and customs.

The final component of Poster's approach is a study of the family in its
structural relation to society. Here the family is conceived as influencing and
being influenced by political, economic, and legal institutions. Since the psychological structure of the family may not be congruent with the formal hierarchies of society, the results of the family's interactions with society are not
predictable and are often a source of conflict.[17]

Poster gives an example of how his critical theory can be used by historians through his analysis of four models of family types: the peasant and
aristocratic families in sixteenth- and seventeenth-century Europe, the bourgeois family in the nineteenth century, and the working-class family during
the early industrial revolution. In each case his analysis reveals a richness of
historical detail along with a conceptual unity which is impressive. In order
for historians to achieve the same level of analysis, they would have to be
thoroughly familiar with a wealth of psychological and sociological literature
on the family. Poster's critical theory of the family is a highly sophisticated
one which can be applied by Chicano historians to capture the continuities
and diversities of family life. Of all the theories discussed it seems the one
best suited for a historical analysis of the Chicano family.[18]

My study of the problem of Mexican-American family theory and
history draws heavily on Poster's critical theory while focusing on what I consider to be the most salient issues in the daily lives of most Mexican Americans, namely, the disruptive effects of industrialization and urbanization, the
continuing dilemmas posed by Mexican immigration, intermarriage with the
non-Mexican-heritage populations, changes in the values surrounding the
patriarchal family, and the problems of family solidarity in a fast-changing

environment. Chapter two discusses the family and society of the second half of the nineteenth century. It provides an overview of urban social history and analyzes the demographic and economic contexts of family life. Chapter three treats the everyday life of the family by looking at patriarchy as both a system of historically developed values and actual practices. Chapter four continues the analysis of everyday life by analyzing the ways in which kinship systems and family structures were changed by cultural and economic forces. Chapter five treats the important issues of Mexican immigration and marital assimilation as they affected family structure. Chapter six attempts to describe the psychological and affective dimensions of family life in the arenas of child rearing, parental discipline, and attitudes toward sex. The final two chapters, seven and eight, seek to bridge the gap between the nineteenth and twentieth centuries. They trace patterns of family life from 1900 to the present, suggest comparisons with the patterns of the previous century, and develop models of family types for the twentieth-century Mexican-American family.

In order to "explain" family change it is necessary to go beyond an ethnographic analysis of practices and customs. Poster's theoretical approach, which has formed the basis for the organization of this book, is not capable of explaining historical changes within the family. The theory is frankly conceived as a descriptive approach.

My views on the dynamics of family change have been influenced by Barbara Laslett's analysis of the conflicts between the family as a reproductive and productive unit. This perspective sees changes in Mexican-American family life as the product of conflicts between ideational and value systems surrounding the family and the capitalist economic system. Thus I am concerned with assessing how the family has been influenced by conflicts between cultural and economic systems. I develop the argument that there has been a persistent tension between the ideals and expectations which Mexican Americans have had regarding family life and the actual conditions of day-to-day reality. The actualities of family life in America have greatly been influenced by economic processes. There has been a conflict between what people have valued and expected and what they have been actually able to achieve in family matters. This conflict between the ideal and the real, I believe, has been central to the history of the Mexican-American family in America. As the American economic system has become more developed over the last 150 years, so too has the intensity of pressures for familial change not only on Mexican-American families but on all families. The experience of the Chicano or Mexican-American family can be taken as a magnified example of the consequences of the dynamic pressures that have been at work in American society in the industrial and postindustrial eras.

CHAPTER 2

Urban Cultural and Economic Transformations

> *Nature abhors immobility. Motion is the normal con-*
> *dition of man as well as of matter. Society is but a*
> *stream, ever seeking its level, ever flowing on toward*
> *the ocean of eternity.*
> –Hubert Howe Bancroft, *Literary Industries*, p. 616.

SAN ANTONIO, SANTA FE, TUCSON, and Los Angeles were four of the most populous Mexican towns in the Southwest when the United States annexed northern Mexico in 1848. Early in the American era they were prominent political, commercial, and trading cities. For Mexican Americans these towns were important social and political centers throughout the nineteenth and well into the twentieth century. The families who populated these urban oases shared a common fate in that they were the first to have to confront the social and political realities arising out of the American conquest. Later generations of Mexican immigrants and Mexican Americans would confront essentially the same problems as their forerunners: racial prejudice, economic displacement, poverty, and marginalization.

A number of historians writing about this period have concluded that most of these Mexican Americans were politically and economically sub-jugated. There were, however, significant regional and class differences in the ways in which Mexican Americans coped with their changing environ-ment. In nearly every town there was a small elite composed of landholding rancheros, merchants, and professionals. For the most part they shared a communality of interest with their counterparts in English-speaking society. The vast majority of Spanish-speaking families, however, were poor and working class. They were increasingly excluded from new opportunities in middle-class and white-collar occupations, discriminated against in religious, political, and educational institutions, and psychologically alienated by the growing dominance of a foreign culture and language.[1] Most Mexican Amer-icans became a disenfranchised ethnic group during the nineteenth century.

This chapter gives an overview of the political and economic conditions which influenced the family life of Mexican Americans living in southwestern towns and cities in the late nineteenth century. It is divided into three parts: a survey of the social and political history of the four towns, an analysis of demographic and economic changes in the urban Southwest, and an appraisal of how these transformations affected the Mexican-American class system.

SAN ANTONIO

San Antonio occupied center stage in an unfolding drama of conflict and accomodation between Anglos and Mexicans. The first violent conflict between these two groups took place in Texas as early as 1819—a result of filibustering expeditions into New Spain led by American and Mexican adventurers. Prior to 1848 San Antonio's history was a saga of political instability, civil war, and foreign invasion. During the period of the Mexican Wars of Independence (1810-1821) the town was captured and recaptured many times, resulting in the mass exodus of families. This pattern continued during the period of the Texas Republic (1835-1845). In 1834 San Antonio was the largest town in Texas with a population of over 24,000. Most of the residents were Mexicans. A year later, however, a large body of the population fled when the city was occupied by Mexican and Texan armies. Additional hundreds of families departed when the Texans finally occupied San Antonio after General Santa Anna's defeat at San Jacinto in 1836.[2]

Even after the conclusion of the armistice and Texas' independence, Mexican armies invaded Texas and recaptured the city twice in 1842. Both occupations forced many American and Mexican residents to temporarily abandon the town. Later, Mexican residents who were suspected of disloyalty to the Texan cause were subject to intimidation and violence. Many lost their lands and possessions through the activities of speculators and squatters. In South Texas the Cavazos family lost their El Espíritu Santo Grant to Robber Baron types like Charles Stillman and Richard King. Juan Seguin, a former mayor and longtime ally of the Texans, had to flee San Antonio and abandon his property because of Texan threats on his life. By 1845, on the eve of the Mexican War, the town's population numbered only about 700.[3]

With the beginning of American, German, Italian, and French immigration into Texas and San Antonio in the 1840s, many of the Mexican upper-class families intermarried with foreigners, joining their landed wealth with new political influence. The Navarro, de la Garza, and de Zavala families had many sons and daughters marry influential foreigners. Foreign immigration gave San Antonio a cosmopolitan flavor, but it also reinforced class divisions between the Mexican rich and poor.

After the Mexican War San Antonio began to rebuild. The town became an important way station for overland immigrants bound for California. Trade resumed with Mexico, and by 1850 the city's population stood at 3,252; by 1860 it climbed to 7,643 free whites and 592 slaves.[4]

The homes of the San Antonio families during the American era were basically of three types. The Mexican poor lived in *jacales*, or huts, made of posts plastered over with mud, a thatched roof, and a dirt floor.[5] They usually had a single room with a kitchen located in an attached *ramada*, or open shelter. The Americans and European immigrant families lived in newer wood and stone homes built according to architectural designs popular in the eastern United States. The American working class built wood frame houses of a frontier style. And the Mexican elite lived in large multiroom stone or adobe houses, which were flat-roofed and covered with shingles. Many of these more substantial homes dated from earlier in the century. Most of them were built around the two plazas, Plaza de las Islas and Plaza de las Armas[6]

San Antonio's prosperity under the Americans depended on military contracts, the coastal and Mexican trade, and ranching. Cart trade with Mexico was profitable, reaching over two million dollars per year during the 1850s. In 1857, however, the Mexicans' control of this lucrative trade was threatened when American merchants forced the independent Mexican freighters out of business through intimidation and violence. Until the 1870s, when the railroad arrived, the main industries were cattle ranching and droving. The high price of wool stimulated massive investments in sheep production during the next decade. Soon sheep surpassed cattle as a major source of income.[7]

Commerce, ranching, and agriculture were the most important sources of living for San Antonio's families. The largest industry was brewing, pioneered by German immigrants. In 1860 the Menger Brewery, the largest factory in town, employed only ten skilled workmen.[8] After the Civil War San Antonio became a modern city because of immigration and improved transportation. It soon boasted a telephone exchange, streetcars, electric lights, and a public water and sewage system. Still, in comparison to the booming commercial cities of Galveston and Houston, the city remained economically underdeveloped well into the twentieth century.

SANTA FE

Six hundred miles northwest of San Antonio was Santa Fe, the oldest of the four Spanish-Mexican pueblos. La Villa Real de Santa Fe was founded in 1610 by Don Pedro de Peralta and some settlers from the nearby pueblo of San Juan. For centuries Santa Fe was the administrative center of New Spain's farthest northern frontier. Located in the midst of the largest settled Indian population in the Southwest, the town served as a missionary, administrative, and trading center for the region. Santa Fe had a long tutelage under Spanish control and as a result developed a distinctively different social

Santa Fe, New Mexico, in 1880 looking northwest, with De Vargas Street and Hispano residences in foreground. Distant structures beyond the trees are Anglo-American homes and buildings. Courtesy Museum of New Mexico, Santa Fe, neg. no. 11364.

Meyer Street, Tucson, Arizona, between 1896 and 1899. Courtesy Arizona Historical Society Library, neg. n. 24329.

Military Plaza, San Antonio, during market day ca. 1880. Courtesy The
Barker Library, University of Texas, Austin.

A view of the Sonoratown barrio, Los Angeles, and the Plaza from Fort Hill
in 1887. Courtesy Los Angeles Public Library, Security Pacific National Bank
Photograph Collection, neg. no. 001-454.

and cultural identity, one more oriented toward Spanish customs and traditions than the Mestizo Mexican.

The northern New Mexicans, or Hispanos, had a long history of resistance to outsiders who challenged their independence and deep attachment to the land. In 1680 the Pueblo Indians staged a successful rebellion against Spanish attempts to stamp out their religion and exact tribute. It took twelve years for the government to reconquer the lost province. Another Indian rebellion took place in 1837, encouraged by Hispanos who were dissatisfied with their Mexican-appointed governor.[9] A decade later the Pueblo Indians again allied themselves with Hispanos to resist the encroachment of the Amerians. In 1847 they overthrew the newly established governor at Taos but were quickly subdued by United States troops from Santa Fe.[10]

The resistance of the Pueblo Indians and Hispanos continued after the end of the Mexican War in 1848. Well into the 1880s Las Gorras Blancas, or White Caps, a Hispano vigilante movement, cut fences, burned barns, and organized politically in attempts to drive out American railroad, lumber, and cattle interests which were encroaching on their village commons.[11] The Penitente movement, a secret religious brotherhood of lay people, arose to defy American authorities. The Penitentes sought to preserve their centuries-old religious autonomy in the face of an increasingly aggressive American government and a non-Spanish-speaking Roman Catholic hierarchy.[12] Other resistance movements sprang up, engendered by American capitalist penetration of the region. In the 1870s the Lincoln County War and the Colfax County Land War attested to the will of the Hispanos to resist forced economic changes in land tenure.[13]

Geographic isolation reinforced the traditions of conservatism in the old ways and resistance to new authority. The New Mexico territory was not as influenced by American or Mexican immigration as was San Antonio. Well into the twentieth century Hispanos were a majority of the population. Consequently the Mexican Americans were more able to maintain their older traditions and culture apart from the American community.

The dwellings of the Hispanos of Santa Fe were adobes of various sizes, depending on the wealth and occupations of the inhabitants. Little change in architecture occurred during the American period. All residents preferred the warmth and functional charm of the larger adobe homes to wood or stone structures. A typical working-class home was easily built following ancient techniques of construction. The materials were practically free and readily available. Poles to support the flat roofs were brought from the nearby mountains. There was never a housing shortage in Santa Fe. Even the poorest citizen could afford to build his own home, with the help of his friends and relatives, if he had land or permission to do so on someone else's. The rich lived in the older sections of the city around the plaza, near the

Palace of the Governors, and to the north. They occupied multistoried spacious dwellings with the traditional patio in the center. The poorer classes lived in smaller but comfortable adobes without the benefit of wood floors or windows; they were concentrated to the west and south of the plaza. The commercial district round Calle de los Burros bustled with mercantile activity, especially when caravans of wagons entered the town, ending their long journey on the Santa Fe trail.

The city's ruling elite in the territorial period were from families who could trace their ancestry back to the early founders of European setttlements in New Mexico, Juan de Oñate and Diego de Vargas in the seventeenth century. The names of Archuleta, Chávez, Vigil, Ortiz, Sánchez, and Martínez appear prominently in the territorial annals as influential leaders. Most of them were related to each other by marriage or *compadrazgo* (god-parenthood). Santa Fe was in reality a village whose native population remained more or less stable, except for a small but significant number of American lawyers, traders, and politicos.

Among these American immigrants were the Missourians Thomas Benton Catron and Stephen Benton Elkins. Together they began to form alliances with other Americans and with the leading Hispano families. In time their loose alliance came to be called the Santa Fe Ring. The Ring, as it developed gradually throughout the nineteenth century, attempted to defraud Hispano landholders by using their control of the surveyor general's office and the legislature and by cultivating key connections in Washington, D. C. Perhaps the greatest significance of the Santa Fe Ring was that it introduced finance capitalism to New Mexico along with monopolistic practices which were being developed to a high art in the industrial Northeast. In bringing the questionable benefits of "modernization" to Sante Fe, the Ring was primarily interested in enriching a small group of entrepreneurs. They laid the basis for a type of colonial society, while assuring that New Mexico would remain subservient to powers outside the territory.[14]

The coming of the railroad in 1880 ended Santa Fe's economic isolation. The railroad meant that it was now possible to open up new rangelands and mines in the hinterlands. The basic pattern of exploitation by the Ring remained substantially unchanged up to New Mexico's admission as a state in 1912.[15] With the rapid growth of Albuquerque to the south in the 1880s Santa Fe became an almost forgotten village in terms of commerce and trade.

TUCSON

The royal presidio of San Augustin de Tucson had been founded in 1776 by a garrison of soldiers from Tubac. The presidio had a history of being an embattled outpost, a walled city, with families of soldiers, ranchers, and traders huddled within to escape fierce Apache attacks. Isolation and insecurity were the main themes of Tucson's early history. Intermittent warfare with Indians forced the *pobladores* to rely almost entirely on their own resources for survival.[16]

The United States incorporated Tucson into the territory of New Mexico with the Gadsden Purchase in 1854. The official purpose of the acquisition was to provide land for a railroad route to California and to settle a boundary dispute arising from faulty surveying of the original border in 1848. Some American officials suspected that the region was rich with copper, gold, and silver.[17] As if to fulfill this possibility, Texan migrants from the nearby Mesilla Valley and the El Paso region soon entered the town hoping to strike it rich in mining, cattle ranching, or trading.[18] In 1862 the Confederates briefly occupied Tucson but soon withdrew in the face of superior forces from California. A year later in 1863 Congress recognized Arizona as a separate territory.

After 1848 the Americans, although a numerical minority, controlled the commercial and political affairs of the city. Charles De Brille Poston, a Kentuckian, emerged as an energetic leader of the mining industry. Mark Aldrich, a wealthy merchant, became the first mayor and was a prime mover in the campaign to have Arizona declared a territory. In a pattern similar to that of the Santa Fe Ring, American merchants and financiers used the political system and alliances with the Mexicano elite in Tucson to enhance their control of affairs. Peonage, or debt slavery, a heritage from the Mexican era, continued to exist even after it was legally abolished by the Fourteenth Amendment. A double wage standard was established for Mexican miners, and Mexican land grants were voided through corrupt manipulation of the courts and government offices.[19] As in New Mexico, the Spanish-speaking elite, most of them immigrants from Sonora, formed business and marriage alliances with the Americans to keep and expand their fortunes. Merchants such as Antonio Contreras, Estevan Ochoa, Mariano Samaniego, and Leopoldo Carrillo acted as intermediaries between the working-class Mexicans and the American establishment. The Arizona elite readily assimilated American ways and further removed themselves from the mass of working-class Mexicanos in Tucson and southern Arizona. They sent their children to private schools in the East and adapted the newest innovations in business methods and technology. Gradually, after the railroad entered the territory, the native elite lost their ownership in large mines and ranches. They had never been very influential in territorial politics.[20]

Perhaps the single most important reality of life in Tucson in the period prior to 1880 was the constant warfare between whites and the local Indians. During the 1860s and 1870s depredations were so frequent that farmers and ranchers came to live within Tucson's walls for extended periods of time. To protect and warn against Indian attacks, packs of dogs were set loose in the streets at night and sentries posted until dawn. Hundreds of soldiers and citizens lost their lives and families in this last great Indian war in the United States.[21]

In Tucson most of the poor classes lived in a section of town called Barrio Libre located on the south side. This included Mexican immigrants from Sonora as well as Indians who were refugees of the Apache wars. Almost all the homes in this section of the town were small one-room adobes with adjoining *jacales*, or small lean-tos. Tucson had a large floating multiethnic population of drifters, gamblers, and fugitives from Mexican and American authorities. They lived mostly in the hotels and rooming houses in the central district. North of this the American and Mexican middle and upper classes lived in large rock, adobe, and wood homes.[22]

The main industries of the Tucson region were trade with Mexico, the shipping of silver and gold ore from local mines and the supplying of government contracts for the army. But in the 1880s Tucson's economy suffered a setback when new railroad connections made the Sonoran trade unprofitable and the U.S. Army began to withdraw its troops.[23] The most long-lasting and profitable enterprises proved to be the copper mines south of Tucson. Most of these mines were owned by large conglomerates in California and New York. Mexican workers, most of them immigrants from Sonora, became the prime labor force for the future growth of this industry.

Like Santa Fe, Tucson remained a small village throughout the nineteenth century. Spanish was the official language of commerce and social intercourse. The early American population quickly accommodated themselves to Tucson's Mexican culture. The Indian wars and a chronic shortage of American women made for political and marital alliances between the two groups. As a consequence there was little overt racial violence in Tucson, at least nothing on the scale of what occurred in Texas and California during the same period.

LOS ANGELES

The last major Mexican urban center in the Southwest in the nineteenth century was Nuestra Señora la Reina de Los Angeles de Porciúncula—or Los Angeles. Founded in 1781 by soldiers and settlers from the Tucson presidio and central Mexico, Los Angeles enjoyed a relatively peaceful and prosperous existence during a short period of Spanish government. Most important changes took place during the Mexican era (1821-1848), largely as a result of the secularization of the mission lands and increased trade with Yankee clipper ships. Hundred of thousands of acres of mission lands were sold or granted to a small group of Mexican soldiers and settlers, thus creating vast ranchos and a new elite class of Californios. The mission cattle stock formed the basis of a thriving cattle industry, which, in turn, led to growing trade with Yankee clipper ships. The mission citrus groves and farms became the stock for the later development of a prosperous agribusiness during the 1880s. But during the Mexican and early American periods agriculture was essentially of a subsistence level.

The Mexican War, followed immediately by the California gold rush, ended the slow-moving pastoral way of life in Los Angeles. Thousands of immigrants from over all the world passed through the town on their way north to the gold fields. Many of them returned when their claims ran out. New residents from Sonora settled in the pueblo as did a variety of Asian and European immigrants as well as migrants from every region of the United States.

Most of the Mexican immigrants and poorer Mexican Americans lived in a ten-block area north of the plaza in a barrio that the Americans called Sonora Town. Here along the unpaved streets the Spanish speaking lived in wood and adobe houses. The plaza itself, once surrounded by the town houses of the landed elite, became a slum area with saloons and brothels, a residence for transient laborers and the Chinese. South of the plaza and near the Los Angeles River some Mexican families lived on small plots of irrigated land where they grew beans, corn, and squash. Americans lived in the newer subdivisions built of wood and brick east of the Los Angeles River or south of First Street.[24]

During the gold rush years the California landholders enjoyed a short-lived prosperity. In the early 1860s droughts and epidemics decimated the cattle herds. The price of cattle fell to new lows when increased stock was driven to California overland from elsewhere in the West. The rancho economy was destroyed in a relatively short time. The Californios began to sell off their lands to meet debts incurred during flush times or to pay for litigation costs arising from a host of prejudicial laws that were passed for the benefit of American settlers.

Like other elites in the Southwest, Los Angeles' upper-class Californios were most anxious to seek a *modus vivendi* with their new neighbors. Until about 1860 the Spanish speaking were a majority of the city's population. Their traditional leaders enjoyed a degree of political and economic power. The families of Coronel, del Valle, Pico, and Sepúlveda figured prominently in local politics. As elsewhere in the Southwest they sought marriages for their daughters with influential Americans. Despite this effort at assimilation periodic violence between Americans and Mexicans punctuated Los Angeles' history. Bandits like Juan Flores and Tiburcio Vasquez carried on a guerrilla war against all wealthy property owners. Often they had the active support of the Mexican working classes. Lynchings of Mexicanos by American and Californio vigilanti committees were common up to the 1880s. Increasingly,

Mexican immigrants who came to the city were imbued with a nationalistic pride growing out of Benito Juarez's struggle against the conservatives and the French in Mexico. Mexican Americans thus developed a new pride in their national heritage.

Unlike Tucson or Santa Fe, Los Angeles developed a barrio culture where Mexican Americans maintained a tenacious hold on their heritage in the face of increasing numbers of English-speaking immigrants. Los Angeles' "conflict of cultures" was similar to that experienced by the San Antonians. The barrio was a society under seige, surrounded by prosperous farms, small-scale industries, and suburbs. As in San Antonio the majority of Mexican Americans in Los Angeles survived by working as low-paid day laborers for the new owners of the agricultural lands and commercial establishments.

After 1865 the main impetus for industrial and commerical growth came from the conversion of rancho lands to agriculture. By 1880 the surrounding farm acreage had increased one hundred times over what it had been in 1850. Small businesses and over a hundred new industries fueled a booming economy. The city built a potable water system, a sewage plant, a gasworks, a telegraph system, railroad connections, and a network of paved roads. Public works construction in turn increased the value of vacant city land and attracted more settlers. Property values rose to an assessed valuation of over twenty million dollars.[25] As a result of these and other changes the basic structure of the modern urban economy was virtually in place by the turn of the century.

DEMOGRAPHIC AND ECONOMIC CHANGE

The social and political history of the urban Southwest in the late nineteenth century provides a background for understanding changes which took place on the family level. A related analysis of economic and demographic change is needed in order to understand regional variations in family patterns. Table 1 shows the total populations of each of the four towns, along with an estimated size of the Mexican-American citizenry. Every town increased in size during the period. Tucson and Santa Fe had the least rapid growth, owing to their more remote geopolitical position. San Antonio and Los Angeles, since they were towns located near waterways and more populated market areas, had the most rapid growth. By 1870 San Antonio surpassed Los Angeles to become the largest Mexican-American city in the Southwest. This was due, in part, to San Antonio's earlier rail connections with eastern cities, the periodic immigration of Mexicans from northeastern Mexico, and the proximity of the town to populous areas in the South. After 1870 Los Angeles' population grew rapidly as well, but the bulk of the growth was sparked by American emigration, not Mexican immigration. Southern California was far removed from proximity to large population centers in Mexico until the advent of the railroad in the late 1870s.

In the 1870s the largest Mexican-American barrio was in San Antonio, and the smallest was in Los Angeles. The numbers of Spanish-speaking residents in San Antonio increased in each census year, while Los Angeles' population remained stagnant. Tucson and Santa Fe had roughly the same numbers of Mexican Americans. Tucson's modest growth was largely due to immigration from Sonora and outlying regions of the territory, and Santa Fe's Hispano population did not increase at all due to immigration. In fact it appears that there was considerable out-migration since natural increases should have resulted in greater numbers than were counted in 1880. By that year Mexican Americans were only 19 percent of Los Angeles' total population.

TABLE 1

Comparative Populations of Mexican-Americans and Anglo-Americans in Four Southwestern Towns, 1850-1880

	1850	1860	1870	1880
Los Angeles				
Total	1,610[e]	4,385[d]	5,728[b]	11,183[b]
Mex. Am.[g]	1,215	2,069	2,160	2,116
Tucson				
Total	n.d.	915[c]	5,716[a]	7,007[b]
Mex. Am.[f]	n.d.	800	4,571	5,605
Santa Fe				
Total	4,832[a]	4,576[a]	4,765[a]	6,635[b]
Mex. Am.[f]	4,445	4,484	4,526	5,838
San Antonio				
Total	3,552[a]	7,643[a]	12,256[a]	20,550[b]
Mex. Am.[f]	1,642	3,286	5,882	8,425

Sources:

[a] U.S. Department of Interior, Census Office, *Ninth Census of United States*, "Statistics on Population," vol. 1 (Washington, D.C.: G.P.O., 1872), pp. 12, 206, 270. The 1870 Tucson population is for Pima County because the census office did not compile the city's population separately.

[b] U.S. Department of the Interior, Census Office, *Statistics of the Population of the United States at the Tenth Census* (Washington, D.C.: G.P.O., 1883), pp. 99, 108, 263, 341.

[c] U.S. Department of the Interior, Census Office, *Population of the United States in 1860* (Washington, D.C., 1864), p. 568.

[d] U.S. Department of Commerce, Bureau of the Census, *Fifteenth Census of the United States*, "Population," vol. 1 (1931), (Washington, D.C., 1931), pp. 18-19.

[e] De Bow, Census Office, *Statistical View of the United States: Being a Compendium of the Seventh Census* (Washington, D.C.: R. Armstrong, 1854), p. 202.

[f] Estimate based on percentage distribution in sample population (see section on methodology).

[g] Based on total count of Spanish-surnamed individuals. See Richard Griswold del Castillo, *The Los Angeles Barrio, 1850-1890: A Social History* (Los Angeles and Berkeley: University of California Press, 1980), pp. 177-184.

San Antonio was 40 percent Mexican American, followed by Tucson with 70 percent and Santa Fe with 87 percent. This represented substantial changes from previous decades. In 1850 Los Angeles' Spanish speaking had been a majority. The San Antonians had become a minority prior to that date. Thus the transition to minority status for the Spanish speaking took place only in the larger cities of the Southwest. The smaller towns of Santa Fe and Tucson retained a large majority of Mexican-born and Spanish speaking.

Urban population growth is one index of the pace of economic modernization. Population increase in the urban areas created larger markets for commercial, manufacturing, and agricultural enterprises. Larger populations also led to increased specialization and investment. Table 2 summarizes the rates of growth in capital investment, agriculture, and manufacturing in the counties served by the four towns.

TABLE 2

Economic Change in Four Southwestern Urban Counties
As Measured by Selected Indicators, 1850-1880

	Los Angeles	Pima	Santa Fe	Bexar
Cash Value of Farms and Ranches				
$ in 1850 (60)	649,900	(151,840)	171,477	209,951
% Increase				
1850-60	249	n.d.	105	282
1860-70	261	n.d.	120	-56
1870-80	284	145	-2	648
Average % Growth 1850-80	264.6	145	74.3	291.3
Capital Invested in Manufacturing				
$ in 1860	316,930	1,699,350	29,000	83,606
% Increase				
1860-70	204	-97	303	-32
1870-80	145	210	-84	550
Average % Growth 1860-80	175.2	56.5	109.3	259
Capital Invested in Farm Machinery				
$ in 1850 (70)	35,900	(18,055)	10,291	14,377
% Increase				
1850-60	124	n.d.	-43	-10
1860-70	169	n.d.	-23	151
1879-80	533	103	154	408
Average % Growth 1850-80	275	103	29.3	183

Sources: U.S. Department of Interior, Census Office, *Tenth Census of the United States, 1850* (Washington, D.C.: G.P.O., 1853); *Schedules of Manufacturing and Agriculture*, 1860 through 1880.

Agricultural investment is measured by the cash value of farms and ranches and the amount of capital invested in agricultural machinery. Generally, the capitalization of farming and ranching was directed by outside investment sources: primarily by bankers in San Francisco for the Los Angeles and Tucson areas, and by investors in the industrial Northeast and Europe for Santa Fe and San Antonio regions. Manufacturing, although not a major source of wealth in any of the towns, generally increased and indicates the region's progressive modernization. Although the data for manufacturing is given for counties, the statistics represent mostly growth within the towns themselves since few manufacturing establishments were located outside the urban areas.

The rate at which increased amounts of capital were invested in both agricultural machinery and lands increased in all four urban areas. Los Angeles and Bexar counties were roughly equal in their rates of growth in the agricultural sector, far outpacing both Pima (southern Arizona, including Tucson) and Santa Fe counties. The decennial rate for the San Antonio region was quite erratic, owing to a depression caused by the Civil War. After 1870, however, Bexar County had a surge of agricultural investment in both lands and farm machinery. The motivating force for this was the rapid growth of cattle and sheep ranching in the South Texas region. San Antonio served as the starting point for the long drives north to the railheads at Abeline and Kansas City. Los Angeles' expansion in the agricultural sector was more even and progressive, the railroad acting as a stimulus for growth in citrus and grain farming. Santa Fe and Pima counties had less change in their agricultural investments than these larger cities. Pima County led Santa Fe in terms of the cash value of agricultural land and investment in farm technology.

Roughly the same patterns can be seen in the manufacturing sectors. Los Angeles and Bexar counties had high rates of investment, while Pima and Santa Fe lagged behind. Pima County's manufacturing consisted mostly of mines and processing plants for gold and silver ore. This industry suffered a depression after the 1860s. Santa Fe's manufacturing was mostly the construction of farming and ranching implements and of wagons and accessories for freighters. After 1870 there was a flight of capital from Santa Fe to other regions, such as Albuquerque which had more direct rail connections with eastern and western markets.

The county-based data on agriculture and manufacturing shows that Los Angeles and San Antonio underwent more rapid rates of economic change than did either Tucson or Santa Fe. Taken together with information on population, it is apparent that San Antonio had the greatest urban industrial change, followed closely by Los Angeles. The smaller towns, Tucson and Santa Fe, were no competitors for these larger cities.

COLONIALISM AND THE MEXICAN-AMERICAN WORK FORCE

In 1970 the anthropologist Joan Moore delineated a useful way of differentiating between the historical experiences of the Mexican-American populations in these towns and their subregions. From her perspective San Antonio and South Texas underwent a type of "conflict colonialism" whereby American control meant the "total destruction of Mexican elite participation" along with frequent violent confrontations between the two ethnic groups.[26] As early as 1850 Mexicans became a numerical minority in San Antonio. Santa Fe and Tucson, on the other hand, had a "classical colonial experience." There the political elites remained intact and cooperated with newly arrived American capitalists and politicians to exploit the riches of their regions. A vital and thriving native society continued to exist, and a majority of the population continued to be Spanish speaking. Economic and political colonization took place more gradually than in either Texas or California. Los Angeles and Southern California underwent "economic colonialism," a mixture of the New Mexican and Texan experience. The gold rush and the rapid economic development of the state effectively destroyed the preexisting economic basis of the Mexican elite. In a short time American emigrants were a majority of the population. Mexicans rapidly became a landless labor force for the burgeoning agribusiness corporations of Southern California. Overall, the Mexican-American population of the four towns became a colonial work force for American commercial and industrial enterprises. The processes by which this came about differed depending on each region's prior history and the nature of external investment.

A more sophisticated scheme for the conceptualization of this process has been offered by the political scientist Mario Barrera. Barrera, in his analysis of the political economy of the Southwest during the late nineteenth century, divided the Chicano work force into four economic sectors, each differentiated by its relationship to the American economic system and social-class level. His theoretical scheme is a useful way of analyzing how the developments discussed thus far related to the working members of families.

In Barrera's terms the "peripheral sector" represented those workers who remained relatively unaffected by the new economic system. This sector was predominantly in rural regions of the Southwest. Neither Tucson nor Santa Fe should be viewed as being part of this sector, despite their more rural contexts. This is because they underwent modest technological and economic change during the nineteenth century: they were not entirely unaffected by the processes of modernization. Tucson and Santa Fe thus are more properly placed in Barrera's segment of the nonperipheral sector since they both had a small Mexican-American middle class of proprietors and skilled workers, although here, as elsewhere, it is not clear that these occupations were fully integrated into the economy on a parity with their American class equals.

The colonized sector Barrera defined as those workers who were "incorporated into the new capitalist economy of the Southwest, but on a subordinate basis."[27] This sector included mostly unskilled laborers who were paid lower wages and had inferior conditions of work compared to their American counterparts. The marginal sector Barrera defined as workers who were displaced from their traditional occupations by the new order. These were mostly unemployed skilled and unskilled workers. The integrated sector Barrera described as "Chicanos who were incorporated into the Anglo capitalist economy on an equal or nonsubordinate basis."[28] This sector included middle- and upper-class white-collar occupations. Since only sketchy information is available regarding the equality of socioeconomic class position and conditions of work for this sector, Barrera concluded that the integrated sector was only theoretically possible, not yet proven by historical evidence.

In each of the four southwestern urban areas the degree to which the labor force participated in the three sectors varied by degree. One would expect, following Barrera's conceptualization, that Santa Fe and Tucson, which were historically more isolated from intensive economic developments, would have a relatively lower percentage of their work force in the colonized sector in comparison to the larger cities. As can be seen in Table 3, this generalization was true except for Tucson in 1870 and Santa Fe in 1880. In those years there were increases in the colonized work force. Tucson, which shared Santa Fe's isolated geographical status, had a decline in the colonized sector from a high of 78 percent of the labor force in 1870 to 58 percent in 1880. At the same time San Antonio had a pattern which supports Barrera's model. In this city there was an increasing proportion of the work force in the colonized sector. But the opposite pattern was true for Los Angeles, where the proletarian work force declined in each census year after 1860. One pattern which seems to contradict Barrera's model is that of the marginal sector. Santa Fe had larger proportions of its Mexican-American work force unemployed than was true in the larger cities, which were undergoing rapid urban and commercial growth. In 1880 Tucson led all the urban areas in the proportion of marginal workers in the work force.

Overall it appears that in Santa Fe and San Antonio the colonial labor system was stabilizing by the 1880s. There was a general rise in the colonized and integrated sectors and a decline in the marginal sector. In Los Angeles and Tucson, however, increases in the marginal sectors meant that the economic situation for Mexican Americans was less stable.

In the urban Southwest the working and employable members of Mexican-American families confronted a dynamic capitalist structure which varied according to economic and financial conditions in each region. The varied patterns of sectorial distribution over time, shown in Table 3, illustrate the importance of considering regional and local history when discussing questions of the family in relation to the economy. It is evident that the colonization or proletarianization of the Mexican-American work force was by no means a uniform or simple process.

Control of the economy meant the power to change the most fundamental aspects of daily life. More importantly it meant the power to mold the lines of authority in society. As the economy of the Southwest came to be dominated by foreigners, it meant that there would be new pressures to change the historical patterns of the Mexicano frontier culture. The colonization process in the late nineteenth century destroyed a preindustrial unity that had existed between the cultural notions of authority and the control of the economy. Thus one of the first challenges Mexican-American families faced was to adjust to new realities of economic domination. The political and economic conquest of the Southwest transformed the material conditions that had supported parental authority within the family. In the late nineteenth century the Mexicano patriarchal family came under attack.

TABLE 3

The Sectoral Distribution of the Mexican-American Work Force
in Four Southwestern Towns, 1850-1880
(Expressed as a percentage of the male work force ages 20-59)

	1850	1860	1870	1880
A. Colonized				
Los Angeles	49.2	76.6	72.6	64.6
Tucson	–	–	78.9	58.2
Santa Fe	79.3	62.1	61.1	77.0
San Antonio	80.0	68.3	72.9	74.5
B. Marginal Sector				
Los Angeles	40.4	14.6	20.3	22.2
Tucson	–	–	12.4	25.2
Santa Fe	17.1	26.3	24.1	12.0
San Antonio	15.8	22.0	22.5	12.2
C. Integrated Sector				
Los Angeles	11.4	5.9	7.1	13.2
Tucson	–	–	8.8	16.7
Santa Fe	3.7	11.6	14.8	11.0
San Antonio	4.2	9.8	4.7	13.0

Source: Computer analysis of manuscript census returns, based on categories as defined by Barrera. In this table and others like it where there were separate N's (total number in sample) for four towns in each census year the sample size has been omitted to make the table more readable. Appendix A has a discussion of sampling procedure used and number of cases for each town in each census year.

CHAPTER 3

Patriarchy under Attack

> . . . *if the man is the head, the woman is the heart,*
> *and as he occupies the chief place in ruling, so she*
> *claims for herself the chief place in love.*
> –Encyclical of Pope Pius XI. Quoted in *The San An-*
> *tonio Express*, January 9, 1931

A NUMBER OF HISTORIANS have studied the impact of economic modernization on families living in individual regions and cities in the American Southwest. While it has been possible for researchers to analyze with some precision the ways the economy has affected family life in one locale, the task is much more difficult when the area of study is expanded to include more than one urban area, for as has been seen, there were many conflicting economic forces at work.[1] Their impact on family life were contradictory and varied.

No single theoretical model can satisfactorily explain the complex relationship between the economy and family change because modernization has occurred on both individual and societal levels and not always at the same rate among different segments of the population. Regional, cultural, economic class, and ethnic differences have influenced the effects of economic and political changes on family life. Yet the family is an institution that has been notoriously resistant to change, and in many instances preindustrial family customs have continued to coexist along with more modern practices.[2] Historically the middle and upper classes have been the first to change, while the poorer classes have retained many of their traditional customs.

The religious and secular ideologies which often surround family life complicate the problem even further. The individual decisions that had consequences for the private life were then as now as much a product of the everyday culture as of the economic system. Whether a person married early or late, sent children to school or to work, or took in boarders or relatives were decisions that often were influenced by prevailing ideals and values about the correct behavior. This ideological culture, including systems of belief, personal values, and social norms, conditioned how individuals responded to their social and physical environment.

For the nineteenth century it is probably impossible to identify a single ideology regarding the family that all Mexican Americans shared. Strictures and customs varied widely from region to region and according to socioeconomic class. Despite this heterogeneity, which still exists, it is possible to sketch broad outlines of the ideals regarding family life. These were beliefs held mostly by the upper classes, who were the most influential and articulate members of Mexican-American society. Because of the lack of sources we may never know the degree to which the working classes upheld these values. But it seems likely that there was always a degree of consensus, reflecting a "downward projection" of familial ideals and practices. There was probably a tendency for the poorer classes to emulate the life-styles and values of the upper and middle classes in both Mexican-American and Anglo-American society.[3]

THE HISTORICAL DEVELOPMENT OF PATRIARCHAL IDEOLOGIES

Most upper- and middle-class Mexican Americans in the Southwest and Mexico shared a common set of expectations about the nature and degree of authority that was owed to the male head of the household. Sylvia Marina Arrom has summarized this patriarchal ideal as follows:

> . . . the *pater familias* exercised his authority without restraints, unencumbered by tradition or competing power; he completely controlled his wife's legal acts, property and person, being able to claim her domestic services, obedience and sexual fidelity (although the double standard granted him sexual freedom); he made all important decisions to enforce his will upon its members using whatever means he deemed necessary.[4]

Ramón Gutiérrez in his history of changing patterns of marriage in New Mexico in the seventeenth through the nineteenth centuries has analyzed the concept of honor in relation to male authority within the family and argued that the patriarchal ideal had deep roots in Spanish racist ideology based on religion. The desire to maintain racial and thereby religious purity (*limpieza de sangre*) lay at the root of patriarchy. The wide-ranging powers of the father and husband were seen as necessary to protect the family, particularly the women, from what they considered pollution, corruption, and shame.[5]

Female honor, not just in Spain but in other Mediterranean communities, was historically related to the social-class system. Different codes of female sexual behavior were thought to be appropriate for different levels of the class hierarchy, with the aristocracy placing the greatest emphasis on female virtue. Reviewing the evidence for nineteenth-century Cuba, Verena Martínez-Alier concluded that while not all hierarchical societies emphasized female purity, "where there is such an emphasis, this is generally related to the existence of status groups."[6]

From Spanish colonial times the church and state, which sought to preserve the structured order of society, supported paternal authority. On the northern Mexican frontier in the early nineteenth century more egalitarian relationships seem to have emerged as a result of increased trade between Mexico and the United States as well as the common poverty endured by frontier families. No doubt the sexual division of labor was more difficult to maintain in a society where everyone had to work to survive in a harsh environment. The divisions in sex roles were more rigid in wealthier, higher status families because within these families women could be liberated from doing men's work. Among the majority of frontier families, however, men and women tended to share the labor of farming, ranching, and household chores.[7] The key to patriarchal values within the family lay not in the division of labor, but more in the authority given to the parents, especially to fathers. Ideally the parents exerted their greatest authority in the selection of marriage partners for their children. Honor, status, property, and family ties were considered to be more important than considerations of romantic love.

Yet even this perogative was eroding well before the American period began. In New Mexico notions of romantic love and individual choice in marriage began to supplant parental control as early as 1800.[8] While attributing these changes in New Mexico primarily to increased capitalist activity, Gutíerrez emphasized that the seeds of romantic love and freedom from patriarchal controls in mate selection were present in Spanish and Mexican culture long before the rise of modern economic activity. The Catholic Church's official doctrine was that all souls were equal before God, and both the church and state in colonial Mexico recognized grounds for divorce, while maintaining the legal identity of women.[9]

In supporting parental authority the church and state helped to maintain patriarchy. Often the authority of the parents to control their children was linked to religion. Respect for elders was cited in Scripture and church teachings, and on the family level children were socialized to look on parents as having religious authority. In New Mexico, for example, the Abeyta family strove to perpetuate the authority of the elders by preparing lengthy written instructions for their children. These lessons, passed from generation to generation, served as a guide for perpetuating a family ideology. In the lesson book the father was seen as imparting moral authority. He was the family priest, dispensing moral lessons and interpreting the word of God. A sample from the manuscript conveys the tone of the lessons:

I have seen Lord your work and I have prostrated myself in your presence because your work sings your wisdom and your Justice. I have turned my eyes to man's work and I have muffled myself in dejection because their work proclaims their ignorance and their evil.[10]

In Tucson families were sometimes led by the father or oldest member of the household in morning or evening prayers. Many families had special prayers that had been passed on through the generations. Carmen Lucero remembered that her family "got up at daylight and, led by the oldest member of the family, said family prayers and sang the 'Alba' or morning song"[11] Francisca Solano Leon remembered that her father regularly led the family in evening prayers "no matter how tired he was, or we were, he had us all together, and we knelt down and said our rosary."[12]

Religious authority within the family was a cornerstone of patriarchal control: it extended beyond the immediate household even to married children. José Arnaz, a Californio, recalled that it was not unusual for "an aged father to whip a married son with children and for his son to receive his lashes on his knees with a bowed head."[13] Another Californio, Antonio Coronel, recorded that "the rule for the family was to particularly preserve respect for the head of the household: in the extreme a son or daughter, although married, was to submit to the orders of the parent."[14]

The church sought to reinforce discipline within the family by its teachings. One example was a marriage manual, *La Familia Regulada*, that was in the library of Antonio Coronel, a Los Angeles ranchero.[15] It cited scriptural justifications for newly married couples to live apart from their parents, yet "the father-in-law, mother-in-law and other elders ought always to be listened to and respected by young people." And a married woman should "have special care to obey, help and be courteous to the parents of her husband." Of all the evils that might infect a marriage, jealousy was the most dangerous, and it was most likely to afflict women. "A poor woman possessed with jealousy does not rest during the day or night," which may result in "the ruin of homes, the wasting of money, the loss of children, the scandal of servants, the bad example to the community and above all, the loss of souls."[16]

An important aspect of the ideal of patriarchal authority involved the subordinate position of women. According to the Iberian Catholic and the pre-Columbian traditions women were supposed to accept absolute male authority in the household. Spanish laws, including the *Siete Partidas*, frequently described the relationship between husband and wife in monarchical terms: "the husband is, as it were, the Lord and Head of his wife." Men were the "rulers," women the "subjects"; husbands were the "absolute monarchs" of the "nation" of the family.[17] During the first half of the nineteenth century some Mexican authors idealized the subordination of women. Sylvia Marina Arrom, reviewing the legal handbooks, didactical tracts, and popular litera-

The Vicente Lugo family standing in front of their home in Bell Gardens, California, ca. 1888. Andrea Lugo, wife of Vicente, seated in center (Vicente Lugo not in photo). Courtesy Los Angeles County Museum of Natural History, Western History Collection, neg. no. 4670.

A Californio family gathering at the Ontivares Ranch near the turn of the century. Courtesy Henry E. Huntington Library, Pierce Collection, neg. no. 4496.

A Hispano family near Mora, New Mexico, representative of those who were forced to leave their communal farms and migrate to urban centers. Courtesy Museum of New Mexico, neg. no. 22468.

Family of Santiago Tafolla and Anastacia Salinas de Tafolla. Courtesy of The Benson Library, University of Texas, Austin, The Tafolla Collection.

ture of that era, concluded: "Throughout this literature women's primary functions in society were regarded as those of wife and mother."[18]

In New Mexico and elsewhere on the frontier a code of honor dictated that men should act as guardians of the purity of the female family members. Gutiérrez summarized the sexual basis of this ideal for colonial New Mexico:

> Because nature created women the weaker of the sexes and rendered her helpless to the whims and sexual desires of men, male authority over them was the only means by which shame and the family's honor could be guaranteed.[19]

In California Ignacio Coronel considered the origin of women's status as having biblical foundations. Undoubtedly the church and his peers supported him in his views. In the 1860s he wrote: "The first woman (Eve) did not have any rivals; nevertheless, she wanted to obtain the apple; and ever since then, in a spirit of imitation, women have not ceased to accuse one another of this desire. . . . Man born before woman is thus more noble than she."[20] Accordingly the sexual vulnerability of women dictated that they be closely cloistered within the home. Contacts between unmarried adults of the opposite sex had to be closely watched.

Kathleen Gonzales, who observed Mexican families in San Antonio during the 1920s, noted the persistence of a rigid male authority over women. She wrote that the husband "dictates to his wife what she is to do at all times and in all matters, their friends, dress and many other personal matters are approved or disapproved by her husband."[21] Ideally the husband's authority was never to be resented by the wife, for she accepted the idea of her inferiority. In Gonzales' words, "Reared with the idea that she is inferior to men, she rather likes to be ruled. Since there is little else to hope for, she had dreamed since childhood of home and a husband."[22] In general the women, marrried and unmarried, were prescribed to live within a restricted world of custom and restraint.

A strict separation of male and female roles within the family did not mean, however, that the wife lacked influence over household matters, especially in the rearing of the children. The ideal wife and mother was supposed to be primarily concerned with the management of the *casa* (home), and the husband was expected to defer to her in mundane domestic matters. His sphere of responsibility lay outside the home as a protector and breadwinner.

EXCEPTIONS TO THE PATRIARCHAL IDEAL

The ideals encompassed in the patriarchal tradition were often contradicted by the circumstances of day-to-day life. In central Mexico women's position varied according to the socioeconomic status of their families, with wealthy women having relatively more freedoms than the poorer. The Spanish legal system, intent on guarding property, family honor, and *limpieza de sangre*, gave women a number of rights which made them juridically equal to men. Women could inherit property and titles, testify in court, and sign contacts. Spanish laws gave married women the right to limit their husband's control of their dowry, and single women, especially widows, had a good deal of economic independence which was supported by the law. Throughout the colonial period women could be found active outside the home in businesses, sharing ownership and management obligations with their husbands or as independent entrepreneurs. This was true for both the upper and lower classes.

Colin MacLachlan and Jaime Rodríguez, while finding that colonial Mexican society was patriarchal and that "once expelled from the protective network of the family women had no place in decent society," concluded that Mexican women probably had more legal rights than elsewhere in the world. In their view:

> Spanish law was progressive and more cognizant of women's rights than most legal systems. As a result, colonial Mexican women enjoyed more rewarding lives than most of their contemporaries in other parts of the world.[23]

While this may have been true in the seventeenth century, it became less true "as Mexican society evolved social mores and legal restrictions circumscribed women's roles."[24] In the nineteenth century, for example, Mexican legistators adopted the Napoleonic code which severely restricted women's rights, and patriarchy found new support.

Mexican and Mexican-American history is full of examples of women who deviated from the submissive ideal. The first novel written in the New World, *La Monia Alferez,* was based on the real life story of Doña Catalina de Erazu, a dropout nun in colonial times who became a famous sword fighter and muleteer (*arriero*).[25]

Mexican authors have produced hundreds of historical biographies of famous and heroic women. A rich folklore and literature has emerged around such women as Doña Marina or La Malinche, Cortez's mistress; Sor Juana Inez de la Cruz, a nun who was an outstanding poet in colonial times; Doña Josefa Ortiz de Domínguez or La Corregidora, a heroine of the Wars of Independence; and Las Soldaderas, the women who fought in the Mexican Revolution of 1910.[26]

On the Spanish and Mexican frontiers there were scores of lesser known women who were historically prominent exceptions to the patriarchal ideal.

In the 1770s María Feliciana Arballo y Gutiérrez, a rugged widow, accompanied De Anza on his second expedition to California. Doña Eulalia Fages, spirited wife of the governor of California in the 1780s, apparently influenced the political history of the province. In the 1820s Doña Josefa Hererra, the wife of the Spanish governor of Texas, drilled troops and debated politics with the pueblo government during her husband's absence. Juana Birones de Miranda was one of sixty Californio women who managed, through their determined efforts, to obtain Mexican land grants prior to 1848.[27]

The pattern of these biographies suggests that there were socially acceptable ways in which women, particularly those of the upper classes, could act outside the rigid limits of the patriarchal family. In reality women's roles were not always circumscribed by family obligations.[28] From colonial times there was limited social support and even an idealization of certain kinds of female involvement beyond the confines of *la casa*. Most often nuns and aristocratic women, held up as models of women, managed to achieve fame and influence in nontraditional ways.

The Mexican Wars of Independence and the chaotic years of the Mexican Republic (1821-1848) did much to liberate women and challenge older patriarchal values. The displacement of large masses of the population by war, famine, and political turmoil increased the likelihood that women would be active in nondomestic arenas. Currents of revolutionary egalitarianism coming from Europe and the United States tended to increase the acceptability of romantic love in personal relations and to weaken the importance of monarchical imagery in marriage.[29]

On the frontier women and men worked and fought side by side out of necessity. A chronic scarcity of marriageable non-Indian women increased the bargaining power of Spanish and Mestizo women, especially those who were emigrants from central Mexico. In New Mexico, after the 1770s, higher rates of illegitimacy and an increasing equality in the ages of marriage partners demonstrate the weakening of parental controls. Among the New Mexican aristocracy and even among the lower classes intermarriage and concubinage with foreigners increased, representing a loosening of the mechanisms of social control. The traditions of patriarchal authority, respect for elders, and female subordination did not disappear, however, but coexisted with new notions of romantic love and individualism.[30]

In California the ideology of patriarchy seems to have undergone significant erosion during the gold rush years due to increased economic opportunities which drew many young adults away from their families and introduced them to new ways of life. The gold rush immigrations resulted in increased violence, gambling, drunkenness, and prostitution. Little wonder the Californios frequently complained that all this was destroying their older ways of life. The social ambience and sudden wealth of these early years of the American era made it increasingly difficult for parents to control their children.[31]

Thus even before the widespread urban and industrial transformations of the American era, the ideology and value system associated with the patriarchal family was hardly a monolithic one. The tradition of the juridical protection of women's rights, the emergence of romantic love, the necessity for frontier egalitarianism, and the idealization of certain female roles outside the home were themes which had their origin in pre-American times.

PATRIARCHY AND HOUSEHOLD STRUCTURE

The data on household organization in the urban Southwest provides a means of measuring deviations from the ideals of patriarchy during the late nineteenth century. Since male dominance within the household depended on the subordination of women and children, it is instructive to analyze the changing patterns of households where women were relatively independent of men. Table 4 illustrates variations in the proportions of female-headed households in Los Angeles, Tucson, Santa Fe, and San Antonio. With the exception of San Antonio, all the urban areas showed increases in matriarchal female-headed households during the thirty-year period 1850-1880 (see Table 4). By 1880 in all towns more than 25 percent of all Spanish-surnamed households were headed by women. By this time there was little geographical variation in the distribution.[32]

Barbara Laslett, in her study of extended households in Los Angeles of 1850, found that females were more likely than men to be the head of augmented families, that is, those who had relatives and others as members. She explained this pattern by noting that California's community property laws guaranteed married women the resources (land) to maintain extended families. Laslett hypothesized that children and older relatives were willing to stay in female-headed homes because of ties of affection as well as the authority the promise of landownership conferred on the mother. By 1870, however, this

TABLE 4

The Percentage of Female-Headed Households among Mexican Americans in Four Southwestern Towns, 1850-1880

	Los Angeles	Tucson	Santa Fe	San Antonio
1850	28.9	–	25.9	36.7
1860	27.4	–	28.4	30.6
1870	37.7	17.6	31.7	33.9
1880	31.1	33.1	27.0	28.8

situation had changed, so that women were more likely to head nuclear families with children. This Laslett attributed to shifts in women's job opportunities; as women's access to wealth, through property and paid labor, constricted, so too did their ability to maintain extended households.[33] A review of the data on female-employment patterns, specifically the employment of female heads of households, indicates that this explanation is only partially true (see Tables 6 and 7). Employment among women heads of household in all four southwestern towns increased after 1860 as did the prevalence of matriarchy (women-headed households) among Mexican Americans elsewhere in the urban areas of the Southwest.

The closest comparison to the pattern of matriarchal families among Mexican Americans is the social history of the black family in the nineteenth century. Various researchers, using federal census data, have found higher percentages of black female-headed households than of European immigrant groups. For example, in 1880 30 percent of black families in Altanta, Georgia, were matriarchal. From 1850 to 1880 in seven cities along the Ohio River the percentage of black female-headed families ran between 27 and 30 percent. United States census figures from 1900 to the present continue to report higher incidences of female-headed households among blacks than among European immigrant groups.[34]

Revisionist historians argue that the institution of slavery did not destroy the black nuclear family and cause these high rates of matriarchy. They point rather to the effects of persistent poverty. Indeed, most black families before and after 1865 continued to be two-parent households as Herbert Gutman and Elizabeth Pleck have pointed out.[35] Gutman found that the matriarchal black family was more common in urban areas and that "most of these father-absent households were the result of the deaths of husbands and the surplus of adult Black women to men." The percentages of female-headed households in the urban southern towns of Mobile, Richmond, Beaufort, and Natchez ranged from 26 to 31 percent of all black households.[36]

There were some immigrant groups, however, whose experience with family-headed households duplicated that of Mexican Americans and blacks. Laurence Glasco found that about 25 percent of the Irish immigrant women who were not living with a husband were heads of separate households in Buffalo, New York, in 1855.[37] When random samples of families are compared, while controlling for economic class, much of the difference in matriarchy by race, national origin, or ethnicity disappears. Among the urban poor, especially those who were immigrants or migrants from rural areas, unemployment and the difficulties and temptations of urban life seem to have been a primary cause of the breakup of nuclear families.[38]

Regardless of the shifts in real and potential wealth among Mexican-American women, they were far from trapped within the confines of a male-

dominated family. As heads of their own households, they were relatively independent of male supervision, even if their husbands were only temporarily
absent.

Declining job opportunities probably caused many married men to
leave their families to look for work. Thus the rates of unemployment for
men are roughly correlated with the patterns of female-headed families in the
four urban towns (see Table 5).[39] The types of jobs available to Mexican-
American men kept them away from their families for long periods of time.
Arrieros (or teamsters), cartmen, wagon drivers, and drovers as well as
miners, vaqueros, and farmworkers could expect, by the nature of their occupation, to be periodically absent from their families. Day laborers might
have to migrate long distances to find work, leaving their families behind until they succeeded in establishing a new residence.

A prime example of this was the case of the Mexican miners in southern
Arizona in the 1880s. The introduction of mechanization in the gold, silver,
and copper mines forced hundreds of men out of work. Many of them opted
to go "placering" along the Gila and Colorado rivers.[40] The entrance of the
railroads into the Southwest in the 1870s and 1880s disrupted the patterns of
work for hundreds of *arrieros*. Many men left their families to search out
short-hauling contracts in areas not yet served by the railroad or to search for
new jobs. Thus the marginalization of the work force, described by Barrera
in chapter 2 above, had a direct impact on family life.

Evidence from Los Angeles in the nineteenth century indicates that differential mortality rates also may have affected the incidence of female-
headed households. During the period 1877-1887 men in the prime age groups,
twenty to forty years, had a death rate almost twice that of females.[41] The
dangers associated with mining and construction work probably created many
widows elsewhere in the Southwest. But abandonments, both temporary and
permanent, were a more frequent cause of the rising incidence of female-
headed families. This, of course, was intimately bound up with the changing
nature of the economy.

TABLE 5

*The Percentage of Males Ages 20-59 Unemployed
among Mexican Americans, 1850-1880*

	Los Angeles	Tucson	Santa Fe	San Antonio
1850	23.0	–	15.9	15.3
1860	6.7	–	23.2	19.7
1870	12.3	13.9	26.0	22.3
1880	11.4	19.2	10.3	10.4

In 1864 María Josefa Bandini de Carrillo, a member of a landholding family in Santa Barbara, described the hard times which had forced members of her family to leave home to look for work. "We cannot live here," she wrote, "There are days upon days that we spend without eating, and without hope of leaving here." She related how her brothers finally set out as migrant workers. "I believe that they will first go to Los Angeles and, if they do not find work, they will go to San Francisco more to the north."[42] But things were not much better for the Californios in northern California. In 1869 Mariano Vallejo, a ranchero who had once been wealthy, explained why he was forced to consider leaving California to seek work in Mexico "not because I want to, but out of necessity. I must earn livelihood and meet my obligations as a father and provider."[43]

One example of how economic necessity forced the temporary absence of husbands from their wives and children is the example of James Tafolla in South Texas. Born in 1837 in Santa Fe and orphaned at a young age, James' first wife died shortly after he was married. In his second marriage he supported his mother-in-law and one child. After a few years a shortage of work forced him to leave home fo several months. He traveled across the border to Mexico where he found work with his brother-in-law. After a period of more than half a year he returned to Texas with a small stake.[44]

Experiences like that of James Tafolla undoubtedly were duplicated elsewhere in the Southwest. In many cases, as was true in Tafolla's, female-headed households were indicative of migration patterns among the males. Albert Camarillo, in reviewing the labor history of four nineteenth-century barrios in Southern California, found that the displacement of workers from traditional occupations forced many men to seek part-time and seasonal work outside the state.[45] This did not necessarily mean, however, that while the men were at home, between harvests or jobs, that they did not expect their women to live up to their patriarchal expectations. But during the male absence the women undoubtedly had wide authority and independence in domestic as well as nondomestic matters.

The Mexican-American experience with matriarchy differs substantially from that of European immigrant groups. Among the Italians the cultural traditions and social pressures within the immigrant community were powerful enough to prevent widespread male desertion of spouses. But again differences in the economic environment seem crucial for understanding this difference. Unlike many Mexicano and Mexican-American men, Italian men found jobs in industrial factories located near their homes. Virginia Yans McLaughlin reported that in 1905 only 4 percent of 2,000 first-generation immigrant families were female-headed. Yet there were some similarities with the Mexican-American experience, since many Italian families were first preceded by the husband's migration to America. The proportions of female-headed households in Italy probably rose during the period of their migration. Only in America, with the family reunited, did it appear that the Italian family was more stable than that of the Mexican American.[46] The arguments that the Italian family was usually cohesive and that this was a cultural manifestation fail to take into account differences in migration and economic opportunities.[47] Among Mexican Americans, poverty, unemployment, and social dislocation were as prominent as among Italian immigrants, yet social control over abandonment was not evident. Perhaps Mexican-American men felt more secure about leaving their spouses and children behind, assured their extended kin and friends would take care of their family while they were gone. Moreover, the Southwest was not a strange and forbidding country to them. As the decades progressed, however, more and more women who were heads of households were forced into the job market. Obviously, the kinship support system increasingly failed to meet their needs.

FEMALE EMPLOYMENT AND MATRIARCHAL FAMILIES

This raises the issue of female employment as a way in which traditional roles expected of women changed. As can be seen in Table 6, only a very small portion of all eligible women in any given census year were employed outside the home. There was, however, a noticeable trend of more and more women entering the job market as the century progressed. A very small number found employment as nurses, owners of small shops, as secretaries or clerks, and in other white-collar jobs. A larger number, but still a small percentage, worked in skilled jobs as hat makers, seamstresses, and cooks. The majority of employed women, however, worked in unskilled jobs as washerwomen, laundresses, or servants.

This pattern of increasing female employment, even on a very modest scale, continued into the next century. Camarillo discovered that in Santa

TABLE 6

The Percentage of Employed Mexican-American Women
Ages 20-50 in Four Southwestern Towns, 1850-1880

	1850	1860	1870	1880
N of Sample	546	760	1129	1230
Professionals	0	.1	.1	.5
Mercantile	0	.1	.1	.4
Skilled	.4	1.4	.3	1.8
Unskilled	.9	7.0	7.0	7.8

Barbara and San Diego in 1910 between 15 and 16 percent of all adult women worked outside the home.[48] It is impossible to determine how many women worked in part-time jobs or in seasonal ones with their families as part of the agricultural work force, but many probably followed the crops with their families.

Women were most obviously part of the casual labor pool in the markets of the public plazas. These *mercados*, a vital part of the economic and social life of the four pueblos prior to the American era, after 1848 continued to be the nucleus of the barrio culture. Many women worked as part-time *vendadoras* selling foods, handicrafts, and a variety of household wares. The Mexican markets in Los Angeles, Tucson, Santa Fe, and San Antonio soon became tourist attractions for the Americans who wanted to partake of the "exotic" life of the Mexican-American population. The "Old Towns," reminders of this era, were places where women were able to earn a few dollars to supplement their family's income. Arnoldo de Leon has described the *vendadoras* of San Antonio: "Young, tastefully dressed *señoritas*, the so called chili-queens, served customers heaping bowls of *chili con carne* and beans, which, with a generous supply of *tortillas* sold for ten cents in the 1880s. . . . Or on occasions *señoritas* performed the Mexican national dances like the hat dance."[49] Some Mexican-American families of that city even converted their homes into restaurants to capitalize on American interest in Mexican cuisine. Their homes became showplaces for women's domestic talents.

The number of women who worked full-time in occupations was surprisingly low, given the increasingly dire economic straits of most families. This was probably because there were only a limited number of opportunities for service-type jobs as laundresses, seamstresses, and the like. Industrial jobs were few and not open to many women, and commercial shops probably had bars against the employment of too many Mexican girls. Moreover, female employment was not really very pronounced, even among European immigrants in eastern cities where there were many more opportunities for full-time jobs. Thomas Kesner, for example, found that in New York in the late nineteenth century only 2 percent of Jewish immigrant wives and only 6 percent of married Italian women had paying jobs. In Buffalo, New York, near the turn of the century, about 25 percent of Polish wives worked outside the home. This was the highest percentage of employment recorded for married women; for other immigrant groups it was much lower. Reviewing this evidence, which seems to contradict the common notion that large numbers of immigrant women were forced into menial jobs, Carl Degler concluded that "at no time did more than 10 or 15 percent of wives of any immigrant nationality work outside the home and usually the proportion was even smaller than that. . . . the propensity of wives to work outside the home is largely an ethnic rather than a class phenomenon."[50]

Among Italian immigrants as among Mexican Americans there were strong prejudices against married women working in jobs which would take them away from their household obligations and give them financial independence, and also cast doubt on their husband's ability to support a family. Mario García, who studied the Mexican immigrants of El Paso during the period 1880 to 1920, found that among married immigrant women "no mothers, and almost no daughters, most being too young, worked outside the home." The same was true for the urban Mexican-American population in other towns of the Southwest before the turn of the century. There were, however, some important exceptions.

Table 7 presents clear evidence of the effect that the economy had on family structure. Women with children but no husband were progressively forced to enter the job market because they lacked a wage-earning spouse or because relatives were unable to provide entirely for their needs. These women were more likely to be employed than either married women with spouses present or single women without families. Surprisingly fewer and fewer women who lived as relatives within extended families became job-holders as the decades progressed. This indicates that the formation of extended families was not entirely related to economic pressures. Female employment was a strategy for the survival of matriarchal, not nuclear or extended, families.

The reality of women working and being heads of families was bound to challenge the traditional male expectations regarding patriarchy. But then it would be wrong to assume that all women were equally affected by these changes. The overwhelming majority were not, and the upper classes hardly at all. The small but significant Mexican-American middle and professional class did not experience many broken families, and, of course, they were the ones to whom patriarchal ideals were most sacrosanct.

TABLE 7

The Household Status of Employed Mexican-American Women Ages 16-59, 1850-1880

	1850	1860	1870	1880
N of Sample	7	66	61	129
Head of HH	28.6	43.9	47.5	39.5
Spouse	14.3	7.5	14.8	3.1
Child (under 21)	14.3	15.1	14.8	23.3
Relative	14.3	10.6	3.3	3.1
Unrelated adult	14.3	22.7	19.7	24.8

Patriarchal values did not disappear under the impact of economic and political changes in the urban Southwest. Men continued to expect their women to be submissive and their daughters to remain cloistered in the home. But in this respect they were not much different from the majority of American men, who had their own kind of patriarchal ideology, sometimes described as the "Cult of True Womanhood." This image of the ideal woman, expressed in the popular and religious literature of the nineteenth century, held that "True Women" had four attributes, "piety, purity, submissiveness, and domesticity." Women were held hostage in the home to all the virtues which men held in high esteem but neglected in everyday life.[52]

The idealization of the domestic woman has been seen as one of the main characteristics of the emerging middle-class American family.[53] In this regard the Mexican and Latin-American families had been "modern" for hundreds of years. For them family life increasingly became a mixture of the old and the new values regarding paternal authority and the proper sphere for women. Increasing poverty and economic insecurity intensified the pressures on Mexican-American nuclear families and led to increased matriarchy and working single mothers. As a result the ideology of patriarchy found less confirmation in everyday life. As a system of values and beliefs, however, it continued to exist.

CHAPTER 4

Varieties of Family Cohesion

> *You didn't have to ask for anyone's help. They would just come to you. Whenever my mother had a child, the house would be filled with other women who would take care of us children, cook for her, bathe her and the baby, help her in every possible way.*
> –Reminiscence of a woman from South Texas in Foley, Mota, Post, and Lozano, *From Peones to Politicos: Ethnic Relations in a South Texas Town 1900-1977*, p. 59

CONTEMPORARY SOCIOLOGISTS studying the Mexican-American family have found that *la familia* among the Spanish speaking is often a broad and encompassing term, not one limited to a household or even to biologically related kin. Close bonds of affection and assistance among members of the family household and a wide network of kinfolk have been found to be one of the most important characteristics of Mexican-American family life.[1] The network of *la familia* usually includes a number of *compadres*, or coparents, established through rituals of *compadrazgo* (god parenthood). This family, conceived in its broadest sense, is often an important source of emotional and economic support. Family members are expected to be warm and nurturing, and to be willing to provide security for one another throughout their lives. Individuals, as members of a family, whether in a nuclear household or as members of an extended network, are expected to place their personal welfare second only to the welfare of *la familia*.[2] While there is some debate over the exact structural form this extended *familia* has taken in present-day Mexican-American society, most experts agree that it is a pervasive characteristic of familial life.[3]

This chapter is concerned with the interplay of economic and cultural forces as they have affected kinship networks and family solidarity. The approach taken here is similar to the one in the previous chapter: it is an attempt to compare the ideology of family solidarity with the empirical evidence of household structures. The Mexican-American experience within the extended family is contrasted with that of Anglo-Americans and offered as a way to evaluate significant differences and similarities between the two groups. Without entering into an analysis of contemporary sociological literature regarding Mexican-American family solidarity and kinship support, my concern here is rather to describe something of this phenomenon in times past. A later chapter will discuss contemporary aspects of Chicano family life in comparison to what we know about the nineteenth century.

THE ORIGINS AND DEVELOPMENT OF FAMILISM

Some have argued that familism, or the values, attitudes, beliefs, and behaviors associated with the Mexican-American extended family, has its roots in the pre-Hispanic social world. The Mexica-Aztec family emphasized the individual's subordination to community-defined norms of behavior. Rigid sex roles were determined at birth, and women were regarded as subordinate to men and morally weak. The emphasis in rhetorical orations was on the family's role in promoting proper ritual behavior, maintaining honor, and fostering self-control.[4] The community *calpulli* system of clan organization and the Aztec-Nahua teachings regarding male and female family obligations influenced the Mestizo family, which emerged as a result of mixture with Europeans.[5] Indeed, in many respects the Mexica-Aztec attitudes surrounding family life closely resembled the Iberian-Spanish. The social transitions under Spanish domination in the succeeding centuries reinforced the older pre-Columbian values, while accommodations resulted in a renewed sense of the importance of the Indian community.[6]

Iberian-Spanish family ideology also influenced Mexican and subsequently Mexican-American values regarding familism. A 700-year-long conflict with the Moors, who invaded and occupied Spain in the eighth century, heightened the importance of family honor and pure lineage. Struggles between Spanish families over the privileges, titles, and lands that were gained during the reconquest reinforced the importance of family solidarity. A close and prolonged contact with the Moors and Jews in Spain loaded a family's claim to *limpieza de sangre*, or pure blood, with religious and political connotations. In the New World the Spanish attempted to preserve their concept of honor and pure descent by regulating racial mixture. By the laws embodied in the *Regim de Castas* they ranked various degrees of race and ethnic mixture with the supposedly pure Spanish. Family status came to be associated with the degree to which its members had intermarried with "inferior" castes.[7]

The psychological and social meanings of kinship and family bonds differed according to a family's class position. For the landed aristocracy in Mexico and in Spain a continuity in the inheritance of real property, titles, and social status was of utmost importance. For the landless poor the extended *familia* served more as a form of social insurance against hard times. On Mexico's far northern frontier the paternalistic hacienda system was less well established, and the benevolent institutions of the church and state were not well funded or organized. For the poor in this agrarian and pastoral society family solidarity was a necessity, involving the widest possible links with members of the community. The extended family was essential to provide for protection in a hostile environment.[8]

One way that families enlarged their ties to others in the community was through *compadrazgo*. The custom of god parenthood made nonbiologically related individuals of a community members of the extended family. *Compadrazgo* evolved in Mediterranean folk custom as a formal ritual sanctioned by the Catholic Church. Godparents were required for the celebration of the major religious occasions in a person's life: baptism, confirmation, first communion, and marriage. At these times *padrinos*, or godfathers, and *madrinas*, or godmothers, entered into special religious, social, and economic relationships with the godchild, or *ahiado*, as well as with the parents of the child with whom they became *compadres* or *comadres*.[9] In the ideal, *padrinos* acted as coparents to their *ahiados*, providing discipline and emotional and financial support when needed. They could expect from their godchildren obedience, respect, and love in return. As *compadres* they were expected to become the closest friends of the parents and integral members of the extended family.

Historical evidence of *compadrazgo* is scattered throughout the letters and reminiscences of the Spanish-Mexican frontier aristocracy in the nineteenth century. In 1877, for example, Antonio Coronel in Los Angeles remembered that "the obligations of the godparents was that they should take the place of the parents should they (the parents) die."[10] In their private correspondence the aristocracy sometimes referred to their *padrinos* and *madrinos* as mother (*madre*) and father (*padre*). They expressed obligations to behave toward these kinfolk much in the same manner as they would toward their biological parents. Frequent visits, celebration of namesake saint days (*mañanitas*), anniversaries, and intimate communications with godparents were part of an *ahiado's* normal family life.[11]

Visiting between *comadres* was an important social activity among women, especially in the more isolated rural regions. They often took care of one another's children and had a good deal of authority over them. A teenage diarist in San Antonio during the 1880s told of numerous visits of her mother's *comadre*. Often the *comadre*, Adina de Zavala, stayed with the girl's family for many days.[12] These visits of relatives, *comadres*, and their families were, for this young girl, high points in what she thought was a drab and cloistered life. And so it must have been for many others in a frontier society where so many were so poor and where there were so few amusements for women outside the home environment. Visiting among the families of friends and relatives was perhaps the major form of recreation. Extended family members including *compadres* and *comadres* also were important during times of crisis. When a woman gave birth or a family member took seriously ill, *comadres* and female relatives automatically came to each other's assistance. Sometimes they even moved their own families into the stricken household on a temporary basis.[13] James Tafolla, living in South Texas during the 1870s and 1880s, recalled that on more than one occasion relatives came to live with his family when he and his wife were sick.[14] And Juan Bandini sadly noted in his diary of having to send his two daughters to live with his sister during a period of personal financial hardship.[15] In these cases and in others it was expected and often true that extended family members would help when needed. Adina de Zavala, a San Antonio matron, expressed this feeling in her journal entry of 1882 when she wrote: "My life is only for my family. My whole life shall be worth while [sic] if I can render happy and comfortable the declining years of my parents and see my brothers safely launched on life's troubled seas."[16]

An important way that families strengthened their support networks outside the immediate kinship arena was through their participation in *mutualistas,* or mutual-aid societies. In both rural and urban areas Mexican Americans sought to insure themselves against the tragedies of death and economic disaster by forming societies where they could pool their meager resources. Most often these *mutualistas* became sources of emergency loans as well. Families often used *mutualistas* like community banks. The mutual-aid societies frequently became a focal point for the community's social life by organizing dances, fiestas, fund raisers, and the like. Occasionally, in conjunction with the Mexican consular offices, they played an important role in helping labor unions during strikes. They also provided help for recent Mexican immigrants by providing temporary housing, food, and job assistance.[17]

The *mutualista* movement among Mexican Americans appears to have been particularly strong in the cities and towns of the Southwest during the late nineteenth century. In Los Angeles La Sociedad Hispano Americana de Beneficia Mutual was established in 1875, and La Sociedad Progresista Mexicana in 1883. In San Antonio Mexicanos organized La Sociedad de la Unión in 1886 and La Sociedad de Protección Mutua de Trabajadores Unidos in 1890. These are only a few examples of the many mutual-aid associations which sprang up throughout the last part of the nineteenth century.

A detailed examination of the books of at least one mutual-aid society, that of La Sociedad de la Unión in San Antonio in 1886, reveals that members paid monthly dues of about one dollar and that the average accumulated savings ran between 80 and 90 dollars. Members of La Unión frequently borrowed small sums against their accumulated dues.[18] Thus, the society and others like it acted as community banks, extending credit to persons who normally would have found it difficult to get loans from banks.

Perhaps the largest and longest-lived *mutualista* was La Alianza Hispano Americana in Tucson.[19] Organized in 1894 by Carlos Ignacio Velasco, editor of *El Fronterizo*, and Mariano Samaniego, a wealthy freighter and rancher, La Alianza grew rapidly from a dozen or so subscribers to over 17,000 members in eight states. Like the other mutual-aid societies of that era, La Alianza was at first exclusively a men's organization, but families also participated in the social activities. By 1913 La Alianza began to admit women to equal membership in the organization.

Mutual-aid societies proved to be very popular among the Mexican immigrants who had regular wage-paying jobs. As fraternal societies they provided the kind of support that was often difficult for poor families to provide—a guarantee of a decent funeral was important for the Catholic immigrants. The societies also provided an important source of entertainment and social activities for members of the working class. They were often a common meeting ground for the immigrant and the native-born Mexican Americans. Not incidentally the *mutualistas* provided status and some economic security for those who were considered aliens by the majority society.

FAMILISM AND THE EXTENDED HOUSEHOLD

Anglo-Americans were frequently impressed by the warmth and closeness they found in Mexican-American families. Frederick Law Olmstead in 1858 observed that "their manners toward one and another is engaging and that of the children and the parents most affectionate." A Protestant missionary in south Texas wrote that the "Tejanos were kindly in home life, particularly to the aged, and clannish to a degree whole families of several generations occupying one hut."[20] A closeness of affection characterized Mexican-American families in the nineteenth century. The roots of this family cohesion, as an emotional reality, lay in religious ideologies and folk customs, as well as in a common poverty.

Family cohesion among the poorer classes can best be studied by analyzing household structures in the nineteenth-century censuses. The surviving documents, letters, and diaries of the Spanish speaking are usually cryptic and incomplete. In any case they reflect the experience of only a handful of upper-class individuals. The degree to which families were willing and able to provide food and shelter for relatives can be viewed as a significant indicator of how families realized, in part, their commitment to a larger extended network. While almost everyone, except the recent immigrants from

Mexico, had kin who lived in the same town, only a few were likely to have, at any given moment, a household which they shared with relatives. Extended family households were a temporary and impermanent creation of circumstance aristing out of old age, sickness, death, or economic misfortune. Nevertheless, the incidence of extended-family household structures in the general population is one way to determine how families interacted with their *familia*.

Mexican-American households may be defined in several ways. Not all households were composed of married couples with or without children (termed "nuclear families"). It was quite common in the nineteenth century for there to be a wide variety of "others" living in households. Boarders, adopted and visiting children, friends, *compadres*, and servants often shared dwellings with married couples. The "extended-family household" was an ideal type, where nuclear families lived with other individuals who were clearly related to the head of the household. These relatives were not always adults, but more often teenagers and children who had come to live with relatives for a variety of reasons. Extended-family households often had "others" such as relatives on the wife's side of the family, servants, boarders, and friends as well as multiple families. Nuclear families who lived in homes without clearly determined relatives but with these "others" may be called the "nuclear-plus-other" type of household. Those households where apparently none of the individuals were related I have termed "no-family" households.

Within these ideal types a good deal of variation in composition and relationship was possible. A couple could be married, sharing the same last name, or live in *unión libre*. Widows and widowers could live alone, with others or with relatives (a stem family in the last case). Older brothers and sisters could live together with or without children from previous marriages. And great variety of adults in varying numbers and related by *compadrazgo* or distant kinship could be present in all types of households.[21]

An analysis of the proportions of extended households in comparison to "no-familly" households is one way to assess the changing patterns of familism. No-family households were groups of individuals who were obviously living separate from their extended families. The members of these no-family households may have participated in an extended-family network located in the same town or a nearby village or farm. Some may have had nuclear families of their own living in Mexico or elsewhere in the Southwest. But their household status, as boarders, travelers, visitors, transients, or simply unattached individuals, meant that they had weaker ties to family than those individuals who reside with kin. Table 8 shows the relative proportions of extended-family households in comparison to no-family households in the urban Southwest.

Generally, the proportions of extended-family households declined throughout the period. A notable exception to this trend occurred in San Antonio in 1860, where extended households exceeded 27 percent, representing a huge jump from the previous decade. A possible explanation for this unusual increase would be the decade of civil strife in South Texas and Mexico. A series of anti-Mexican riots, the Cart War of 1857, the Cortina rebellion in the Matamoros-Brownsville area in 1859, and the wars of the reform in Mexico (1857-1862) displaced hundreds of families from their ancestral homes in Mexico and the South Texas region.[22] Many Mexicans fleeing the violence in the surrounding countryside may have sought safety with relatives and friends in the comparative security of the large city of San Antonio.

Los Angeles also had a slight increase in extended family households in 1870. This was probably caused by the sudden collapse of the ranching industy in Southern California, which increased unemployment and put pressures on families to consolidate their resources.[23] Barbara Laslett in her study of Los Angeles has found that by 1870 those families that owned real and personal property were more likely to live in extended households than in any others. This had not been the case earlier, indicating that economic pressures were at work.[24]

It should be noted that in Los Angeles and Santa Fe the extended-family household remained about as prevalent in 1880 as it had been in 1850 despite the very different socioeconomic histories of the two towns. Only in San Antonio and Tucson was there a big decline in extended-family households. The expected effect of variations in regional economic development thus did not appear to have an influence on extended-family formation. Indeed, no single set of variables appears to account for these patterns; this underscores the

TABLE 8

The Proportions of Extended and No-Family Households, 1850-1880

	1850	1860	1870	1880
Los Angeles				
No-Family	14.4	26.9	20.6	22.8
Extended	11.5	10.1	15.2	10.2
Tucson				
No-Family	–	–	23.9	16.2
Extended	–	–	15.3	10.3
Santa Fe				
No-Family	11.8	21.7	30.9	14.4
Extended	15.8	15.2	9.4	13.3
San Antonio				
No-Family	17.0	17.8	11.1	18.7
Extended	14.0	27.7	13.2	3.7

truism that family solidarity was a complex of beliefs, attitudes, and customs that varied often irrespective of the economic cycle.

The pattern of no-family households presents a similar problem of explanation. Generally, at any given census year there were proportionally more unattached individuals than people living in extended families. San Antonio, Santa Fe, and Los Angeles had a net increase in no-family households over the forty-year period. There were progressively more unattached "family-less" individuals in the Mexican-American population. This suggests a probable decline in the cohesiveness of the family unit, especially when seen in conjunction with the net decline in extended-family households.

The pattern could also have been caused by increased geographical mobility and by economic pressures. Young men and women left their families of origin to seek adventure and fortune or perhaps in the hope of helping their families to survive. The patterns of the two types of households, the no-family and the extended, seem to have been related. The number of no-family households rose when the proportion of extended households declined. No-family households declined in years when extended households were increasing. It appears that familism, as measured in terms of household organization, acted as a safety valve for temporary dislocations. In Laslett's theoretical view (see chapter 1) the formation of extended families was a strategy for family survival.

THE FORMATION OF EXTENDED-FAMILY HOUSEHOLDS

The formation of extended-family households among Mexican Americans was influenced by a number of factors: socioeconomic class, nativity, age, sex, and marital status of the head of household (see Appendix, Table 29). Over the forty-year period most extended families were headed by married, lower-working-class, native-born men under the age of twenty-five. As the decades progressed, Mexican-born immigrants established more and more extended families, and this indicated a progressive stabilization of immigrant family life. Little wonder that extended-family living was most prevalent among the poor and young: both were more likely to be dependent on relatives for support. The stem family, with young newly married couples living with older parents, existed hardly at all among the Mexican-Americans. Early in the American era single parents with children did not tend to live in extended families. The majority of extended households were of heads of nuclear families with children. A noticeable trend later in the century was for more and more extended families to be headed by single, unmarried individuals without children. Obviously, the nature of family solidarity changed during the decades—away from the nuclear core families to other more complex family relationships.

One case history points out this process. In 1860 Francisco Solano lived
in Tucson with his wife Ramona. The census marshall in that year recorded
that they had six children. Four years later the territorial census taker listed
them as having thirteen children, all with the same last name as the father.
Six years later, in 1870, the Solanos had only seven children, a housekeeper,
and a married son with his common-law wife.[25] Without an exhausting and
probably fruitless geneological search we will probably never know how the
Solano family mysteriously expanded and contracted during these years. In
only ten years the Solanos had progressed from being a purely nuclear family
to being one more complex.

In analyzing the question of why individuals entered into extended-
family relationships, it is useful to compare the Anglo-American population
with the Mexican American. Through this comparison we get a better idea
of the role of culture in family solidarity.

Table 9 shows the decennial proportions of household types in the four
towns for Mexican Americans and Anglo-Americans. As might be expected,
given the value of *la familia* in Mexican culture, Mexican Americans regularly had larger proportions of extended-family households and fewer no-
family households than did the Anglo-Americans. There was very little difference, however, with regard to other forms of household organization.
Anglo-Americans as well as Mexican immigrants, most of whom were recent
arrivals to these southwestern towns, were unlikely to have many extended-

TABLE 9

The Distribution of Mexican-American (MA) and Anglo-American (AA) Households,
1850-1880
(expressed as a percentage)

| | 1850 | | 1860 | | 1870 | | 1880 | |
	MA	AA	MA	AA	MA	AA	MA	AA
N in Sample	(385)	(106)	(687)	(218)	(756)	(376)	(986)	(299)
No-Family	14.5	34.0	24.9	28.0	21.4	30.3	19.8	27.1
Nuclear Family	50.2	42.4	40.9	43.5	45.6	44.7	48.4	45.8
Nuclear plus Other	22.3	17.9	20.8	20.2	19.2	17.0	18.4	20.1
Extended	13.0	5.7	13.4	8.3	13.8	8.0	9.9	7.0

Note: Nuclear-family households are summaries of household types 1-3, and extended-family
households are types 5-8 given in Table 12.

family members and more likely to be single and unattached. The native-born Spanish speaking, however, had historic kinship ties in the region. For them extended-family households accounted for a significant proportion of all types of households until 1880. Over the decades Mexican Americans and Americans became more similar in their family structures. This was largely due to the fact that more and more Anglo-Americans formed extended families, while the proportions of Mexican Americans who lived in these kinds of households remained the same.

Notwithstanding the possibility that it was more difficult for Anglos to create large extended families on the frontier, their proportions of these types exceeded the national averages in the rest of the country except in 1880 (see Table 10). Carl Degler, studying the families who migrated west in the late nineteenth century, found some evidence to show that many Anglo-Americans either brought kinfolk with them or financed a serial migration of relatives from back east.[26] During the late nineteenth century the eastern seaboard cities underwent rapid urbanization and industrialization. The industrial Northeast had the highest percentages of extended families in the nation.

Rudy Ray Seward, who studied this unusual occurrence, believed that economic and residential pressures in these eastern cities sometimes forced families to lure wage-paying relatives to come and live with them.[27] The population east of the Mississippi also felt the demographic effects of the Civil War, which created many broken households and resulted in higher incidences of extended households. Moreover, in the industrial cities newly arriving European migrants tended to cluster along Old World family and town lines, often sharing the same tenements, apartments, or neighborhoods.

TABLE 10

*Mexican-American and Anglo-American Extended Households
Compared to National Trends, 1850-1880*

| | Extended/Multiple Households National Sample* | | | Extended Households | |
| | North East | North Central | South | Southwest | |
				Anglo	Mex. Am.
1850	6.1	2.6	3.4	5.7	13.0
1860	6.8	3.1	5.8	8.3	13.4
1870	7.9	5.2	6.0	8.0	13.8
1880	13.5	9.4	10.5	7.0	9.9

* From Rudy Ray Seward, *The American Family: A Demographic History* (Beverly Hills: Sage Publications, 1978), pp. 130, 131.

By 1880 the proportions of extended families east of the Mississippi reached high levels. These same high levels had existed among Mexican Americans in the urban Southwest for thirty years prior to that time. It is not at all clear that the prevalence of extended families among the Spanish speaking was due to the same factors that were operating in the East. Of all the forms of household organization the extended family in the southwestern cities was most related to ethnicity.[28]

CULTURAL FACTORS IN EXTENDED-FAMILY FORMATION

In considering why it was that Mexican Americans tended to have more extended households than did Anglo-Americans, inevitably the problem of cultural determinism arises. The question of causation is not easily dismissed by simply arguing that because of their cultural traditions Mexican Americans preferred to live with their kin rather than alone or in other types of arrangements. If this were indeed the case, we should have trouble explaining why it was that at no point in the late nineteenth century did the majority of the Spanish speaking live in extended family households. Most lived separate from kin.

One would expect that the kinship organizations of both Americans and Mexican Americans would be disrupted by geographical mobility. Evidence from nineteenth-century western towns on this point suggests that both groups tended to be highly transient. In San Antonio only 32 percent of the total population continued to live in the town between 1880 and 1890.[29] Geographic mobility was most related to socioeconomic status, with the laboring classes being the most geographically mobile. Alwyn Barr, who studied San Antonio during the period 1870-1900, found that only 7 percent of the skilled and unskilled workers continued to live in the city. The rates of persistence were much higher for the middle and upper classes.[30] In Los Angeles only about 11 percent of the Spanish-surnamed population remained in the town during the twenty-year period 1860-1880. Only twenty-two heads of households remained in the town between 1850 and 1880.[31]

There were systematic differences in the composition of Mexican-American and American extended families. Mexican Americans differed most from Anglo-Americans with regard to age and occupational status. After 1860 young Mexican Americans tended to be overrepresented in extended households. For Anglos age was not as important. The young were as likely as the aged to be the relatives residing in households. As can be seen in Table 11, the overwhelming majority of Mexican-American extended-family members were under twenty-nine years of age in every census year. This was not the case for Anglo-Americans.

Unidentified Hispano children ca. 1900. Probably from the upper classes. Courtesy Museum of New Mexico, neg. no. 53813.

A family gathering at a baby's funeral in Tucson, April 21, 1890. Left to right: Feliciano, Librada, Ysidro (kneeling), Leonardo Jr., Diego, Ramona, ???, Leonardo Romero, Sr., and two other children. Courtesy Arizona Historical Society Library, neg. no. 64313.

Refugio (Ruth) Brown, Alejandro Brown, and Refugio Carrizo Brown in a mining camp near Tucson in the late 1880s. Courtesy Arizona Historical Society Library, neg. no. 63025.

Tucson Mexicano children standing with their mother (back turned) by the rear of their home. Note the kitchen which has been added onto the house. Taken March 5, 1899. Courtesy Arizona Historical Society Library, The Reynolds Collection, neg. no. 13295.

That so many young people should have been relatives in these Spanish-speaking families seems unusual given our contemporary notions about the family as a collective source of economic support. Few of these young people could contribute much in the way of wages to the households. Some of the older teenagers and young adults worked outside the home to supplement their family's income. But in the census the majority of the young adults were classified as unemployed. Of course there were other ways a young person could help the family, even though not employed in a full-time occupation. He or she could take part-time care for younger children and perform housework, freeing others to enter the job market.

Some of these young relatives probably were newly married spouses who were just starting out and who needed a place to live. In the Spanish and Mexican eras it had been a custom for newlyweds to reside with the bride's parents for a period of time.[32] Other young members of extended households were probably relatives who may have been visitors or orphans.

Indeed, visiting was probably responsible for a significant number of these child relatives. The great distances which sometimes separated extended family members led to protracted visits whenever they got together. In the early 1900s, for example, Dolores Aguirre sent her daughter to visit relatives in El Paso, Texas. Lupe stayed with her aunt Dolores P. de Bennet three weeks and then was sent to visit her cousins in Juárez for another month.[33] Many of the wealthier families had guest rooms that they used to put up friends and relatives during their stays. The Ochoa family in Tucson, for example, had three or four rooms set aside for this purpose. The house was reportedly always full of friends and relatives, who visited for long periods of time.[34] A general ethic of hospitality and sharing was traditional in Spanish-speaking society. This had the domestic result of reducing isolation and integrating family members with a great variety of others. Mutual respect and formality insured a degree of privacy. By and large the family's home was available

TABLE 11

Age Characteristics of Mexican-American and Anglo-American Relatives Living in Extended Households, 1850-1880
(expressed as a percentage)

Age Categories	1850		1860		1870		1880	
	MA	AA	MA	AA	MA	AA	MA	AA
1-19	55.2	25.0	57.5	56.5	58.6	19.2	57.9	50.0
20-29	23.2	37.5	24.6	21.7	14.8	19.2	22.2	7.1
30-49	17.3	37.5	11.0	13.1	19.5	34.6	11.1	14.3
50-	4.3	0	6.0	8.7	7.1	27.0	8.8	28.6

and open to almost everyone of good will. To be sure, the ability of a family to support visitors depended on its economic resources, although even the poorer classes were quick to share their meager food and humble abodes with visitors and relatives.

It may be stretching the point to call these households "extended" when many had this structure only because of the presence of young visitors, cousins, siblings, adopted children, stepchildren, and distant kinfolk. The presence of these youthful relatives also suggests that some nuclear families were unable to provide a supporting home environment for children.

Judge Benjamin Hayes recounted one example of how children came to be displaced from a nuclear family. In 1856 he told the story of a native California woman who came to him for legal advice. Months earlier she had applied for a divorce from her husband, who had been mistreating her. At this time the husband along with the children moved into his mother's home. Subsequently the couple had been reconciled, but the mother-in-law refused to forgive her son's wife, and she would not allow her to have her children back. "This mother (the mother-in-law) fired with wrath whenever the subject was mentioned, and warned the son that if he received his repentant wife she would give him her maldiction, a mother's curse, a wish that he might go out upon the earth in rags, with neither bread to eat nor water to drink, a dire maldiction dreaded by the son with a terror he cannot overcome, for it appears that Religion had no exorcismal value."[35]

The story of the wrathful mother-in-law indicates how much influence parents in Mexican-American society had over their married children's lives. From the mother-in-law's perspective, her son's wife had violated a taboo against divorce and thus was not worthy of raising her own children. Stories like this illustrate the importance of tradition and ideology in family life. It also points out the occasional role that culture, and not incidentally emotion, played in breaking up nuclear families.

COMPARISONS WITH OTHER EXTENDED HOUSEHOLDS

Economic factors seem to have been relatively more important in the formation and maintenance of Anglo-American extended households. Most relatives in Mexican-American extended households were unemployed or under the age of 19. But in every census year except 1880 proportionally more Anglo relatives tended to have wage-paying jobs (see Appendix Table 30). Thus American extended households tended to benefit economically from the incomes of their relatives. This was not true of the majority of Mexican-American households. For Anglo relatives, joining a nuclear family appeared to be more a matter of individual choice and, perhaps, negotiation.

Both the individual and the receiving family stood to benefit. The American extended families appeared less to be the result of crises than economic and perhaps residential convenience.

This point of view is strengthened by evidence from studies of extended families in industrial cities in both America and England during the late nineteenth century. Howard Chudacoff and Tamara Hareven studied Essex County, Massachusetts, between 1860 and 1889 and found that it became progressively more difficult for young people to find inexpensive housing. Newly married couples and young people who were anxious to leave home were pressured by the difficulty of finding suitable housing. For economic reasons they continued to live with their parents. During their prolonged stay they contributed to the family by having jobs. The "empty nest" syndrome was less common among Americans in these cities than later in the twentieth century.[36]

In a separate study of Providence, Rhode Island, during the periods 1864-1865 and 1879-1880, Chudacoff found that more than one-half of the newly married couples either lived in extended families or resided nearby.[37] During the period of their residence with the parents the newlywed couple contributed economically to the household in exchange for cheap lodging. In the Southwest this same process was probably less pronounced, since housing was not as expensive or hard to locate as in eastern cities. For the Anglo-Americans in the fast-developing frontier extended families may well have served as temporary rest stops on the way to new opportunities rather than as a holding pen for frustrated youth. As such the American extended household in the trans-Mississippi West took on more the character of a boarding house.

In his study of English industrial towns during the nineteenth century Michael Anderson found large proportions of "parentless" children living in extended households. The proportion ranged from 28 percent of all kin in the city of Preston to 42 percent of all kin in rural hamlets. Most of these children, Anderson found, were either orphans or from families where the mother had died, for relatives often assumed the raising of orphaned children. "Most of these young men and women," he found, "were already earning and would be thus already keeping themselves and indeed, probably made some useful contribution toward family finances. . . . Many more would soon be doing so in a society where child labor was the norm."[38] This was in contradistinction to the Mexican Americans in the urban Southwest, where much larger proportions of the young were without occupations outside the home.

The evidence surrounding family solidarity among Mexican Americans suggests that the kinship network functioned primarily as a support system during times of crisis. It seems to have served the same function among blacks. In Herbert Gutman's view "extended and augmented families were important 'adaptive strategies' to deal with the poverty most Blacks knew."

Indeed the proportions of extended and augmented families among blacks seem to have increased when more and more families moved to the cities. In 1880 approximately 36 percent of all black households in Mobile and Richmond were extended or augmented. By 1900 samples from the same urban areas showed rates of family extention as high as 59 percent.[39]

In the nineteenth century the extended-family household among Mexican Americans was an important institution, much more so then than now. It functioned primarily as a place to take care of displaced children. Contrary to the contemporary ideal conceptualizations of the Chicano family, there were very few aged *abuelos* and *abuelitas* (grandfathers and grandmothers) who lived with nuclear families. In fact, the probability that the aged would find shelter with the families of their children was greater for Anglo-Americans than it was for Mexican Americans.

Extended households among the Spanish speaking were more important as emotional support systems than was true for other Americans in the West. They were vital to insure the proper rearing of children and were less important as a means of economic security for adults.

THE DIVERSITY OF HOUSEHOLD ORGANIZATION

Neither the majority of Anglo-Americans nor of Mexican Americans lived in extended or in nuclear households. In fact, a great diversity of living arrangements characterized both groups. Table 12 illustrates nine different types of households found among Mexican Americans and Anglo-Americans. Throughout the decades there were few differences between the two groups with respect to the proportions of households containing nuclear, nuclear-plus-other families, or "no-family" households. The most important differences, those that relate how the culture and the economy affected Mexican Americans, were the higher numbers of female-headed households and extended households among the Spanish speaking. The former seems to have resulted primarily from economic pressures, while the latter, the extended-family household, from cultural patterns.

Given the wide diversity of household types and a lack of geographical stability for both Anglo-Americans and Mexican Americans, it seems likely that family solidarity was realized in a great variety of settings, not just in extended-household situations. Fluid and dynamic family structures changed to meet the needs of individuals. The kinds of support and degree of interaction between kin and the members of households varied according to a great variety of factors: the residential proximity of kinfolk, the social status and economic class of the family in relation to kinfolk, the type of relationship to the head of household (biological or fictive), generational differences, and the personality preferenes of individuals.

In sum, it appears that the economic changes in the nineteenth-century urban Southwest did not clearly alter the role of *la familia* as a support network, particularly among the working classes. In fact, for the poorest members of Mexican-American society economic insecurities may have resulted in strengthened bonds of family unity. This was despite the fact that the economy also worked to disrupt traditional familistic behavior, mainly by creating broken homes. The existance of extended housholds which had little economic support from resident kin was evidence that cultural ideals of familism continued to provide strategies for survival during hard times.

TABLE 12

Mexican-American (MA) and Anglo-American (AA) Households
in Four Urban Areas, 1850-1880
(expressed as a percentage)

Household Type	1850	1860	1870	1880
1. Nuclear household with or without children				
MA	27.3	22.9	29.0	33.0
AA	26.4	28.0	32.4	31.8
2. Male-headed household with no wife present, with children				
MA	8.3	6.6	5.0	5.2
AA	11.3	12.8	6.4	8.0
3. Female-headed household with children				
MA	14.3	11.5	11.6	13.8
AA	4.7	2.8	5.9	6.0
4. Nuclear household plus others				
MA	22.3	20.8	19.2	18.4
AA	17.9	20.2	17.0	20.1
5. Extended households				
MA	5.7	7.4	7.8	4.7
AA	3.8	5.0	4.5	4.0
6. Male-headed households without a spouse but with relatives				
MA	2.1	1.7	1.5	1.7
AA	.9	1.4	1.6	.3
7. Female-headed household with relatives				
MA	3.6	2.2	2.2	1.7
AA	0	1.4	1.3	1.7
8. Related adults, no children				
MA	1.6	2.0	2.2	1.5
AA	.9	1.4	1.3	1.7
9. Unrelated adults				
MA	14.5	24.9	21.4	19.8
AA	34.0	28.0	30.3	27.1

CHAPTER 5

Mexican Immigration and Intermarriage

Que dices, chata, nos vamos	*What do you say, snub-nosed;*
Pa' los Estados Unidos	*Shall we go to the United States*
Donde gozan las mujeres	*Where women have a good time*
Al lado de sus maridos?	*Living with their husbands?*

–La de la Nagua Azula (corrido of the 1920s) in
Manuel Gamio, *Mexican Immigration to the United
States* (New York: Dover, reprint, 1981). p. 90.

Y el que niega su raza	*But he who denies his race*
ni madre tiene,	*Is the most miserable creature.*
pues no hay nada en el mundo	*There is nothing in the world*
tan asqueroso	*So vile as he,*
como la ruin figura del renegado	*The mean figure of the renegade.*

–El Renegado (a corrido of the 1920s) in Gamio,
Mexican Immigration to the United States, p. 94.

MEXICAN-AMERICAN FAMILIES were by no means uniform in the ways in which they responded to the many historical changes that transpired after 1848, for the individuals within families have always interpreted and reacted to their social and economic environment in varied ways. Both the Mexican culture and the American economic environment impinged upon the family's structure and ideology. The previous chapters have described how the economy affected the realization of ideals of patriarchy and family solidarity. This chapter examines two important phenomena that were also related to economic changes in the Southwest: Mexican immigration and intermarriage. Immigration from Mexico after 1848 along with shifting patterns of intermarriage with other groups began to create a rich diversity in the social history of Mexican-American families.

The Mexican-immigrant family's experience, with the attendant problems of generational conflict and pressures for assimilation, was an issue of growing importance in the everyday life of Spanish-speaking families in the late nineteenth century. Mexican-immigrant families were likely to be the least Americanized group in Mexican-American society. Segregated by language, residence, and occupation, their family life was more Mexican in ambience than that of the native-born second and third generations. At the opposite end of the cultural spectrum were those families that emerged from intermarriage between Mexican Americans and other groups. These mixed families were a staging ground for new generations of marginal individuals who often lacked a firsthand experience with the language and traditions of Mexican culture. Together the *Mexicano* families and the "mixed" families represented the entry and exit points for individuals within the Mexican-American subculture.

MEXICAN IMMIGRATION IN THE NINETEENTH CENTURY

No reliable estimate exists of the number of Mexican immigrants who came to the United States before the turn of the century. It is almost certain that large numbers crossed the unmarked and unpatrolled border to visit relatives, search for jobs, engage in illicit trade, or escape political and economic oppression in Mexico.

Mexican immigration into California during the gold-rush years was sizable. More than 25,000 crossed the border to enter the golden state between 1848 and 1852. Most of these immigrants and their families came from Sonora and other regions of northern Mexico. In the middle 1850s violence and restrictive laws in northern California forced many of these immigrants to go elsewhere to seek their fortunes. A sizable contingent of Sonorans settled in Los Angeles in the late 1850s and 1860s. This group was so large that the old pueblo became a Mexican barrio, often called Sonora Town by the Anglo-Americans.[1] There are no valid estimates as to how many of these immigrants later left California and became part of the migration of miners into the silver- and gold-mining regions in Nevada, Arizona, and Colorado during the 1860s and 70s. Those who remained in Southern California became a primary source of labor for the rapidly expanding agricultural and construction industries, especially so after the 1882 Chinese Exclusion Act.[2]

The expansion of the silver, gold, and copper mines throughout the nineteenth century increased Mexican immigration to southern Arizona. Charles Poston, a local mineowner, estimated in 1856 that several thousand Mexican miners crossed the border and settled in the mining camps around Tubac, south of Tucson. Mine operators like Poston preferred to recruit whole Mexican families in order to avoid the problems associated with labor transiency. Mexican miners with families were less likely to protest long hours, low wages, and dangerous working conditions. During the 1860s Mexican immigrant miners and their families moved into and out of Arizona following the cycle of mining booms and bursts. By 1870 more than 3,700

Mexican immigrants had settled in the area south of the Gila River.[2] In the next ten years mechanized deep-shaft mining created a new demand for large numbers of Mexican workers, and the Mexican immigrant population of Arizona more than doubled, going from 4,348 to 9,330. Many of the immigrants came from the state of Sonora, and most were peons who sought to escape the debt slavery of the haciendas and mines in Mexico. In 1879 the *Arizona Sentinal* commented:

> Sonora seems to be undergoing a labor crisis. . . . Ten years ago she paid her peons 7 to 10 pesos per month and cotton clothes. Now due to American influence, they want shoes, pants, flannel shirts for which the *hacendado* puts them deeper into debt. But the peons run away.[3]

Wages in the American mines were much higher than in Mexico, averaging between twenty-five and thirty dollars a month along with rations of food. American employers, however, retained the essence of peonage through their control of the company stores and housing.

By the turn of the century the demand for Mexican immigrant labor in Arizona had reached massive proportions, the result of open-pit copper mines and increased farming activity in the Phoenix-Tempe region. In 1901 the editor of the *Bisbee Daily Review* estimated that between 60,000 and 100,000 immigrants were crossing the border annually. *Enganchadores*, or labor contractors, operating out of Tucson did a thriving business through providing workers for the mines and farms. The inflow of these workers into Arizona followed the rail lines. From El Paso they went west by the Southern Pacific Railroad, and from Sinaloa and Sonora they moved north by the Guaymas Railroad. Many of those who first came to work for the railroads or mining companies soon drifted off in search of better jobs in Tucson, El Paso, or Phoenix. Much of the Mexican immigration was thus of a transient sort. In 1901 Arizona's Governor Kirby reported that the immigrants "are passing to and fro all the time between Sonora and Arizona. . . . Most of them work a few months and return to Mexico, but numbers stay from year to year."[5]

Texas shared the longest border with Mexico being adjoined to the populous states of Tamaulipas, Nuevo Leon, Coahuila, and Chihuahua. In the 1860s chronic border violence between Juan Nepumecenio Cortina's followers and the Texas Rangers made life miserable for the Mexican families in South Texas. During the 1860s Cortina waged war on the Confederate Texan forces in the Bownsville area, and after the Civil War his band continued their raids aimed at restoring *Mexicano* control of the region. This violence probably limited the numbers of immigrant families who settled in that region. During the 1870s, however, with the Cortina wars over, a small but steady stream of immigrants began to enter South Texas to escape the increasingly repressive policies of General Porfirio Díaz's government in Mexico.[6] In 1875 the Mexican government lodged a formal complaint alleging that thousands of *peons* were fleeing Mexico to seek refuge in Texas. A Mexican commission found that in a single year a total of 2,572 individuals comprising 812 families had immigrated illegally into Texas. This, they said, had caused a net loss to their Mexican employers of over a million dollars.[7] The illegal immigration of which Mexico complained in 1875 increased in later years as conditions worsened for the *campesinos* and peones.

One example of the impact of Mexican immigration on the cities of the Southwest was the rapid growth of El Paso, Texas. In 1850 El Paso was a sleepy village of fewer than 200 persons located across the Rio Grande from the more populous city of El Paso del Norte (Ciudad Juárez). In the late 1880s the development of commercial businesses and especially of large industries like the American Smelting and Refining Company and the Southwest Cement Company attracted thousands of Mexican laborers to the American side of the river. Oscar Martínez estimated that in the early 1900s over 2,000 Mexican immigrants crossed the border each month during the summer and that by 1907 the figure had climbed to more than 9,000 a month. El Paso's Mexican-born population grew steadily from about 150 persons in 1850 to 321 in 1860, 2,115 in 1870, and 8,848 in 1900.[8] Many of these immigrants moved north from El Paso and settled in the Mesilla Valley in New Mexico. In the latter part of the century Mexican workers were in great demand in construction and rail maintenance. They were the backbone of the sheep and cotton industries in South Texas long before the turn of the century.

The Mexican government grew alarmed over the exodus of its skilled workers into Texas. Since 1877 the official policy had been to encourage the repatriation of Mexican workers from the United States. The continued flow of migration embarrassed the government. Between 1880 and 1910 González Navarro estimated that more than 100,000 Mexicans left their country and that only a few returned to settle on the colonization lands promised by the government.[9] Hoping to stem this flow the Mexican government placed ads in newspapers to publicize the bad treatment given Mexican workers in the United States. The government tried to popularize slogans such as "No vayas a El Paso, porque es dar un mal paso" (Don't go to El Paso, for to do so is to make a bad move) and distributed corridos which emphasized the dangers of leaving Mexico.

No vayas al gringo
no traspases la frontera
buscando el honrado pan.

Si trabajo te dan
te aventarán un centavo
te golpearán como esclavo
y a tu patria humillarán.

Don't go to the gringo
don't cross the border
searching for honorable work.

If they give you work
they will toss you a centavo
and will beat you like a slave
and humiliate your country.[10]

Even the Mexican Catholic Church entered the campaign. In 1904 *El Pais*, a church-oriented newspaper, accused the United States of trying to depopulate the frontier by drawing workers from northern Mexico into Texas, Arizona, and California.[11]

Historical demographers have provided rough estimates of the total number of Mexican immigrants who found their way into the United States in the nineteenth century. Richard Nostrand concluded that about 54,000 came to the Southwest between 1820 and 1900, with most immigrants coming after 1880. Elizabeth Broadbent calculated that 90,000 immigrants entered during the period 1850-1900. Oscar Martínez, arguing that both estimates may have been conservative by a factor of as much as 40 percent, suggests that anywhere between 54,000 and 126,000 Mexican immigrants may have come to the United States by 1900.[12] Ironically, contemporary statistics regarding Mexican immigration in the 1980s are not much better than those which we have for the previous century. In calculating immigration statistics, then as now, a constant source of error has been the fact that many workers and their families crossed the border more than once and were temporary residents in the United States.[13]

MEXICAN-IMMIGRANT FAMILIES: THE ROOTING PROCESS

There was considerable variation in Mexican immigration into the southwestern towns according to geographic region. Santa Fe, which did not have the dynamic economy to attract Mexican immigrants, had the lowest forty-year average of Mexican immigration. In northern New Mexico most of the farming was done on small family or communal plots. Traditionally the *Nuevo Mexicanos* of the Rio Arriba region did not welcome newcomers to their ancestral lands. In the other three towns—Los Angeles, San Antonio, and Tucson— Mexican immigrants comprised a significant portion of the total Spanish-speaking population, ranging from 18 percent in Los Angeles in 1850 to 73 percent in Tucson in 1870. Table 13 summarizes the percentages of Mexican-born in each of the four towns during the forty-year period after 1848. While the proportions varied from town to town and in each census year, there was a similar pattern in the immigrant flow: the Mexican-born population steadily increased up to about 1870 and then fell off slightly by 1880.

Twentieth-century studies on Mexican immigration have suggested that most Mexican workers usually have come to the United States intending to stay only for a short period of time.[14] In the nineteenth century temporary immigration was also prominent owing to the seasonal nature of agricultural and construction work. The most interesting question about this phenomenon, then as now is what has caused these "temporary" workers to remain and become permanent residents.

Part of the answer can be found in the ways in which Mexican immigrants become rooted in the United States through the establishment of kinship and family ties. While an immigrant may have intended to stay only a short time in the United States, he was less inclined to return if he married and had children in the United States. For the twentieth century this "rooting" process through marriage and the raising of a family has been documented in Chicano historical novels and in the autobiographies of the immigrants themselves.[15]

To answer the question of the permanent versus the temporary residence of Mexican immigrant families in urban areas, we can analyze their household composition. The family structure was related to increased Mexican immigrant residence in the United States. Those immigrants who lived in nuclear and more complex types of households were those either who had married and established families in the United States or who had brought their families with them from Mexico. Those immigrants who lived as unmarried individuals in households with relatives or with unrelated adults were undoubtedly more mobile. They were a more temporary group than those living in family situations.

THE HOUSEHOLDS OF MEXICAN IMMIGRANTS AND NATIVE-BORN MEXICAN AMERICANS

The increased number of Mexican immigrants in the Southwest after 1848 corresponded with their establishing more permanent kinds of families. In Los Angeles and San Antonio during the forty-year period progressively increasing proportions of Mexican immigrants lived in families with children. In 1850 only about one Mexican household in four was nuclear in composition. By 1880 this ratio had increased to almost one out of two. Throughout the decades the Mexican immigrant's proportions of extended households and other complex living arrangements were similar to those of the native-born (see Table 14).

Most Mexican immigrants tended to be men between the ages of twenty and fifty working in skilled, laboring, or mercantile occupations. In comparison to the native-born they were poorer and owned less real and personal property. Yet in their family life they shared many characteristics with the second-

TABLE 13

The Percentage of Spanish Surnamed Born in Mexico, 1850-1880

	1850	1860	1870	1880
Los Angeles	18.0	30.6	27.9	19.9
Tucson	–	–	73.4	68.3
Santa Fe	5.3	2.8	3.5	.5
San Antonio	29.9	39.5	40.7	35.1

and third-generation Mexican Americans. They had approximately the same numbers of children per family. They tended to have about the same proportions of nonrelated individuals within their households. And, like the native-born, their wives and daughters did not tend to have wage-paying jobs outside the home. As the century progressed, the socioeconomic differences between Mexican immigrants and the native-born Mexican Americans became less pronounced (see Table 31, Appendix C).

The main differences between the Mexican immigrant families and the native-born Mexican Americans lay in the area of the relative numbers of broken households. The natives had larger proportions of female-headed

TABLE 14

The Household Organization of Native-Born Anglo-American,
Native and Mexican-Born Spanish Surnamed
in Los Angeles and San Antonio, 1850-1880

(expressed as a percentage of all household types)

Type of Household	1850	1860	1870	1880
1. Nuclear (both parents)				
Anglo	26.7	27.2	36.5	36.4
Native SS	26.7	18.8	24.5	30.4
Mexican SS	27.5	26.8	28.0	41.0
2. Male-headed HH (no spouse, with children)				
Anglo	9.3	11.7	5.9	7.1
Native SS	6.3	3.8	3.7	4.1
Mexican SS	13.8	10.1	9.3	8.1
3. Female-Headed HH				
Anglo	4.0	3.1	7.4	7.1
Native SS	18.8	14.7	20.8	16.5
Mexican SS	9.2	9.4	12.1	10.5
4. Nuclear plus Other				
Anglo	21.3	21.6	18.2	19.6
Native SS	22.5	19.5	17.6	16.2
Mexican SS	21.1	19.5	20.1	11.3
5. Extended HH				
Anglo	5.3	7.4	6.4	6.5
Native SS	9.9	12.0	13.9	7.2
Mexican SS	12.8	10.5	11.2	7.7
6. Related Adults				
Anglo	0	1.9	1.5	2.2
Native SS	2.1	2.7	2.8	2.3
Mexican SS	.9	1.4	2.3	.8
7. Unrelated Adults				
Anglo	33.3	27.2	24.1	21.2
Native SS	13.6	28.4	16.7	23.2
Mexican SS	14.7	22.6	16.8	20.6

Note: The category "Anglo-American" includes the native-born and European immigrants.

households than the Mexican immigrants. This pattern may be understood in terms of differences in kinship support systems. The native-born Mexican Americans were better able to provide for women whose men had died or were temporarily absent. Because of their historic ties to the southwestern towns and kin relations, native-born Mexican-American women probably were better able to remain independent of men. Mexican immigrants, however, lacked familiarity with the social environment and an established kinship network, at least in the early years of their migration.

As the decades progressed, native-born Mexican-American women increasingly entered the job market. Mexican women, however, had a more traditional frame of reference. They did not work in occupations outside the home in any great number. In rural Mexico it was less socially acceptable for women to live independently of men, and as a result, in the United States very few Mexican-born women lived alone or without a husband.

Throughout the last part of the nineteenth century the native-born Mexican-American women faced a marriage crisis. There simply were not enough native-born men to go around, and they increasingly sought mates from outside their generational and ethnic group. Perhaps this is one reason why the Mexican-American women were more likely than Mexican immigrant women to have broken marriages. Toward the end of the century the proportion of female-headed households among Mexican immigrants increased. This signaled that they were beginning to experience the same kind of marital problems as the rest of the Mexican-heritage population. By the 1880s Mexican immigrants had established a network of extended kin, and this enabled relatively more women with children to survive independently from their spouses.

Another noticeable difference between the immigrant and native-born families was the higher incidence of male-headed "motherless" households with children. In every census year Mexican immigrants had twice as many single male-headed households with children as the native-born Mexican Americans. The rates of single male parenthood among Mexican immigrants paralleled those of Anglo-Americans. Thus the pattern cannot be explained as being caused primarily by ethnicity or even by low socioeconomic status. Nor can it be understood as arising from serial migration. It would have been highly unlikely for a Mexican husband to have migrated to the United States with his children while leaving his wife behind. The most obvious explanation for this phenomenon would be the death of the wife in childbirth combined with the lack of kinfolk. While the death rates for women nationwide declined throughout the century, in the Southwest, the scarcity of doctors and more primitive living conditions made childbirth particularly dangerous. Moreover, the mortality rate for Mexican Americans both native and immigrant was substantially higher than for Anglo-Americans.[16] The death of a wife for a Mexican immigrant as well as for an Anglo-American meant that they would have to go it alone until they could remarry or send the children to live with relatives. Not having relatives nearby meant that a relatively larger proportion of men would have to endure widowhood with children. Overall, Mexican immigrant families became more like those of the native-born Mexican Americans. The meaning of the patterns of household composition was that the immigrants became more permanent and less temporary residents of the urban barrios. The major differences in their household structure seem to be explicable in terms of the proximity and availability of kinfolk.

MARITAL ASSIMILATION: ENDOGAMY AND EXOGAMY

At the other end of the cultural spectrum from the Mexican immigrants were those individuals who assimilated into non-Mexican cultures, sometimes attempting to improve their social and economic status in the process. Marriage between persons of Mexican heritage and native-born Anglo-Americans or European immigrants was often the most important way that assimilation took place. Historically marriage strategies sometimes have reflected economic pressures on submerged groups. For some Mexican immigrants marriage with higher-status individuals was a way out of poverty, and for the native-born a similar route was open through intermarriage with non-Mexicans.

Milton Gordon, who has written extensively about the social meaning of intermarriage, has identified a number of categories for an analysis. Intermarriage goes by a variety of names in the literature: "exogamy," or out-marriage which follows social norms, and "cacogamy," or out-marriage which violates social norms. Within intermarriage there is the potential for "hypergamy," or a person out-marrying in order to achieve a higher social status, and "hypogamy," when a person out-marries into a lower social stratum.[17] Social class standing and racial prejudice are important factors affecting exogamy. Generally high rates of racial or ethnic intermarriage have been associated with social and geographical mobility, increased education, age (older persons tending to higher rates), birth position (the youngest child tending to intermarry), and religious beliefs (Protestants intermarrying with Protestants and so forth).[18]

Interethnic marriages among Mexican Americans and Anglos can be interpreted as an important measure of the degree to which assimilation occurred. But the mere fact of intermarriage did not always mean a loss of cultural ties to the Mexican culture. Two examples of mixed families illustrate this point.

In 1870 Nathan Appel lived with his wife and six children in the dusty town of Tucson. He was a German immigrant from Prussia who, at age forty-eight, worked as a freighter hauling ore for the local miners. His wife, Victoria, age forty, was a native New Mexican. Originally they had met and married in New Mexico, where they had lived for more than sixteen years raising three children: Adolfo, Viviana, and Honasio. During the Civil War Nathan moved with his family to Sonora to seek his fortune in the new mines that were being opened up there. The Appels lived in Mexico for six years, where three more children—Amelia, Soledad, and Sara—were born. Sometime in the late 1860s Nathan moved to Tucson and bought a wagon to begin his own business.[19]

Ten years later in 1880 an Englishman, Michael White, owned a home on Fort Street in Los Angeles. He lived there with Maria, his native Californio wife and four of their grown children: Jane Courtney, a 46-year-old widow; Jane White, 26; James, 24; and Ester, 22. The elderly father still worked as a farmer on a small plot but the family depended mostly on the wages of the eldest son, James, who worked as a carpenter, and Jane Courtney, who had a job as a hat maker.[20]

These two sketches, taken from the census returns, illustrate the real-life complexities that were involved in interethnic marriages. In the Appel household the first names of the children and the long residence of the family in Mexico suggest that its cultural orientation was more Mexican than Anglo-American. Indeed Nathan Appel himself was an immigrant who probably had not fully given up the language or culture of his European ancestry. In the Appel household German food, language, and traditions mingled with the Mexican culture. More than likely they spoke Spanish in the home. They probably had kinship ties to other Mexican-American families in the Tucson barrio. The Whites, however, were probably more Americanized. Three of their children had English given names, and one of the older children had married a man with an English surname.

Differences in time and place were important for sustaining ethnic identity within mixed marriages. Tucson was culturally a Mexican village in 1870. Los Angeles, however, was a booming commercial city with only a tiny Spanish-speaking population. In Los Angeles there was little support for maintaining the native Californio language and traditions.

The examples of the Appels and the Whites point out the importance of differentiating between the various subgroups in the "Anglo-American" population (see Appendix B). Anglo-Americans in the Southwest included a sizable multiethnic population of European immigrants in different stages of acculturation. The true Anglo-Americans, the American-born and English speaking, were a majority of the non-Mexican population in all the cities of the Southwest after 1848. They controlled the political and economic life of the towns and interacted with the Mexican-American population on different levels, of which intermarriage was perhaps the least important. The European immigrants, on the other hand, were undergoing the same processes of subordination and cultural conflict as were the Mexican Americans. Both the Spanish speaking and the European immigrants had to compete with the native-born Anglo-Americans for cultural and economic hegemony. Hence intermarriage between European immigrants and Mexican Americans was relatively more common than with the native-born Americans. After 1848 streams of Mexican and European immigration met in the Southwest.

ETHNIC ENDOGAMY IN THE MEXICAN ERA

Before the Mexican War Mexican women of upper-class standing entered into marriages with native-born Anglo-Americans and some European immigrants. Jane Dysart, in a study of upper-class Tejano families in San Antonio, found that there were many arranged marriages between Mexicans and high-status Americans. The upper-class Mexican families hoped that inter-ethnic marriages would protect them from loss of political and economic influence.[21] Despite the much stronger family ties of the Mexican women who married Americans, there was a pronounced tendency for the children of these mixed marriages to adopt the language and culture of their American fathers. The second-generation children of these unions were increasingly assimilated, but racial discrimination prevented some of these women and their children from achieving full equality. As Dysart indicated, "Only women and children with Anglo surnames, light skins and wealth had a reasonable chance to escape the stigma attached to their Mexican ancestry. Judging from their actions many of them considered it important, perhaps even necessary, to do so."[22]

Rebecca Craver's study of intermarriage in New Mexico during the period 1821-1846 found a somewhat similar process at work. In New Mexico almost 75 percent of the male foreigners, mostly Anglo-American, resident in the province before 1850 married native Hispano women. Most of these men were American-born. They sought to promote their business and political standing by marriage to natives, but few of them married into aristocratic families. After 1850 the majority of the children of these mixed families married Anglo-Americans and were assimilated. But prior to that time the husbands as well as the children were considered an integral part of Hispano culture.[23]

Those mixed marriages that did occur were occasionally fraught with cultural conflict, but, as Leonard Pitt observed, "The bride's people, especially her father, usually liked their Yankee relative (although they might despise the rest of his "race"), so long as he behaved as a good family man." By the mid-1890s almost every Californio family had daughters and occasionally sons who had married Americans. As in San Antonio the main reason in these marriages was the desire of the Mexican elite to hold onto their social and economic status or of the families from the lower classes to improve their socioeconomic standing.[24]

ETHNIC ENDOGAMY IN THE AMERICAN ERA

As the American population in the Southwest grew and as Mexicans became more and more a numerical minority, racial and ethnic prejudices became more of a barrier to intermarriage. Mexican women, especially those who were dark-skinned and Indian in appearance, were widely regarded by Americans as being of easy virtue and not desirable as marriage partners. Beverly Trullio, in researching the attitudes held by Anglo-Americans toward New Mexican women, found that "the women of mid-nineteenth-century New Mexico failed to escape the stigma of Anglo cultural, political and racial bias. To their Anglo judges, Mexican ladies merely constituted the more attractive element of a quaint and backward populous."[25]

Arnoldo de Leon discovered much the same kind of pejorative feelings about dark-skinned Mexican women among the Anglo-Texans. They regarded Mexican women as being morally defective. The Americans stereotyped them as voluptuous, ardent, promiscuous, and passionate beyond restraint, especially when American men were involved. Mexican women were held to be suitable for passing alliances but not for respectable marriages.[26] At the same time American men generally drew a distinction between "Spanish" and Mexican women. The former they considered as being almost the equal of white Anglo-women or southern belles. These *rubias*, or light-complected Mexican women, were acclaimed as "SUPERB SPECIMENS OF WOMAN-HOOD" in editorials appearing in California as well as Texas.[27]

The sex ratio of men to women was a factor that favored intermarriage between Mexicans and Anglos. During mining booms in California, Arizona, and northern New Mexico thousands of single men flooded the Southwest. In New Mexico and Texas the opportunities to make a quick killing in land speculation and in cattle and sheep raising drew thousands of single "men-on-the-make" from the deep South and Midwest.

Everywhere in the West there was a shortage of American women, at least until the railroad made travel easier and safer. Some women's under-standable dislike of the difficult journey west is well documented. A few of their diaries are peppered with comments like that of one woman who thought that the West was "a heaven for men and dogs but hell for women and oxen," or another who wrote, "I am weary of this journey, weary of myself and all around me. I long for the quiet of home where I can be at Peace once more."[28]

In the urban and settled areas of Los Angeles, Tucson, and Santa Fe, which were on the peripheries of mining and ranching frontiers, there were sizable surpluses of American men to American women (see Table 15). In Los Angeles and Santa Fe Anglo-American men outnumbered women by 2 to 1 until the 1880s. In Tucson the ratio was even higher, 9 to 1. San Antonio, which was less influenced by the mining booms, had the most equal ratio of three American men to every two American women. By 1880 parity between the sexes existed in the larger cities of San Antonio and Los Angeles. But in Tucson and Santa Fe there were still many more men than eligible women.

EUROPEAN IMMIGRANTS AND INTERMARRIAGE

Demographers and sociologists have long regarded differences in the sex ratio as important for understanding interethnic intermarriage.[29] Virginia Yans McLaughlin's study of the Italian immigrants in Buffalo, New York, found that among Italian immigrants a surplus of marriageable men over marriageable women resulted in higher rates of male exogamy. Six percent of all marriages in Little Italy were of a mixed type, and "80 percent of those marrying non-Italians were men; only 20 percent were women."[30] She hypothesized that Italian men married outside their ethnic group in the hopes that they would achieve greater socioeconomic status. But it is also true they were forced to do so by virtue of demographic pressure.

McLaughlin's findings suggest that racial prejudice toward working-class Italian men may have been less than it was for Mexican-American men, who did not marry Anglo-American women in any significant numbers. It also points to the effects of declining parental controls over marriage and mate selection among Mexican Americans. The erosion of patriarchal and community social controls had the consequence of freeing more women to marry outside their ethnic group.

Native-born Anglo-Americans intermarried most with those immigrant and ethnic groups that were least different from them: the British, Germans, Scandinavians, and Irish. Outside the Southwest southern European immigrants and other dark-skinned peoples had low rates of intermarriage with the native-born. Ruby Jo Kennedy in a longitudinal study of native intermarriage

TABLE 15

The Percentage of Unmarried Men to Unmarried Women:
Anglo-Americans Ages 16-59, 1850-1880

	1850	1860	1870	1880
Los Angeles	93.8	70.2	73.9	50.0
Tucson	–	–	91.7	89.5
Santa Fe	90.9	100.0	68.3	82.6
San Antonio	74.7	62.2	53.9	50.0

with European immigrants found that ethnic exogamy was highest for the northern European immigrants and lowest for Jewish and southern European immigrants. By 1900 the rates of exogamy were 45 percent for German immigrants, 28 percent for the British, 26 percent for the Irish, and 18 percent for Scandinavians. The lowest out-group marriage rates were among the Jewish and Italian immigrants, with 2 and 3 percent respectively.[31] Over a longer period of time, from 1870 to 1950, religion as well as ethnic similarity influenced intermarriage. Native-born Protestants married immigrant Protestants, and native-born Catholics married immigrant Catholics.

PATTERNS OF INTERMARRIAGE IN THE FOUR TOWNS

After 1848 a complex of social and demographic as well as cultural and ideological forces were at work: imbalances in the sex ratio, the size of the ethnic population in relation to the Anglo-Americans, racial prejudice, economic class standing, and cultural and linguistic barriers formed a complex grid of opposing normative forces.

One way to measure the rate of intermarriage for the nineteenth century is to study the proportions of couples appearing in the manuscript census schedules (see Table 16). The proportions of mixed couples varied according to geographic location. San Antonio had the lowest rates of intermarriage, and the other three towns had relatively higher rates. The much lower percentage of mixed couples in San Antonio is understandable, given the lower numbers of single Anglo-American men relative to women. In Los Angeles the decennial proportions of interethnic couples appear to have slightly declined, from 12.2 percent in 1850 to 8.7 percent in 1880, while the percentage of mixed couples in Tucson, Santa Fe and San Antonio rose. The high rates of intermarriage in Santa Fe and Tucson appear to have been related to the higher sex ratios of single Anglo-American men to available women. Overall the pattern was one of gradually increasing or relatively stable rates of mixed marriages.

TABLE 16

Intermarriage: Mixed Unions as a Percentage of All Couples in Four Southwestern Towns, 1850-1880

	1850	1860	1870	1880
Los Angeles	12.2	12.3	12.0	8.7
Tucson	–	–	9.1	13.9
Santa Fe	5.7	5.8	18.5	12.5
San Antonio	0	3.9	3.6	4.7

CROSS-GENERATIONAL ENDOGAMY

But intermarriage was, in reality a more complicated phenomenon than the proportions of exogamous Mexican-American unions would suggest. Endogamy, or marriage within the ethnic group, also produced a kind of assimilation. Marriages between generations were likely to promote an economic as well as a cultural leveling effect within Mexican-American society. Cross-generational marriage was greatest for Mexican-born men prior to 1870 and for native-born women after that date. In the early years of the American era male Mexican immigrants married native-born Spanish-surnamed women in large numbers. Forty-one percent of all Mexican immigrant marriages in 1850 were with native women. But by 1870 this percentage had dropped to 34 percent (see Table 32, Appendix C). The high rate of cross-generational marriage for the Mexican-born men was related to the fact that prior to 1870 there were fewer Mexican-born women in relation to men. In addition, proportionally more Mexican immigrants than native-born were upwardly mobile, skilled workers, and merchants with property. Many native-born women seem to have sought economic security and higher status by marriage to promising immigrants from Mexico.[32]

After 1870 it was the native-born Spanish-surnamed women who were the most likely to marry outside their generational cohort or ethnic group. Most of their out-group marriages were with Mexican immigrants, as has been noted, but increasingly they tended to marry European or Latin American immigrants. In comparison to her Mexican-born sisters the native-born Spanish-surnamed woman had much higher rates of exogamy and cross-generational marriage. Despite impressionistic evidence to the contrary, neither native-born nor Mexican-born women were very likely to marry American men. They were much more likely to marry within their own ethnic group but cross generational boundaries.

An imbalance in the sex ratio for Mexican men and women can explain these patterns of ethnic endogamy. As the sex ratio stabilized (by about 1880), the proportions of cross-generational marriages decreased. For the native-born women the sex ratio was also crucial for understanding why so many married outside their generational group. There were just not enough eligible men of their generation. After 1860 the imbalance between native-born men and women increased steadily. So too did the rates of cross-generational endogamy.

The native-born Spanish-surnamed men who married exogamously tended to do so with European and Latin American women. Mexican immigrant women, however, had the lowest rates of ethnic exogamy. Here again the sex ratio was important. An eligible Mexican woman had many partners of her generation to choose from. At the same time it appears that the barriers to exogamous marriage were least for the native-born, both men and women, indicating the effect of cultural assimilation, mainly in language ability, on their ability to find mates from outside their ethnic group. Overall, intermarriage with Anglo-Americans remained quite low for all generational groups. It was relatively more common for a man or woman, whether a Mexican immigrant or native-born, to marry a German, Polish, Chilean, or Spanish immigrant than to marry a migrant from Missouri, New York, or Massachusetts.

ASSIMILATION, PATTERNS OF INTERMARRIAGE, AND MIGRATION

Superficially the increasing rates of intermarriage within these urban towns would seem to indicate that a Mexican-American population was destined to follow the trajectory of marital assimilation that some other immigrant nationalities were to experience. But this was not to be the case. The assimilation that did take place, in terms of marriage, was predominantly with groups that had yet to enter the American mainstream.

One could argue that increased Mexican immigration inhibited the tendency toward exogamy. As the pool of eligible marriage partners grew, so too did the cultural and socioeconomic distances between Mexican heritage and Anglo-American populations. This in fact was a pattern in the southwestern cities. Los Angeles and San Antonio had growing numbers of Mexican immigrants and falling rates of intermarriage. In the towns of Santa Fe and Tucson declining rates of Mexican immigration were related to patterns of increased intermarriage.

Exogamy was related to the immigrant flow. Later in the twentieth century Mexican immigrants flooded the southwestern cities, and the rates of intermarriage remained relatively low. It was not until World War II that rates of exogamy began to rise. This phenomenon was mostly related to the easing of ethnic barriers and a growing number of Mexican Americans of the third generation. Prior to about 1945, however, marital assimilation did not bring about the "Americanization" of Mexican Americans. This was because a large and growing stream of Mexican immigrants assured that the pool of Mexican-heritage families would grow faster than the outflow of those who had assimilated through intermarriage. Segregation, poverty, and cultural ethnic prejudice, as well as the preferences of Mexican Americans themselves, insured that most would never be "Americanized," at least to the degree desired by the Americanizers. The patterns of intermarriage and Mexican immigration were thus part of a dynamic and complex social process which resulted in the persistence as well as the diversity of the Mexican-American ethnic family.

CHAPTER 6

Child Rearing, Discipline, and Sex

> *Your parents have looked after your happiness but,
> instead of listening to their counsel and respecting
> their authority, you consort with evil company. Some
> day you will shed tears of blood for having dis-
> regarded their venerable advice.*
>
> –*El Clámor Público*, February 2, 1856

THE PURPOSE OF THIS chapter is to assess the relationship between ideals and behavior in the realms of child rearing and sexual expression. That these two subjects are related is obvious to all who have lived through the post-Freudian age. Incest taboos and Oedipus complexes not withstanding, one of the most fundamental lessons all humans seem to teach their children is the proper way to love, and these lessons have complex and hidden consequences for succeeding generations. The complex psychological dimensions underlying the socialization of children in relations between the sexes could be a good topic for a more lengthy study. I leave it to others who are more trained in psychoanalytic analysis to assess the obscure meanings of the historical record. My central objective here is rather to trace, as best I can, given the scattered and imperfect evidence, what I think are the basic outlines of the emotional fabric of one of the most sensitive and important areas of family life.

The control of passions has always been a central problem for civilizations and cultures. It was a very human problem which occupied the energies of the Protestant as well as the Catholic authorities in the nineteenth century. In the two hundred years before the American westward movement Anglo-Americans had developed a Puritan tradition as a means by which exterior biblical-based authority was internalized by individuals.

By the time of the American Revolution Americans had succeeded in constructing what Ronald Takaki has called a republican "iron cage."[1] The individual was solely responsible for controlling his instinctual needs. The key to maintaining self-discipline, the work ethic, and sobriety was an internalized and essentially unmitigable sense of guilt. In the process the self became fragmented into compartments of reason and passion, "the bodies half-dead; genitals dissociated from heart; heart severed from head; head dissociated from genitals." The result was that the Puritan "had to curtail the range of experiences he could have in republican society. This meant that he had to devote his life to work, frugality, and sobriety, and to be master of his passions and instinctual needs."[2]

The Catholic-Mediterranean tradition of authoritarian external control, the importance of shame in the community's control of behavior, and the socialization of guilt through Catholic ritual resulted in quite different kinds of attitudes toward the control of passion and spontaneity. Rather than leaving the individual to police himself, appointed authorities, secular and religious, discovered, punished, and forgave, enforcing adherence to explicit moral standards.

The Counter-Reformation in Europe in the sixteenth century sought to harness the very same passions that had been condemned by the northern Protestants and to turn them to religious expression. The sensual madonnas, the religious ecstasy, the tactile and evocative religious art, the soaring architecture of the Baroque period were evidence that Western Catholicism had tapped a new psychological source. The religious orders specialized in asceticism and discipline. Ordinary citizens were expected to be more human.

The Catholicism of Spain and Latin America held that lapses in personal morality were not so much the fault of the individual as that of the authorities—heads of families, priests, and political officials—who were supposed to be examples, supervisors, and instructors in good behavior. Hence in Spanish America the idea of personal guilt as a driving and all-consuming force was not prominent in the individual psyche. In fact, guilt was regarded as a form of pride, an evil to be erased through contrition, confession, and absolution.

Thus an unruly child in a Mexican family was a "hijo mal criada," or a badly reared child. Parents who had failed to set proper examples, exercise vigilance, and instill discipline were blamed for errant children. Indeed, "disciplina" in the home, church, or school was the linchpin in the child's socialization process. By "disciplina" Spanish-speaking Catholics did not necessarily mean a vague personal self-discipline, but more a prescribed ritual of behavior, for example, the rote memorization of the catechism or unvarying forms of formal address. "Disciplina" was that which was enforced from without and obeyed because of superior moral authority.

After political independence from Spain in 1821 Mexicans faced the same dilemma that confronted the Founding Fathers of the United States: How does a nation control the unbridled passions of the body and maintain civilization in the absence of traditional royal authority? Both in the British colonies and in Latin America there was a progressive secularization of society.

Sex and sin came to be separated as the church lost most of its functions in regulating social morality. To take the place of a declining religious presence, Mexican society reinforced the authority of the family as a mechanism of social control. The family filled the gap left by the failure of the old religious and political order. Catholic-Mexican families became more self-centered. The romantic idealization of motherhood, child rearing, and family life, while originating prior to the Independence period, intensified throughout the nineteenth century.

In the American Southwest the Victorian-American middle-class family faced the Catholic-Mexican family and found points of mutual agreement. Due to their distance from centers of power and control in Mexico, families, in their struggle for daily survival on the Mexican frontier, had tended to be cohesive and self-reliant, depending on small villages and kinship links. The villages of northern New Mexico are a good example. There for hundreds of years families had formed tightly woven enclaves; they turned inward for protection against hostile Indians and an unforgiving environment. After 1848 the frontier family's solidarity was challenged by the influx of new populations with radically foreign cultural traditions, by the Anglo-American political system, through laws facilitating divorce and civil marriages, by secular mixed education, and by new economic developments that vitiated the older generation's patrimony and authority.

The Catholic Church remained as a support for family authority, but less directly so since it was in the hands of non-Mexican prelates. Thus, the Mexican-American family found itself forced to accept new external authorities, and in the process the old colonial unity of home, church, and government was shattered. The changes had consequences for the socialization of children and for the most intimate aspects of personal life. Aspects of the older unities remained: the emphasis on *dignidad* (dignity) and *respeto* (respect) in personal relations, the emphasis on ideals of virginity and chastity in women, and the sacred authority of the husband over the wife.

CHILD REARING AND DISCIPLINE

Child-rearing practices among Mexican Americans cannot be studied primarily as quantitative phenomena, although some family historians have successfully mined a good deal of information from statistics dealing with premarital adolescent sexuality.[3] But these kinds of historical data are not readily available for Mexicans as a subgroup within American society after 1848. There is scattered evidence of a literary type about the middle and upper classes' attitudes and values regarding the problems surrounding the socializations of children. In using this evidence there is still, as one writer put it, "a nagging fear that a history of childhood may well be impractical; for to know what a relatively few articulate individuals thought about these problems, in contrast to what the majority of people actually did, makes for a highly speculative history."[4]

An analysis of child rearing according to socioeconomic classes is almost impossible given the lack of reliable sources. We may assume that there were different styles of child rearing among Mexican Americans, depending on their generational distance from Mexico, socioeconomic status, and degree of assimilation into American society. Only a handful of diaries, letters, novels, and handbooks disclose something of how these differences affected the rearing of children. In commenting on the experiences and attitudes of the middle and upper classes it is important to emphasize that childhood for the working classes may have been quite different.

Rare evidence is provided by a diary kept by a teenage girl during a three-year period, 1889-1892. She lived on a farm located on the outskirts of San Antonio, and she was related to Adina de Zavala, a matron historian of the city who came from a respected Texas family.[5] The girl was part of an English-speaking Mexican-American family, and thus she wrote her diary entirely in English—referring to her relations as "speaking Mexican"—yet sometimes calling her older brother "Carlos" or disparagingly "Don Carlos." Her daily entries reveal a feeling for the routine of her life.

Through the years she and her brother (there appear to have been two children) helped with the housework. Her brother was responsible for helping with the family's laundry and chopping wood. The parents allowed "Don Carlos" much more freedom than the girl, for she led an almost cloistered life. Carlos was allowed to go into town on errands and to travel around the countryside on his horse. The girl lamented on Tuesday, January 12, 1889: "Papa and Carl went to the ranch to get wood. I wanted to take a ride today but they were too mean to let me. I don't go anywhere."[6] During a four-month period she had only one chance to escape the house when a chaperoned dance was held in town, but she was not allowed to go. In a six-month period she went to only one social event in town, on Christmas when her family traveled into town to visit her aunt Adina, received presents, and returned to their home. On many occasions the girl's parents left her alone as mistress of the house. Her mother frequently left home alone for overnight visits with friends or relatives and did not take her daughter with her. The men, her father and brother, were frequently away from home chasing cattle, in town on business, cutting wood, or visiting neighbors, but the girl never accompanied them. She did not attend school during the period of the diary, but her ability in written English indicates that she must have had some formal instruction when she was younger. Occasionally Adina de Zavala would come to visit and bring her daughters to the home, providing companionship for the girl. The mother, on her own birthday, left the girl alone and went into town for several days.

This diary gives us an intimate glimpse of an acculturating middle-class Mexican-American child. While her views and experiences cannot be regarded as typical of all Mexican-American children, there were patterns which may have been found generally among families of Mexican-Anglo intermarriage or among middle-class Mexican Americans. These were that (1) young girls were severely restricted in their contacts with others, (2) boys had relatively more freedom than girls, but they also did housework and chores which might have been labeled "women's work," (3) married women with older children were quite independent of home life and frequently traveled about alone without their husbands, and (4) relatives may not have been as important in children's lives as has sometimes been suggested by contemporary research on the Mexican-American family.

Another kind of evidence informs our views of upper- and middle-class child rearing. There were a limited number of nineteenth-century manuals on the proper ways of rearing children that were published in Spain, Mexico, and the Mexican-American Southwest. In New Mexico the Catholic Church published booklets such as a *Catecismo* and *Los protectores de la juventud*. *La revista católica* in Las Vegas, New Mexico, published periodic editorial pieces in its weekly magazine such as "Sobre deberes de los niños," or "On the Obligations of Children." In California Antonio Coronel kept a small booklet in his library entitled *Avisos saludables para los niños que para su bien espiritual,*or *Good Advice for Children's Spiritual Welfare.*[7] This book demonstrates how adult Spanish society of that era viewed children. It provides a sample of the ideals that may have been influential among the upper-class *Californio* families.

Avisos saludables depicted children as being innocents, subject to corruption from the malicious activities of the devil. Children were capable of sin primarily because their reasoning powers were not fully developed. Most inportantly they were not to blame for sin; it was entirely the devil's actions which produced evil. *Avisos saludables* expounded on five principles or lessons which children should learn: (1) "Love God above all things"; (2) "The most valuable thing in the world is your soul"; (3) "Love with all your heart the Virgin Mary"; (4) "Avoid mortal sin"; and (5) "Meditate upon death in order to give meaning to life." Notably, in the portion of the book dealing with mortal sin, the writer advised, "If by some disgrace you fall into mortal sin, do not suffer your conscience, but repent well and beg God for pardon all your day."[8] The writer compared sin to a broken leg that could be mended by the expert application of contrition, confession, and absolution. Sin was not to be internalized but projected outward and erased through accepted

Carolina Villalongín (third from left) and three other actress members of the Villalongín company, June 3, 1900. Courtesy of The Benson Library, University of Texas, Austin, The Tafolla Collection.

Children in front of Hilario Ybarra's residence on upper Main Street in Sonoratown, Los Angeles, ca. 1900. Courtesy Henry E. Huntington Library, The Pierce Collection, neg. no. 1333.

Phoeby, Anita, and Sara Tafolla in San Antonio ca. 1900. Courtesy The Benson Library, University of Texas, Austin, The Tafolla Collection.

ritual. The final lesson on the importance of death emphasized that life had only one purpose, the attainment of afterlife: "Think often that we are soon to die and after death we will have to be eternally with the devil in hell or with God and his angels in heaven, depending on our good or bad works."[9]

Death and childhood were indeed close companions for Mexican Americans. By Catholic custom and teaching it was believed that baptized children, if they died, bypassed purgatory and went directly to heaven without sin. Their death was thus an occasion for rejoicing, not sadness. As was the custom, children served as pallbearers and a small orchestra played a happy tune as a coffin was carried to the cemetery. English-speaking Protestant observers were taken aback by the festive funerals which Mexicans held for their deceased children. Edward Carlson, a soldier stationed in Los Angeles during the Civil War, once attended a gay fiesta in town. Not until the end did he discover that it was in reality a wake and that the corpse of a small infant was prominently displayed and surrounded by flowers.[10] Benjamin Hayes and Harris Newmark reported the same customs existing at other times and places in California. Hayes remarked that the fiestas died out by the 1880s, probably the result of the American Catholic Church's disfavor. Generally death was not held out as a threat to children; it was interpreted more as an unexpected prize than a punishment.

Further evidence regarding child rearing among the Mexican-American middle class in the nineteenth century may be drawn from the writings of Joaquin Fernandez de Lizardi. In doing so we must be cautioned that his observations were based on the society of central Mexico. It would be wrong to assume that his views were representative of all Mexican Americans in the Southwest during the middle part of the nineteenth century. Most likely his views on aristocratic childhood applied to those upper-class individuals who migrated to the border region or to those Mexican Americans of the middle and upper classes who continued to be influenced by the culture of central Mexico.

Lizardi is known as "El Pensador Mexicano." He wrote numerous plays, poems, novels, and essays criticizing the customs and politics of his time. He is regarded as one of the keenest observers of middle-class family life in Mexico during this era. His famous novel *El periquillo sarnieto* is largely autobiographical. It reveals that servants had almost as much influence on aristocratic children as the parents. When Periquillo, the hero of the novel, was born, he was immediately swaddled to prevent him from being unruly in later life. His mother sent him out to a wet nurse since the nursing of children was considered lower class. Thereafter servants surrounded Periquillo and his brother Pomposa; in effect the servants raised them, teaching the children ghost stories, legends, tales of the devil, and folk beliefs. Thus the servants provided them with an informal education in the culture of the masses even while their tutors and parents sought to instill in them the manners of aristocracy. By the time they were twelve the children learned their place. They began to order the servants about as miniature masters. Their parents indulged them in almost all their desires.[11]

In contrast to the relatively permissive atmosphere surrounding the rearing of upper-class aristocratic boys, one of the main lessons lower-class children were taught was *dignidad* and *respeto* (dignity and respect). In California parents took their children to public executions (until the 1870s when they were banned) to teach the fatal consequences of evil acts. Rafael Prieto, in Monterey, California, remembered being whipped after one such execution so that he would always remember its moral lessons.[12] The teaching of *respeto* included such customs as addressing your parents in the *Usted*, formal voice, removing hats in the presence of elders, asking permission to smoke, dance, or take leave. Ethel Shorb, who married into the Yorba family, remembered the Del Valle family's table, where "much formality was observed . . . and the routine of the day was never interrupted. . . . The household sat according to their rank."[13] This formality, observed by all, was a means to teach mutual respect and dignity among family members.

The rote memorization of ritual played a role in the socialization of children. They learned the most important lesson, *La doctrina católica*, by heart at a tender age. Mariano Vallejo remembered how, as a student, he had been forced to memorize long passages from the catechism and then to repeat it for the edification of his father's guests. He had a low opinion of this socialization process. For him it was "a heaping up of horrors, a torture for childhood." The old school system, he felt, was detrimental to the free spirit. "In it the souls of a whole generation were innoculated with the virus of a deadly disease . . . extinguishing the light of reason in the new born man."[14] The "disease" Vallejo referred to was the blind acceptance of religion and the resulting rejection of free thought.

The custom of teaching through rote memorization was not uniquely Mexican or Spanish but was common throughout the elementary education of the United States until the reforms of the early twentieth century. In American schools Mexican children were taught English by rote, but they no longer had to learn the *Doctrina*.

Discipline in the American schools was at least as strict as in the Mexican schools prior to 1848, with beatings being a common means of punishment. But even this did not always intimidate willful students. In the 1860s Juan Bandini remembered that a whole school of Mexican-American children had "bothered, frightened and generally worsted" a new school teacher in San Diego and that as a result a special committee of parents had to be set up to monitor the students' possession of knives and other weapons.[15]

The socialization of children occurred primarily through parental example and teachings. Throughout the Southwest prior to 1848 public schooling was irregular and badly organized. In the American era, particularly after the 1880s when the states began to pass compulsory school attendance laws, public schools began to encroach on the prerogative of the family and the church. This tended to fragment authority. Increasingly Mexican Americans were presented with models for proper behavior which conflicted with their traditional culture. Mexican-American families sometimes reacted to this dilemma by withdrawing their children from the schools or protesting the curriculum and methods of instruction.

In general more Mexican-American children remained under their parents' care for a longer period of time than was true for other American children. Table 17 shows the percentages of children who were over the age of twenty and who continued to reside in their parents' household. In every census year more Mexican-American children than Anglo children over the age of twenty remained with their families. The bulk of these older Mexican-American children were from middle-class native-born families. Robert McGlone has argued that in the nineteenth century a modern middle-class child-centered family began to emerge in America. An important characteristic of this new family model was that the period of chilhood was prolonged, and a new emphasis was put on adolescence. This appears to explain the increasing proportions of American children over twenty years of age who resided in their parents' homes. At the same time, however, the trend could have been

TABLE 17

Proportions of Children over the Age of 20 Remaining in Households by Ethnicity, Socioeconomic Status, and Nativity of the Head of Household, 1850-1880 (expressed as a percentage of total)

	1850 % (N)	1860 % (N)	1870 % (N)	1880 % (N)
1. Ethnicity				
Anglo-American	3.4 (3)	5.2 (14)	6.9 (34)	7.3 (30)
Mexican American	11.2 (86)	11.6 (108)	11.6 (106)	11.6 (154)
2. Socioeconomic class				
Mexican American Upper and Middle Class	25.0 (20)	21.2 (17)	19.7 (18)	24.3 (32)
Mexican American Working Class	15.5 (28)	18.5 (54)	12.2 (41)	14.9 (64)
3. Nativity				
Mexican-Born	9.1 (2)	8.9 (5)	8.3 (8)	12.0 (15)
Native-Born Mexican American	10.3 (84)	10.4 (103)	10.6 (98)	10.6 (139)

due to economic and demographic factors that promoted a later age at first marriage, to a sexual imbalance among Anglo-American males and females, or to changing inheritance practices. It is important to note that Mexican-American families had long been child-centered. Moreover, the Mexican-American families firmly believed in childhood as a special protected stage of development and in the importance of motherhood as an idealized role. This, of course, implies that some of the features of "the modern nuclear family" were already present in preindustrial Mexican-American families.[16]

The families of the Mexican-American native-born middle and upper classes seemed to be the most child-centered of all families sampled. Within their households they had the largest proportions of children over the age of twenty. This indicates that the more affluent families were more able to keep their elder children at home in a dependent status. Then too these older children may have stayed at home to calculate the prospects of inheriting land, wealth, or social position. In working-class Mexican-American families children left home earlier in their life cycle. Despite the probability that most of these working-class children had wage-paying jobs, they still did not continue to live with their parents. In comparison to the upper- and middle-class youth they were more independent of family ties. Of course, it is likely that the vast majority of working-class children had no choice in the matter and may have been forced by economic necessity and parental poverty to leave their families.

There were important ethnic differences in the patterns of children leaving home. Even the poorest Mexican-American families had higher proportions of elder resident children than the affluent non-Mexican-American families. The increased proportions of Americans who had older dependent children gives a limited support to McGlone's thesis that these families were becoming more child-centered. It is limited in that it is based on the questionable assumption that residence with parents automatically produced a special emotional quality which can be called "child-centered."

Given the more prolonged period of childhood in the Mexican-American family's life cycle, it is probable that the socialization process had more pronounced effects. As in other American families, the mothers of Mexican-American families had the responsibility of rearing the children. Thus, for both Mexican and English-speaking Americans the women's suffrage movement in the late nineteenth century presented a poignant threat to traditional ideals of motherhood and family stability.

WOMEN AND CHILD REARING

The debate over women's suffrage was particularly heated in New Mexico, where Hispano society was more bound by ancient Catholic customs and attitudes. Father Donato M. Gasparri, a Jesuit priest who published *La revista católica* in Las Cruces, New Mexico, led in the fight against women's suffrage. His position on this issue and that of secular education found support from Spanish-language editors in Taos, Santa Fe, and Albuquerque.[17] Father Gasparri's jeremiad against women's suffrage on March 24, 1877, was typical of the parade of horribles being circulated at the time: "How absurd it is, how repugnant to the sentiments of respect which we all hold for the gentle sex, to see a woman who abandons household work to present herself before the ballot box!" Suffrage would reverse traditional roles, he argued, so that "the merchant will have to leave his store, the lawyer the office, the worker his workshop, the laborer his plow, and go to the house to take care of the crib!" Women's suffrage threatened the very foundations of the family and civilization: "If women are given the vote, the family will be destroyed, it will lead to juvenile delinquency and increased abortions and eventually to the destruction of the human race."[18]

It appears from scattered evidence gathered in New Mexico, Arizona, California, and Texas that Mexican Americans thought that special discipline was necessary for girls in order to mold them into proper mothers. In all the didactic essays and *consejos* (advice) which appeared in the popular media, in newspapers, in plays, and in folk songs, the overwhelming concern was that little girls be taught restraint in love and learn how to be good mothers and wives. Ignacio Bonillas, editor of Tucson's *El fronterizo*, reflected a common view when he wrote (in 1882): "The mother is the priestess, the mother has a great mission to fulfill on earth, to form souls through her virtue." Women were held generally to have an undisputable dominance over the spiritual welfare of their charges, and over men as well. Mothers were "deified by affection, illuminated by love." The mother was a refuge for her husband and a "balm for his cares, a counsel for all his worries, surrounding him with her tender sisterly soul."[19] Writing in another issue, Bonillas continued on the same theme: "Mothers, be exemplary so that your children will follow your example . . . be virtuous so that your children will reflect your virtue." Mothers were "the soul of society" and the "balance of the universe." As keepers of the "soul of the family" mothers should be particularly careful not to destroy children's happiness. "Without interrupting their happiness, a good mother can engrave serious ideas and noble examples in the hearts of adolescents." Mothers were solely responsible for the heart and soul of children, and this was a "sublime destiny . . . which society and nature has imposed on her."[20]

In all this, religious education, especially that of girls, played a particularly important role. Writing in 1883, Bonillas spoke in an editorial entitled "A Mother's Advice to Her Daughter": "Above all follow the path of religion and nurture your heart with the sentiments which religion inspires."

The Catholic Church was seen as a source of female hope, love, and respect. Even so, women were destined to experience sin through the sexual temptations offered by men: "You are destined to suffer a certain amount of disgrace, poor girl! Very vain are the pleasures of this world, with its memory it disturbs us, position and status doesn't satisfy us, its loss casts us into dispair." True happiness for women lay in their accepting their duty as mothers with a "peaceful soul." Thus: "Live in your house; do not get involved in any business except that of your family; be simple, just and modest." Any other course of life risked eternal damnation since "all pleasure is danger." The world was a minefield for women, and Bonillas advised self-abnegation, self-control, religion, and discipline as the only means of preventing sure destruction.[21]

One of the worst accusations that could be made of a child was that he or she was *malcriado*, or badly brought up, for this reflected on the family and in particular on the virtuous example of the mother. Carlos Tully, another Tucson editor, wrote many didactical articles on child rearing and on the responsibilities of parents, especially of mothers. For Tully "The greatest science of mothers should consist of forming modesty in the hearts of her daughters, even though they may not know it, because they will have gained much for the world and also for God." His advice to mothers in the rearing of children seems quite modern in light of today's fashion of "Tough Love." "All the science of the education of children can be reduced to very little," he wrote. "Above all, firmness of character; when they commit an error, reprimand them with prudence, without recurring blows or brutal threats; because that which you tolerate today, you will have to put up with tomorrow and all your life." Children were not assumed to be completely innocent, for they had "nascent vices" and many faults. Among the evils to be corrected in children were indolence, pride, and disobedience. The latter was the most important to correct since "Obedience is the first and most important of all the good qualities of children. . . . It is the most beautiful of virtues."[22] Thus in the area of child rearing the Mexican Americans of the nineteenth century still relied on a good deal of Catholic pedagogy, which had been inherited from the Spanish era. In fact, it appears that these formalistic attitudes and values had remained relatively unchanged by contacts with English-speaking Protestants.

ATTITUDES ABOUT SEX

Mexican-American attitudes toward sex and marriage were probably as diverse as those of other Americans and most likely differed according to socioeconomic class. But as with the study of childhood, we are confronted with the problem of insufficient evidence for a thorough discussion of working-class attitudes in sexual matters. All that we have are the writings of the upper and middle classes. Basically their views can be divided into three categories that are not necessarily discrete and are somewhat overlapping: (1) religious and moralistic indoctrination, (2) romantic, idealistic, and secular views, and (3) playful, ironic, and ribald attitudes.

Attempts by church authorities and moralists to control sexual behavior has provided us with a rich if neurotic history. Catholic preachments and dogma as well as popular folk beliefs and customs sought to instruct individuals on the proper comportment and relations between the sexes. A basic and pervasive view expounded in the pulpits and the press was that marriage was good because it controlled the sexual appetite within an institution sanctioned by God. In an editorial Francisco Ramírez, editor of *El clamor público* and himself a bachelor, argued that adolescent passions were propelling too many youth into early marriages. "It is truly sad to contemplate the immorality which reigns during puberty," he wrote, "Young men who hardly know how to put on their pants are dreaming of illusions of love and matrimony." Early marriages, he reasoned, were deleterious to physical and mental health: "When undertaken by those without experience or age . . . (early marriage) destroys the constitution, weakens the intellectual faculties and results in children with more imperfections than their parents."[23] Latent in this popular view was the belief that women were naturally more passionate and unrestrained in their sexuality than men. They had enormous powers over men and children because they were the "heart" of the family and should be taught to "sing with the seductions of her soul."[24]

The Catholic Church's position about sexual conduct in the late nineteenth century was unambiguous. The debate over secular education in New Mexico revealed a host of clerical assumptions about the evils of uncontrolled passions of the heart. Father Gasparri, strenuously opposed to secular education, entered the fray with a series of editorials vigorously opposing the education of girls and boys in the same classroom. The proposal for mixed, secular education he thought "ridiculous and dangerous," bound to lead to "corruption and perdition."[25] The separation of children and young adults of the opposite sex and religious education had been the "fundamental principles for educating our children, young people and especially our young girls!" The proposal for secular coeducation, Gasparri felt, would "remove any brakes to contain the passions of the human heart . . . add fuel to the fire, stoke the flame." This kind of education he saw as endangering the virtue of young girls. He cited as evidence cases in England where secular education had supposedly led to prostitution.[26]

In 1874 Archbishop Lamy in a pastoral letter threatened to withhold the sacraments from children who attended these coeducational secular schools. The separation of the sexes in education had been a traditional Catholic practice for centuries. In Mexico there were even regulations covering the distance a girls' school had to be located from a boys' school. The New Mexicans were thus voicing their opposition to a dramatic change in the *status quo*, one that threatened their most cherished assumptions about the purity of childhood and sexual distance. Ironically, the bill which had caused all of this furor had been introduced by Jacinto Armijo, a member of one of the venerable native families in New Mexico.[27]

The romantic and secular notions of sexual relations mixed distinctly non-Victorian sensual images with ideals of purity and innocence. The love poetry of the period, which appeared periodically in the Spanish-language press, was racy, at least in comparison to the journalistic standards of the English-language press. The poem "A una niña" appearing in *El clamor público* in 1858 was characteristic of this romantic genre. It reflected mixed images about the opposite sex:

> I want to gaze at your rising bosom
> Showing the agitation within your soul.
> And I want to see your colored cheeks
> When you awaken with divine calm.
> . . . .
> By your side in the silent countryside
> I want to look at your purple aurora.
> I want to see, by your side
> In the repose of the night,
> The seductive moon.[28]

The title "A una niña" literally meant "To A Young Girl," which implied an innocent virgin, not a mature woman. This kind of love was, of course, the most highly valued, for it combined the ecstasy of religious imagery with the challenge of sensual conquest. The author of this poem, Francisco Ramírez, had a richly deserved reputation as a neoromantic nonconformist. But poems like this one appeared elsewhere.

El ranchero in solidly conservative San Antonio printed numerous poems about love and boundless passion. These were probably more in the mainstream of Mexican upper-class sensibility. "El primer amor," written in 1856, was a lengthy epic poem detailing the subtleties of the psychological passions engendered by a first love. The first passions, according to the anonymous writer, soon gave way to vague memories, then to feelings of lost love, and finally to profound melancholy.

> Death and suffering are the ultimate fate of lovers.
> First love, like all love is fleeting and impermanent.
> Death is the only end of man.[29]

In a later paper the editor devoted almost the entire issue to "la vida del corazón," or "the life of love," with poems and essays on the passions and sensibilities of lovers. All of this was framed in the highest and most respectable romantic imagery. Love was an "eternal spring, a noble passion, and a torment."[30]

A more detailed exposition of love and relations between the sexes, aimed more at the teenage audience, was given in an 1855 Spanish translation of a French "Catechism for Matrimony," which appeared in *El clamor público.* The writer recommended that beautiful girls should marry when they reach their eighteenth birthday, "so that nothing will happen to diminish your honor." Young girls should live by four commandments if they would hope to get a man: "(1) Be reticent and modest, (2) Know all the obligations of a housewife and apply yourself to work, (3) Take care of your clothes and room, and (4) Do not dress more luxuriously than your state in life." If girls were to hold on to their lover they should "love him honestly; avoid disrespectful or improper words; always be in a good humor; do not make him jealous by flirting with others." Finally, there were detailed instructions on how a young girl should behave on her wedding day: "You should maintain a modest appearance and show respect for your parents. . . . Take care not to laugh if someone proffers some words with double meanings contrary to purity; try not to cause a scandal."[31]

The popular plays, which were performed throughout the Southwest in the late nineteenth century, also demonstrate attitudes toward sex. Peripatetic groups of actors in northern Mexico and in the American Southwest performed locally authored dramas, tragedies, and comedies. The Carlos Villalongín Company, a prime example of one of these traveling companies, operated out of San Antonio. Generations of the Villalongín family presented hundreds of plays between 1848 and 1930.[32]

Plays, a popular folk art among Mexicanos, furnished cheap recreation for barrio residents. They were written in a popular style, and the people identified with the language as well as the stories that were enacted. They had the same appeal as the *telenovelas,* or "soap operas," have today. Like their modern successors, the dramas depict the ideals and mores of the Spanish-speaking community.

Three plays from the Villalongín collection exemplify contemporary values regarding women and love in the nineteenth century. *Hija y madre* (*Daughter and Mother*), a melodrama by Manuel Farmago y Daios written in 1872, involves a mother's attempt to protect her daughter from the unworthy attentions of various suitors. The father and extended family do not appear in the play. It was clearly the mother who was most responsible for upholding a standard of decency in love. *La mujer adultera* (*The Adulterous Woman* by Juan P. Vázquez) was a tragedy about a married woman who was

cleverly seduced. Although no date is given for this play, it appears to have
been written in the late nineteenth century. In it the married woman is
helpless to resist the onslaught of her passions. The relentless ardor of her
suitor results in uncontrollable thoughts. When discovered, her final solution
is to commit suicide, a reprehensible act in the eyes of the church but a noble
solution in terms of the play. Here Vázquez shows how familial standards of
honor and shame had triumphed over religious morality. *Me inconviene esta
mujer* written in 1888 by D. Enrique Zumel y Caballero, was a comedy about
a romantic triangle involving a timid, ineffective bumpkin, a suave courtier,
and a duchess. Most evident in the play is the fact that the decision to marry
is left entirely to the whims and feelings of Rosa, the heroine, not her family.
In fact, the family is nowhere to be seen.

Together these three plays — a melodrama, a tragedy, and a comedy —
illustrate varieties of attitudes toward love. The underlying unity of all three
is that all were individualistic and secular. Neither the church nor the extended
family had a significant role to play. In only one play, *Hija y madre*, did a
family member have a mediating role in upholding proper standards of sexual
conduct. In all three plays sexual relations were seen as chaotic, dangerous,
and ultimately beyond moral control.

It was a Mexican-American folk belief that women, not men, were the
ones who had to learn control, but this was difficult given woman's naturally
more passionate nature. Men were not responsible for trying to corrupt
women because they were merely following their instincts. "Men unninten-
tionally, because of their nature, can destroy a woman's modesty," argued
Las dos repúblicas: "They are like boys who encounter brilliant and beautiful
butterflies and jubilantly celebrate running after them. But when they touch
them, they destroy their wings . . . and kill them."[33] Consequently women
had to beware. It was their responsibility to maintain modesty and virtue in
sexual relations.

The ideal of male superiority and the double standard was not always
accepted by the women themselves. In a rare public proclamation of protest
an anonymous woman writing in *El fronterizo* (Tucson) in 1883 struck back
at the " traditional roles" expected of women. She rejected the biblical argument about men being created first and thus being more perfect than women
and argued that the Bible itself was written by men and, since "all men were
liars," it could not be trusted. In a satirical voice the essayist related the story
of creation according to a woman's point of view. "Adam was the first coward
because when God asked him, 'Have you eaten of the forbidden fruit?' Adam
answered while hiding behind Eve." Ever since men have been corrupt and
irresponsible. They are "like birds, often they search out the dirtiest corners
to build their nests. . . . Men are like lit cigars, they show more smoke than

fire." In a rousing conclusion she wrote: "If you have committed enough foolishness and have become conceited enough and have mocked and cursed women sufficiently then hold your nose animal!"[34]

Many observers have commented on the more liberal standards of sexual conduct among Mexican women. In 1827 one American visitor at the San Gabriel mission noted: "The women here are very unchaste; all that I have seen and heard speak appear very vulgar in their conversation and manners. They think it an honor to ask a white man to sleep with them."[35] English-speaking travelers in Texas and New Mexico thought that Mexican society was given over to sensual pleasure and immorality. They were shocked to see women smoking, gambling, swearing, and dancing in uncorseted dresses.

Janet Lecompte has argued that before 1848 women in New Mexico were free from the rigid pruderies of Victorianism and that after their Americanization they adopted the moral attitudes of middle-class America.[36] In the Mexican era women in San Antonio and Los Angeles bathed together in communal pools, exciting the interest of accidental strollers-by. Low-cut and short dresses that showed the bosom, ankles, and legs shocked the Americans who attended the fiestas in New Mexico. In Lecompte's view, "Because of earlier maturation of New Mexican girls and lack of shame surrounding sexual activity, girls were frequently living in concubinage or indulging in illicit relations at early puberty."[37]

Lecompte believes that before the American occupation the double standard was less pronounced and that "standards of behavior were essentially the same for both sexes." Frontier conditions indeed tended to make for more equality of the sexes, and Mexican court records show that men were prosecuted as much as women for violation of the public morality. Under the laws of the United States Mexican-American women lost a degree of juridical independence. Under Mexican law women could "own, inherit, loan, convey or pawn property," the rights of married women to do this were undercut by American laws.[38] But other evidence from literary sources seems to point to the formal expectation that women would have less freedom than men in Hispanic society (see chapter 3). Moreover, it is highly questionable that Mexicans learned the double standard from Americans. What probably happened was that Victorian morality emanating from both central Mexico and the United States created a new emphasis on prudery at least among the middle and upper classes. Polite society, both Mexican and American, tolerated prostitution until the late nineteenth century, mainly because it was limited to the poorer sections of town and because rich and influential men wanted it. More liberal attitudes about sexual behavior were more likely to appear in the cities and towns among the working classes than in rural areas. A fast-growing, highly mobile population tended to break down older social controls within the family and community, and in the American era individuals had relatively more freedom from close supervision by the church and polite society.

COMMON-LAW MARRIAGE AND BARRAGANÍA

A major cultural difference in attitude toward sexual relations between the English-speaking Protestant American and the Spanish-speaking Catholic was the acceptance of free unions between unmarried adults and illegitimacy. Common-law marriage as well as concubinage were common throughout Latin America in the nineteenth century. While marriage was both a religious sacrament and civil status regulated by law, over the centuries a folk custom of common-law union and *barraganía* developed. Technically, free-union, or common-law, marriage was a form of *barraganía*, or concubinage, and in the nineteenth and twentieth centuries *barraganía* came to be associated almost exclusively with marital infidelity. In Spain and Latin America free-union marriages were widespread, so much so that the practice was recognized in statutory law. *Las siete partidas*, drafted in the thirteenth century, stated: "Holy Church forbids that any Christian man have *barraganas*, for to live with them is mortal sin. But wise men of old who made the laws permitted that some might have them without civil penalty, for they held that it was a lesser evil to live with one woman than many, and that the paternity of children would be more certain."[39]

In practice many men and even priests took common-law wives, violating church laws but following age-old customs. In Mexico church and state officials tended to be tolerant of informal unions between unmarried adults, especially of Indians and the lower castes. They were less so when it came to the secular clergy and adulterous liaisons between married men and single women. For the upper classes *barraganía* was part of the double standard, one aspect of the male's prerogative within the patriarchal family, although there were instances where aristocratic women also enjoyed this privilege. But these were illicit and temporary relations, not morganatic marriages. The upper classes had more to lose by illegitimacy in terms of questions of inheritance and political status. For the poor, however, *unión libre* was fairly common. For them the double standard melted into a single one because of the lack of money to pay for church marriage ceremonies and a general apathy about religious and civil laws.

Woodrow Borah and Selburne Cook's study of colonial Mexican marriages found that the percentage of adults living in *unión libre* in Mexico City and in other urban areas was much lower than in most of the countryside. Common-law marriages in the urban centers ranged between 15 and 30 percent of all couples, whereas in the southern rural areas of Mexico they ranged from 30 to 50 percent. This was caused mainly by a chronic shortage of priests and a larger Indian population in the remote areas of Mexico.[40]

There is evidence that the folk customs supporting *barraganía* and common-law unions went north from Mexico and were part of the daily family life of the frontier. Gutíerrez found three types of concubinage existing in colonial New Mexico: extramarital sexual partners mostly taken by men in unhappy marriages, partners taken by men from among Indian and Mestizo servants, and cohabitation of unmarried single adults. Using illegitimate births as an index of free unions, he found that between 1690 and 1846 the percentage in both the Rio Abajo and Rio Arriba regions, going from 25 to close to 50 percent of all births.[41] The majority of these illegitimate children were of unions between members of the lower classes; the aristocracy was understandably reluctant to claim illegitimate offspring. One factor often cited by the authorities for the prevalence of common-law couples among the poor was the high fees charged by priests for marriage ceremonies. While the church set a fixed, low fee for the performance of marriages (the *arancel*), many priests ignored it.

In California, José Arnaz recalled that free-union couples were quite common before 1848 and that there was little social stigma attached to them. He said: "There were others . . . . who had the reputation of living in concubinage or in being available to men, and nevertheless they were admitted to polite society."[42] The free and easy acceptance of concubinage and free unions sometimes shocked more prudish individuals when they encountered it. Even urbane Madame Calderón de la Barca living in Mexico City in the 1840s recorded her surprise when her hostess, a lady of the aristocracy, unthinkingly played with the illegitimate child of one of her servant girls.[43] Also in the 1840s Reverend Juan Marie Odin, the new vice-prefect of the Catholic Church, visited San Antonio and reported that two of the local Mexican priests, Father Refugio de la Garza and Father José Antonio Valdéz, were living with women and their children. The two priests justified their concubinage to the population by claiming that the Council of Trent had permitted priests to marry. Odin reported that one of the priest's daughters lived in concubinage with an American lawyer.[44]

In 1879 Padre José Antonio Martínez, the famous priest from Taos, New Mexico, was accused of keeping a concubine, as were several other New Mexican priests, among them Vicar Juan Felipe Ortiz of Santa Fe. According to the complaint Father Ortiz had provided a woman a house adjacent to the convent for easy access. William Ritch, the territorial secretary wrote, "the Old Mexican clergy, in the light of 1879 . . . might and undoubtedly would be charged as indecent adulterers and audacious gamblers." Yet they could also be excused because, in Ritch's words, "the old priesthood was a kind of patriarch, acknowledged his bastards (and) was manly in the case of giving them as good advantages and education as the country afforded."[45]

Unión libre circumvented paternalistic controls over marriage and the family, at least in those cases where it occurred between unmarried adults. The children and spouses of such unions had no legal rights to inheritance or titles except as granted by the courts or on an *ad hoc* basis. Paternal authority in such families probably was qualitatively different from what it was for those families where the father had the support of the legal institutions. Parents living in free union would find it difficult to reconcile their children's illegitimacy with the moral laws of the church. Parish records indicate that free-union couples did baptize their children, but it is likely that they avoided calling on the church for support in their role as parents. They could not expect the church or the government to uphold their rights as parents, and they probably avoided formal involvement with these authorities.

Table 18 shows the incidence of common-law unions for the urban areas of the Southwest after 1848 as computed from the manuscript census returns. Unfortunately these statistics exclude those women who were concubines of married men. The table shows that the rates of *unión libre* tended to be higher in the more rural towns of Santa Fe and Tucson than in the metropolitan cities of San Antonio and Los Angeles, a pattern that parallels that reported by Borah and Cook for Mexico. Nevertheless, this is a surprising finding. In small rural towns, public and religious sanctions should have kept concubinage low. In cities and urban areas, secular places by definition, the moral and ethical constraints on concubinage should not have operated with as much force. One factor which may have played a role was the conflict between the Mexican and European priests in the territory of New Mexico. Bishop Lamy provoked a civil war with Father José Antonio Martínez and other priests. As a result many couples may have been torn in their loyalties and confused as to the legitimacy of the clergy, which would discourage them from seeking a church wedding. The pattern can also be explained by the diminishing influence of the church in the larger urban centers and in the persistence of traditional practices—namely, of priests charging high fees—in

TABLE 18

Free-Union Couples, 1850-1880
(expressed as a percentage of all Mexican-American couples)

	1850 % (N)	1860 % (N)	1870 % (N)	1880 % (N)
Los Angeles	11.7 (14)	11.1 (29)	8.1 (19)	8.4 (28)
Tucson	–	–	17.0 (17)	18.2 (30)
Santa Fe	4.9 (5)	13.5 (7)	29.0 (36)	8.2 (6)
San Antonio	6.6 (6)	4.6 (7)	3.6 (6)	1.3 (2)

the more isolated villages and towns. In the fast-growing cities there was more of a secular attitude toward marriage. By the 1880s increasing numbers of Mexican Americans appeared before justices of the peace and paid only a nominal sum for a quick ceremony. Then, the replacement of a number of the more venal Mexican clergy who had been extorting high fees took place more rapidly in these cities than in the countryside. Also the increase of *barraganía* in Santa Fe and Tucson may have been related to the persistence of community norms, since for much of the territorial period the church's presence among Mexican Americans suffered a decline, so that couples were not under great community pressure to seek a church wedding.

The surprising jump in *unión libre* in Santa Fe during the 1870s is difficult to explain. It corresponded with increasing numbers of female-headed households and an exceptionally high male unemployment rate (over 25 percent) and a drop in female employment (see chapter 3). By 1870 the Santa Fe Ring was in full operation, dispossessing numerous families from their lands. Lawlessness and violence were rampant in the territory, especially in nearby Colfax County, where the Maxwell Land Grant War produced numerous lynchings and murders.[46] Economic uncertainties probably caused a larger than usual number of Hispanos to put off legitimizing their marriages. But ten years later the proportion of free-union couples fell to its lowest level in forty years, indicating that conditions had improved. The same pattern, of increasing rates of free-union couples during times of political and economic upheaval, appears for Los Angeles during the period 1860-1870 and for San Antonio during the period 1850-1860.

SEXUAL MODERNIZATION

In some respects the nineteenth-century Mexican Americans appear more liberated in their sexuality and its expression than their middle-class Victorian contemporaries. Edward Shorter has suggested that the sexual revolution occurred first among the working, not the middle, classes. Middle-class family authority, he argues, "remained inviolate," and fewer middle-class youth were able to "break out of the web of familial custom and control."[47] In his view the lower working-class family had become less effective as an agency for the social control of the young, and this resulted in a "liberated libido."

In the case of the Mexican Americans, as has been argued by Gutiérrez's work on New Mexico prior to 1848, the liberation of sexuality occurred much earlier than its American counterpart and had little to do with the decline of family solidarity. It was linked more to older cultural and religious patterns of socialization. It was a paradox that a society predicated on authoritarian control resulted in emotionally liberated individuals. Specifically, behavior seemed at odds with the formal preachments. This can be explained in terms of traditional Catholic attitudes toward authority and the individual. To be sure, Victorian values made inroads into middle- and upper-class Mexican-American society, since these were the classes which acculturated most rapidly. Naturally the upper classes' view of sexual repression, education, and discipline reflected their propertied interests in inheritance. But it can also be argued that inasmuch as older values about child rearing persisted, so too did attitudes about proper sexual expression. In the twentieth century Mexican Americans came increasingly into contact with commercial mass advertising and marketing and new modes of dress and behavior. The enlargement of the government's role in compulsory secular education and the growth of social welfare and service organizations in the twentieth century eroded the family's control over the socialization of their children. Increasingly the home, for all groups in American society, was less a "haven in a heartless world," to borrow Christopher Lasch's expression, and much more permeable to policy decisions made by the local and national "experts."[48]

CHAPTER 7

Mexican-American Families, 1910-1945

> *The manifestations of family organization in individ-*
> *ual behavior are the effects of the subject's attitudes*
> *and of the social conditions; these social conditions*
> *must be taken, of course, with the meaning which*
> *they have for the acting individual himself, not for*
> *the outside observer.*
> –William I. Thomas and Florian Znaniecki, *The*
> *Polish Peasant in Europe and America,* vol. 2, p.
> 1168.

AFTER 1900 THREE TENDENCIES became more pronounced in the American Southwest: rapid industrial and commercial growth, progressive urbanization, and large-scale Mexican immigration. As we have seen, the origins of these changes lay in the nineteenth century. The essential dynamics of family life in the first half of the twentieth century changed but slowly. Perhaps the most pervasive force making for continuity in family life was the grinding poverty endured by the majority of Mexican families whether immigrant or native-born. The basic problems which had influenced Mexican-American family life in the previous century, those of marginalization, discrimination, and economic insecurity, remained. Overcrowding in large cities, the massive influx of new immigrants and migrants, the proliferation of low-paying industrial jobs, the impact of new technologies, the superheated nationalism and nativism spawned by World Wars I and II, and the economic disasters of the Great Depression all affected the daily lives of Mexican-American families.

The complexities of Chicano social history during this period are only now beginning to be examined.[1] There are volumes of information gathered by government agencies, libraries, and social scientists which can be used to elaborate on this history. The purpose of this chapter is to sketch in broad strokes an outline of some of the major continuities and discontinuities in family life in the first half of the present century. The major forces affecting family life in this period were industrialization, urbanization, and Mexican immigration.

INDUSTRIALIZATION AND URBANIZATION

Rapid industrial growth in various regions of the historical Southwest after 1880 had the effect of intensifying the dependency of families on wage-paying jobs and of removing them from agricultural ties. Industrial growth was greatest in California and Texas and much slower in Arizona and New Mexico. The automobile and the development of the oil industry had a major influence on industrialization by providing both a new mobility for the labor force and cheap energy. The huge increases in the population of Southern California was directly related to new and better transportation networks. The population of Los Angeles alone increased more than tenfold between 1900 and 1940 (see Table 19). This fueled the growth of numerous consumer industries in textiles, food processing, furniture making, and construction. In Texas the oil industry created a boom economy, particularly in the Dallas-Fort Worth area. In San Antonio and South Texas, where the bulk of the Mexican-American population lived, industrial growth was more related to improvements in agricultural technology and food processing as well as to the construction of new highways and rail lines. San Antonio's industries were based on the availability of cheap labor—mostly new Mexican immigrants— cheap energy, and the development of the Winter Garden area of South Texas. San Antonio remained the largest Mexican-American city in Texas. New military installations and advertising promotion of the region added to the growth of Anglo migrants from the Midwest and other regions of Texas.[2]

During this period there was an increasing specialization in laboring occupations, and large numbers of Mexican laborers entered the industrial work force.[3] In San Antonio, for example, 47 percent of a sample of Chicano workers during World War I held semiskilled and skilled jobs in construction, shipping, and manufacturing. Industrial growth and the specialization of labor meant that Mexican-American wage earners, as heads of families, were increasingly integrated into the urban economy, much more so than had been true in the previous century. This also meant that they and their families were subject to technological unemployment and more intense job competition. As was true in the nineteenth century, the economic development of the southwestern cities acted as a magnet, not only for Mexican immigrants but also for hundreds of thousands of others including, to a lesser extent, black migrants.

Before World War II approximately one-half of the Spanish-speaking population became urban dwellers in towns and cities of over 10,000 population. The 1930 census reported that 50.8 percent of all Mexican-heritage families lived in urban regions.[4] El Paso, Albuquerque, San Antonio, and Los Angeles became depots for newly arrived migrants and Mexican immigrants. The mobility engendered by the promise of new jobs and the increased ease of transportation heightened the temporary nature of Mexican-American urban society. Many industrial workers in Texas and California followed the harvest as migrant workers during periods of unemployment or in order to supplement their low-paid jobs in the cities. Other Mexican immigrants arrived in these cities only to move to the rural areas in search of jobs. It was not unusual for Mexican families to migrate as far north as the state of Washington, Chicago, or western Pennsylvania in search of temporary work. Many families opted to settle in these regions, thus founding

TABLE 19

*Mexican-Born, Mexican-Heritage, and Total Urban Population
in Four Cities and Counties, 1900-1950*

	Los Angeles	Tucson	Santa Fe	San Antonio
1900				
Mexican-born	1,613	3,520*	48	4,752*
Total population	170,298	14,689*	5,603	69,422*
1910				
Mexican-born	11,793	4,457*	103	13,226*
Total population	504,131	22,818*	5,072	119,676*
1920				
Mexican-born	29,757	4,261	138*	28,444
Total population	576,673	10,354	7,236	161,379
1930				
Mexican-born	53,684	1,199	14*	1,745
Mexican-heritage	97,116	10,235	834	82,373
Total population	1,238,048	32,506	11,176	231,542
1940				
Mexican-born	36,840	2,874	102	22,530
Total population	1,504,277	35,752	20,325	253,854
1950				
Mexican-born	71,620	2,220	106	33,831
Total population	1,970,358	45,454	20,325	408,442

Note: Only the 1930 census distinguished between the Mexican-born and the Mexican-heritage populations. In that census they enumerated "all persons born in Mexico or having parents born in Mexico." This excluded almost all third-generation Mexican Americans, including a large number of Hispanos who were enumerated with the white population. *Fifteenth Census: Population*, vol. II, p. 27.

Source: U.S. Department of Commerce, Bureau of the Census, Twelfth to Seventeenth Censuses, volumes on population as follows: *Twelfth Census*, vol. I; *Thirteenth Census*, vols. II, III; *Fourteenth Census*, vol. III; *Fifteenth Census*, vol. III; *Sixteenth Census*, vol. II; *Seventeenth Census*, vol II.

(*) County-based data.

some of the first Mexican *colonias* ouside of the Southwest. Low wages, periodic unemployment, and frequent migrations were nothing new to the family experience of Mexican Americans, for these same patterns had been in evidence in earlier decades. What was new was the magnitude of the population involved, the decreasing availability of agricultural lands in the Southwest, and the rapidity of economic change.

CLASS AND GENERATIONAL VARIATIONS

Mexican-American family history during this period continued to be characterized by persisting regional, socioeconomic, and generational differences. Conceivably there were at least four different kinds of family experience corresponding to complexities in the social and economic life, although more can be imagined.[5]

The families of the working-class Mexican immigrants in the cities were predominantly monolingual Spanish-speaking, and hence not acculturated. They were the most disadvantaged segment of Mexican-American society. A very small but socially and politically important portion of Mexican immigrant families were from the middle and upper classes in Mexico. They brought with them the cultural ideals of their class but usually, owing to their social status, accommodated themselves more easily to American society than did the working-class immigrant. The native-born families of laboring and semiskilled occupations were the core populations who lived in the urban barrios. They lived alongside the Mexican immigrant working class and shared, for the most part, the social and economic world of the immigrant, although they had the distinct advantage of being bilingual and more accustomed to life in the United States. The upper-class native-born families, of which the Hispano aristocracy in New Mexico was the most visible element, had their own familial environment. Usually they lived apart from the working classes and had values which shadowed those of the majority middle class. Sometimes they joined with the Mexicano upper-class immigrant families in social and political activities. Within this group the Hispano upper class considered themselves to be set apart by their Spanish heritage from the Mexican-born and Mexican-heritage populations and probably were more a part of American society than any other group.

There is a natural inclination, on the part of social historians, to emphasize the experience of the laboring classes in the cities, since they were the majority of the Mexican-heritage population. This emphasis should not obscure the fact that there were Mexican-American upper and middle classes and that their family experience was distinctly different from those of the immigrant and native-born working classes. Most often these differences lay in the degree to which these families had achieved success in the process of biculturalization, that is, the adaptation of their family lives to the American economic and social environment.

MIDDLE- AND UPPER-CLASS FAMILIES

Perhaps the most detailed information on the middle- and upper-class families of this period has been gathered by Richard García in his study of the intellectual history of San Antonio's Mexican-American population. García estimated that between 1,000 and 1,200 middle- and upper-class families lived in San Antonio during the 1930s. They tended to be more acculturated than the families of the working class. In these families, "Both Mexican and American cultures co-existed." They had their own circle of clubs, schools and churches. Bilingualism within the family was more pronounced and social controls over girls' activities were more strict. While patriarchal family values pervaded all strata of Mexican society of San Antonio, the "Ricos" and "Los de Clase Media" (rich and middle class) contradictorily tended to emphasize the theoretical equality of men and women within marriage. Thus, "For the 'Ricos' the woman was equal but marriage was still her personal 'salvation'." In practice the middle- and upper-class women had more freedom than working-class women, but this was due primarily to their class position. Otherwise "emotionally and intellectually she was reared to 'please, comfort and know her place'." The more affluent families of San Antonio nevertheless felt themselves to be set apart from the masses. They lived in a separate section of the city and only superficially interacted with the multitudes of Mexican immigrants and Mexican-American workers. Throughout the 1930s and 1940s, however, the upper classes maintained a cultural continuity in their practice of Mexican culture.[6]

García's treatment of the nuances of culture and life-style among the various class sectors of San Antonio's Mexican families is a model of how a rich ethnographic detail can inform Mexican-American family history. One of the main differences between the ambience surrounding the lives of these middle- and upper-class families and that of the working class lay in the area of security. The more affluent Mexicanos felt more confident in their daily lives, while insecurity pervaded the lives of the poor. It is probable that the issues of assimilation, biculturalization, and intermarriage were more important for the small numbers of upper- and middle-class Mexican Americans, and less so for the working classes who were more isolated from the Anglo population by language and culture. Similarly, the problems associated with poverty—frequent migration, juvenile delinquency, the breakup of homes, and lack of eduation—were issues more relevant to the family experience of the urban workers than to the Mexican-heritage bourgeois. Among the Mexicano upper classes fewer women and children worked outside the home since there was no economic necessity for them to do so. And in any case it was regarded as being degrading to the family's honor to have them employed for wages outside the home. Needless to say, having steady, well-paid employment or being self-employed meant that they did not have to rely on relief, part-time work, or migration to supplement jobs. The middle-class families were thus able to maintain more stability in their day-to-day lives. Their children's lives were not subject to the periodic disruptions that characterized the lives of working-class poor.

After 1945, due to increasing national prosperity and new pressures for cultural conformity, Spanish-speaking middle- and upper-class families became more important statistically as well as culturally. In the post-World War II period familial diversity as well as an economic stability characteristic of the middle class became more pronounced for Mexican Americans.

WORKING-CLASS MEXICANO FAMILIES

The bulk of the historical and social scientific literature in this period was generated to document the problems of the laboring-class Mexican immigrants as part of a national concern over the effects of unlimited Mexican immigration into the United States. In the arena of family life the tendency was to focus on the social disorganization and pathologies suffered by family members. The lack of the Mexican's acceptance of American family values — specifically the incidence of Mexican-American juvenile delinquency, gang behavior, and crime — became front-page news, especially in the 1940s during the so-called "Zoot Suit Riots" in Los Angeles. While this kind of information is important for illustrating the negative effects of urbanization and industrialization as well as the dynamics of nativism and prejudice, this emphasis obscures more positive aspects of family experience. Instances of poverty and family disorganization mask the fact that for many working-class Mexicanos and Chicanos life within families continued to be a source of support and succor within an oppressive environment. Conceptually what is significant are the strategies these families used to survive despite hardships.

Nowhere were the effects of industrial urban life more pronounced than among the families of the pecan shellers of San Antonio. The Mexican workers, both immigrant and native-born, in this industry were among the lowest-paid industrial workers in America, averaging between one and two dollars a week in 1940. Most often whole families worked for the 400 or more subcontractors in San Antonio. They worked at home or in small, badly lit, unventilated shops for a piece rate. The average annual income for a family of four in 1940 was 251 dollars.[7] This poverty-level income meant that more than one quarter of the 12,000 workers and their families had to migrate periodically to other areas of Texas to supplement their income by picking

Estelle and Fred Quiroz, ca. 1915. Courtesy Arizona Historical Society Library, neg. no. 62692.

Santa Fe woodvendor's children in front of the Hudelson home, ca. 1922. Courtesy Museum of New Mexico, neg. no. 56518. Photo by Sam Hudelson.

Children with their mother on the porch of the old Juan Seguin house near San Antonio, ca. 1930. Courtesy The Barker Library, University of Texas, Austin.

Santa Claus handing out presents at a San Antonio orphanage for Mexican children in the 1930s. Courtesy The Benson Library, University of Texas, Austin.

cotton or working in the sugar-beet fields. A large number of the pecan shellers' families were on relief. In 1939 about half the Mexican workers in San Antonio received public assistance. The economic consequences of all this on family life were summarized by a 1940 government study.

> Crowded into old shanties with an average of more than two persons to the room, three-fourths of the pecan shellers could not afford electric lights and almost nine out of ten did not have inside plumbing. Overcrowding and malnutrition contributed to the high death rate prevailing among Mexicans, particularly from tuberculosis and infant diseases. Migratory work patterns and lack of money for clothes and shoes tended to discourage school attendance.[8]

In order to live it was necessary for everyone within the family over the age of twelve to work. Large families meant more family income. Sickness or unemployment were disasters to these families that had no health insurance or savings. The case summary of the Juan Flores family, gathered by government researchers, tells of the effects of poverty and racial discrimination on family life:

> Juan Flores came to San Antonio in 1918. He never had work other than odd jobs paying $2 or $3 a week until 1923-1925, when he worked for two years at the local water works, earning $2 per day for "pick and shovel work." From 1925 on he and his family spent part of each year in the cotton fields. When crops were good the family usually ended the cotton season with $50 to $60 in cash to last them through the winter. When WPA was started, Juan was assigned a job paying $35 per month. Lack of citizenship caused his termination. Late in 1936 he began working in the pecan plants, where he never earned more than $2.50 to $3.75 per week. His wife also worked in the shelling plants when she could get away from the children. The family's total income was only about $240 in 1938, so that when the plants shut down the family was dependent on Federal surplus commodities and on an occasional loaf of bread obtained from the Salvation Army. Within a month the family was threatened with eviction, because they were already behind with the $4-a-month rent which they paid for their three room shack.[9]

Profiles such as those of the Juan Flores family could be replicated hundreds of times in the cases collected by Manuel Gamio and Paul Taylor, an anthropologist and a labor economist who studied Mexican laborers in the 1920s and 1930s.[10] The standard of living endured by working-class Mexican-immigrant families can also be documented through the statistical profiles gathered by social scientists during this period.

Most researchers agree that laboring conditions were better in California, where the economy was more diversified and wages were higher. But, regardless of urban location the conditions surrounding the family life of Mexican immigrant laborers were oppressive: overcrowding, high rates of infant mortality, substandard housing, malnutrition, juvenile crime, and economic insecurity were prominent features among the Mexican workers of Los Angeles as well.

In 1930 the governor of California commissioned a fact-finding committe to investigate the conditions of labor and family life among the Mexicans of the state.[11] The majority of "Mexicans" studied were immigrants. California had had an enormous increase in the Mexican-immigrant population prior to 1930. There were, however, a significant number of Mexican Americans, native-born citizens who were also the subject of the study. In fact the term "Mexican" in the federal census of 1930 as in the state report referred to all persons of Mexican heritage. In 1930 the Federal Census Bureau reported that 97,116 Mexicans lived in the City of Los Angeles. This was an increase of 92,505 from 1910. Yet in 1930 the census also reported that only 53,684 persons were Mexican-born, meaning that the balance, 43,432 or 44 percent of the city's Mexican-heritage population in 1930, were native-born[12] (see Table 19). Most of the native-born were included in three groups: the children of immigrants, the adult native-born of California, and native-born migrants from other regions of the Southwest. These qualifications being made, it is also true that there was little difference between the socioeconomic standing of the Mexican immigrants and that of the native-born. Both groups were predominantly poor and working class.

Of great concern to nativists and immigration restrictionists throughout the 1920s had been the rising birth rates of the Mexican and nonwhite immigrants. The 1930 California report seemed to confirm their darkest fears. In Los Angeles 22.7 percent of all births were of Mexican-heritage couples. Mexicans made up only 11 percent of the city's population. Nativists tended to overlook the fact that a high death rate, particularly for infants, worked to offset the high birth rates. Infant mortality for Mexicans in Los Angeles County in 1929 was well over 104.5 per 1,000 live births. This compared to 39.6 infant deaths per 1,000 for the white population. As bad as this situation was, it represented an improvement over previous decades. In 1919, for example, infant mortality had been 170 per 1,000 for the Mexican-heritage city residents.[13] It is evident from this that many Mexican-immigrant and native families suffered personal tragedies each day. Poor diets, caused by poverty, was a major cause of infant death; most infants died during premature delivery or succumbed to gastrointestinal diseases, symptoms of malnutrition in the mother's diet (see Table 20).

One of the effects of poverty and migration on family life was to produce orphans that could not be cared for by kin or families. In the nineteenth century the tendency was for families to take in orphaned or unwanted children. The increasing numbers of Mexican-heritage orphans being institutionalized within Los Angeles indicated that the extended-family network was breaking down.[14]

The commission found living conditions similar to those among the pecan shellers in San Antonio. "Two sometimes three shacks built on one very small lot. . . . The shacks are flimsy shells, usually constructed of scrap lumber, old boxes or other salvage." Most of the homes in the Maravilla Park district on the outskirts of the city limits were dilapidated, averaging 4 to 5 persons per house. Only 10 out of 317 homes had flush toilets, 9 out of 158 homes had refrigerators, and 64 out of more than 300 homes had little or no food in their cupboards.[15]

In Los Angeles the large family was not economically advantageous, since the kinds of industrial jobs available did not employ child labor. Still, children worked part-time after school in a number of low-paying jobs. A study of 788 Mexican families in Southern California in 1929 reported that one-fourth of the children had part-time jobs but there was no correlation between a family's income and the numbers of children. In comparison to the pecan shellers of San Antonio, the Spanish-speaking families of Los Angeles had a higher income, averaging $1,500 a year. But this was still at or below the poverty level for a family of four.[16]

TABLE 20

Infant Mortality Rates (per 1,000 live births)
for the Mexican and White Populations of Los Angeles County
(unincorporated area), 1916-1929

Year	Infant Mortality Rate	
	White	Mexican
1916	70.0	265.0
1917	67.4	255.1
1918	71.3	348.1
1919	61.9	170.0
1920	60.2	186.7
1921	57.6	179.0
1922	78.4	243.4
1923	80.5	250.6
1924	61.3	163.2
1925	58.5	166.1
1926	41.9	124.6
1927	45.4	96.9
1928	51.7	116.8
1929	39.6	104.5

Source: *Report of Governor C.C. Young's Mexican Fact-Finding Committee*, Table 7, p. 183.

Like the Mexican pecan shellers, the Mexican families of Los Angeles experienced a great deal of transiency, a continuation of patterns begun in the previous century. Less than 21 percent of the skilled and unskilled workers and their families continued to live in Los Angeles during the period 1921-1928. Transiency was related to the proximity of the Mexican border, which made it easy for Mexicanos to travel back and forth according to the economic cycle. In addition a large number of Mexicans in the city moved on to the agricultural areas, lured by higher wages and the opportunities for family income as farmworkers. Like San Antonio, Los Angeles' barrio "functioned as a depot or 'stepping stone' for Mexican immigrants recruited to work in the Midwest and other areas of the Southwest."[17]

NATIVE WORKING-CLASS FAMILIES

It seems likely that the conditions surrounding family life for the native-born adults of long residence in the Southwest were better than for the Mexican immigrants, if only because they were more likely to be fluent in English and hence be more able to get better-paying jobs. There were only a few studies of the Mexican-American native-born, as a group separate from the Mexican immigrant, during the 1920s or 1930s.

A special census report published in 1933 provides a rough outline of the major characteristics of the native-born Mexican-heritage families (see Table 21). Nationwide, the natives were more likely to live in rural regions than was true for immigrants. Fifty-five percent of all Mexican immigrants lived in urban settings, while only 41 percent of the natives lived in cities in 1930. The families of the native-born were a minority of the Spanish speaking in all the largest cities of the Southwest, ranging from 16 percent in Los Angeles to 33 percent in San Antonio. Compared to the immigrant families, the natives were more likely to own their own homes, but there was little difference between the two groups with respect to the values of these dwellings. Roughly the same proportions of Spanish speaking, regardless of nativity, lived in substandard ($1,500 and below), middle-class ($3,000 to $4,999) and affluent ($10,000 and over) housing, which suggests that the native families were not necessarily better off than the immigrants (see Table 21). The native-born had a smaller family size, fewer employed adults per household, and lower proportions of lodgers than did the Mexican-immigrant families. Overall, however, the differences in living conditions were not as great as the similarities.

There were ideological and cultural differences between the native-born and the Mexican-immigrant groups. Intermarriage between Mexican immigrants and Mexican Americans was quite common, and there were occasional, superficial, conflicts between the two groups. Ironically, the native-born

TABLE 21

Characteristics of Native-Born and Mexican-Born Urban Families in 1930

1. Urban/Rural Proportions of Mexican-Heritage Families in the U.S.

	Urban		Rural		
	N	%	N	%	Total N
Native	31,022	41.5	43,592	48.5	74,614
Immigrant	112,819	55.5	90,267	44.5	203,086

2. Families by Nativity in Selected Southwestern Cities

	Native-Born		Mexican-Born	
	N	%	N	%
a. Belvedere (L.A.)	89	23.7	286	76.3
b. El Paso	1,339	24.2	11,091	75.8
c. Los Angeles	3,007	16.0	15,771	84.0
d. San Antonio	5,634	33.4	11,226	66.6
e. Tucson	670	31.6	1,451	68.4

3. Percent of Families Owning Homes

Native-born	31.7
Mexican-born	25.2

4. Urban Home Ownership by Value

	Substandard ($1500–below)	Middle Class ($3,000–4,999)	Upper Class ($10,000–above)
Native-born (N = 9,826)	59.4	10.4	1.0
Mexican-born (N = 28,420)	58.4	10.3	1.1

5. Median Family Size

Native-born	4.14
Mexican-born	4.24

6. Families Having Gainfully Employed Workers

	None	1	2	3 or more
Native (N = 31,022)	4.7	64.4	19.2	11.7
Mexican-born (N = 112,819)	3.8	62.7	20.5	13.0

7. Families Having No Lodgers

Native-born	92.2
Mexican-born	88.6

Source: *Fifteenth Census of the United States: 1930, Population: Special Report on Foreign-Born White Families by Country of Birth of Head with an Appendix Giving Statistics for Mexican, Indian, Chinese and Japanese Families* (Washington, D.C.: G.P.O., 1933).

called the Mexican immigrants "Chicanos" or "Cholos," while the immigrants sometimes referred to the native-born as "Pochos." Evidence indicates that the native New Mexican Hispanos and the Mexican immigrants seemed to be the most at odds. There was "a more deeply seated prejudice between the Spanish Americans and the Old Mexicano Mexicans (immigrants) than . . . between Anglos and Spanish Americans."[18] Nevertheless Mexican immigrants as well as Hispanos felt that same kind of racial and cultural prejudice by Anglos.

Perhaps the most thorough studies of Hispano families during this period were conducted in the small pueblos of northern and central New Mexico.[19] Indeed, the plight of the rural Hispano villagers has continued to be a subject for intensive study among social scientists, while this concern has tended to overshadow the research that has been done on the urban Hispanos in the cities. The village researchers were concerned about the increasing migration of families to the larger cities in New Mexico, Colorado, California, and Arizona. They found that once the families had moved to the city, Hispanos frequently retained close kinship ties as well as property in their native villages.[20]

New job opportunities created by World War II accelerated Hispano migration from the rural villages to the cities. Large numbers of the younger generation moved to Albuquerque, Phoenix, and Southern California to work in the war industries plants.[21] Mexican immigrants made up only a tiny fraction of the Spanish-surnamed urban populations of Albuquerque and Santa Fe during these years. In 1940 only 629 persons of Mexican birth lived in Albuquerque, and only 115 in Santa Fe. Most of the Mexican immigrants who lived in New Mexico settled in the counties of the Mesilla Valley and worked as agricultural laborers. This pattern, of a predominantly Hispano migration into New Mexican cities, was typical of previous decades as well.[22] The Hispanos who lived in these cities were there because they were unable to earn a living on their traditional lands, and this was a direct result of decades of outside encroachment, especially that of the National Forest Service. Small family farms could not hope to compete with the large modern agribusiness corporations in the Mesilla Valley and elsewhere in New Mexico. Increasingly they were forced to migrate in search of jobs to supplement their meager incomes. In this repsect the dynamics of New Mexican Hispano family life closely paralleled that of Mexican immigrants.[23]

Even though many Hispano migrants in the cities may have retained their familial ties to relatives back home, and this became easier to do with the construction of modern roads and telephones, there were differences between their family lives and those of the rural villagers they left behind. Cleofas M. Jaramillo, a descendant of an old Hispano family, conducted a series of interviews with long-time New Mexican residents to record their remembrances of fast-fading customs. One old-timer lamented, "The younger generation, finding the strangers' customs new and attractive, began to adopt them and forget their own. The quiet reserve and respect has gone. . . . The old Spanish courtesy and hospitality has also changed, to the regret of the elders, who have found it hard to get accustomed to the new ways. . . . The land of *Poco Tiempo* has become the land of haste and hurry."[24] Jaramillo's subject was probably reflecting on the life-styles of the Hispano youth who had moved to the larger towns and cities.

In Albuquerque the San Jose barrio was composed almost entirely of Hispano migrants. Frank Moore, who studied this barrio in 1941, found an increasing tendency for children to leave home at an early age, "thus destroying the old family solidarity."[25] Laura Waggoner, who also studied this barrio in the 1940s, found that many Hispano migrants moved to this section of the city because of the availability of low-cost housing. Within their enclave Hispano family life was characterized by a mixture of urban and rural patterns. Community social controls, fiestas, dances, and religious celebrations commingled with periodic unemployment, public relief, and transiency. Waggoner believed that poverty acted as a buffer preventing a more rapid change in family life. "The effects of disorganization and instability by unemployment in the developing slum character of San Jose have been ineffective in creating rapid social change in people whose lives and traditions have been geared to low standards of living that privation and further reduction in standards are not able to materially disturb their equanimity."[26]

In 1943 Sigurd Johansen was pessimistic about the villagers' ability to maintain their old family traditions in the cities. He wrote: "Family solidarity is decreasing. Lack of parental control and dissatisfaction with prevailing conditions have developed too rapidly for adaptation to take place, and disintegration has started."[27] Undoubtedly the sense of extended-family solidarity was stronger for Hispanos who had ancient roots in the region. Nancie González suggested that the Hispano immigrants in Albuquerque probably felt less *anomie* and had less social disorganization in their lives than did the Mexican immigrants farther to the south in Las Cruces and El Paso. She found that the urbanization of Hispanos resulted in more ethnic exogamy (with Anglo-Americans), more educational opportunities for children, and increased juvenile delinquency. At the same time there was a tendency for Hispanos to retain their traditional Catholic religious affiliations. No clear pattern of Protestant or secular marriages emerged among the urbanizing Hispanos.[28]

Hispanos, the long-term residents from established families, should have been more likely to experience upward socioeconomic mobility than would Mexican immigrants. A few examples of Anglo-Hispano joint business ventures in the nineteenth century would seem to promise greater upward mobility in the twentieth century for Hispanos. A study of upper-class Hispano families in urban areas of New Mexico found that skin color was an important feature of their status. Individuals with lighter complexion were more often monolingual English speaking, even while retaining a pride in their Spanish heritage.[29] But before World War II limited evidence for urban areas of New Mexico indicates that remaining linguistic, cultural, and educational barriers prevented most Hispanos from achieving middle-class status. The 1907 *Albuquerque City Directory* did not list any Spanish-surnamed professionals, and few Hispanos were able to afford a college education until the G.I. Bill of World War II. Most of the economic and educational progress of the New Mexican Hispanos occurred after that war.[30]

Thus it appears that in many respects the working-class Hispano family experience may well have resembled that of the Mexican immigrant. Large numbers of Hispanos were themselves uprooted migrants who had been forced to leave their traditional village cultures. In the cities they were subject to the same kinds of discrimination, job competition, and poverty as were the Mexican immigrants of San Antonio and Los Angeles. Once in the urban environment, both Hispanos and Mexican immigrants retained strong ties to their family and kin back home. And Hispano urban dwellers, because of low wages, were forced to pursue a migratory existence, often competing with Mexicano migrant labor.

INTERMARRIAGE 1900-1945

The higher rate of intermarriage between persons of non-Mexican heritage and Hispanos was one very important difference from the Mexican immigrants. The rate of intermarriage for Hispanos with out-group members increased steadily, with the greatest jumps coming after World War II (see Table 22). Within urban areas like Albuquerque the rate of intermarriage was

TABLE 22

Intermarriage of Hispanos and Anglos in Bernalillo County (Albuquerque), 1915-1964

Year	Total Marriages Involving Hispanos	Percent Mixed Marriages
1915-1916	108	14.3
1926	209	10.0
1936	313	17.9
1945-1946	430	21.6
1953	535	23.4
1964	815	32.5

Source: Data compiled by Nancie González in *The Spanish-Americans of New Mexico: A Heritage of Pride* (Albuquerque: University of New Mexico Press, 1969). Taken from Table 7, p. 170.

somewhat lower. A student of exogamy among Hispanos in Albuquerque between 1924 and 1940 found that only between 6 and 9 percent of the Hispano population married outside their ethnic group.[31] But five years later in 1945 another study found a substantially higher rate in Bernalillo County. Over 20 percent of all Hispano marriages were, by then, exogamous, and the vast majority of these unions were by civil ceremonies. Thus in the period 1900-1945 older patterns of intermarriage prevailed, with noticeable changes taking place after World War II. In the nineteenth century, marriages between Mexican immigrants and the native-born Spanish speaking were much more pronounced than exogamous unions. This pattern of intragroup acculturation by marriage continued to be notable in the twentieth century, as was noted in a 1931 study.[32] A study of ethnic exogamy in Los Angeles during the period 1924-1933 found that 116 per 1,000, or less than 12 percent, of all Mexican-heritage unions were exogamous. Of these out-group marriages three-fourths were with Latin Americans, Filipinos, Spaniards, and Italians.[33] This was a continuation of a pattern that was first noticeable in the previous century.

The very limited historical data on intermarriage indicates that the barriers of poverty, culture, racial discrimination, and geographic isolation were still important during the first half of the twentieth century. Studies of intermarriage in the postwar period (after 1945) suggest that intermarriage has increased dramatically. This has been attributed to reduction in these same barriers.[34]

THE IMMIGRANT EXPERIENCE AND THE ETHNIC FAMILY

For the Spanish-speaking population of the urban Southwest history was indeed process and change as each year thousands of new immigrants entered the barrios and colonias in the cities. These immigrant families underwent increased pressures to conform to majority cultural mores, in the factories, in the schools, and in the social environment. This drama of adaptation has been a central theme in American history, and none has moved the popular imagination as much as that of the millions of European immigrants who came to the United States during the period 1880-1924. In some ways the experiences of Catholic European immigrants paralleled that of the Mexican Americans in the first half of the twentieth century.

The Irish immigrant experience dates from the seventeenth century, with the largest waves coming to America during the tragic potato blights in the first half of the nineteenth century. The majority of Irish immigrants settled in cities and worked in low-status industrial laboring jobs. There was little upward mobility between the first and second generations. Nevertheless, by 1900 there developed a heterogeneous family class system which was expressed in the colloquial expressions "real lace" Irish (upper class), "lace curtain" Irish (middle class), and "shanty" Irish (working class).

A major factor in the history of the Irish American family was the importance of the Irish Catholic Church as a basis for social organization and normative control. In the period 1900-1945 the parish became the focus of community life replacing the ethnic neighborhood. According to one ethnographic description of family life within a Massachusetts parish during the period 1920-1950, the Irish Americans recreated a kind of village community.

> The parish was compact enough that some of the children knew almost everyone and at least half the adults knew one another personally and knew more by sight. People with problems and children with handicaps were enveloped in a relatively closed community. Priests were a familiar sight on the streets talking with adults and watching the young. Older teenagers and young adult men would gather at the shops in the evenings and teenage girls in groups would find some reason to shop or to visit the church. There were informal cliques among all age groups and, harking back to Ireland, most of these were age and sex graded. The pace of life was not fast. Small talk passed back and forth. Those in need were visited by the priests. Women individually and voluntarily helped other families at times of crises.[35]

Irish-American families adapted to the American environment through their control of parish affairs and the local Catholic church. Many of the ethnic traits associated with being of Irish descent were ultimately linked to this fact. The celebration of Sunday masses and holy days were community as well as family events. The church's doctrines, as interpreted by the Irish-American clergy, molded the way children were socialized, reinforced the husband's authority in the home, supported the traditional kinship obligations, and sanctioned the rites of passage.

In comparison to Mexican-American families, Irish-American families were more successful in entering the middle and upper classes during the twentieth century. Mexican Americans, while Catholic, did not control their community parish churches, and, moreover, after the Mexican Revolution a significant number of Mexican-immigrant men were profoundly alienated from the church as an institution. Ethnicity for Mexican Americans was less related to the Catholic religion. For the Irish Americans the native church was of fundamental importance in everyday life.[36]

One of the earliest attempts by sociologists to study the immigrant family experience was that of William I. Thomas and Florian Znaniecki in their book entitled *The Polish Peasant in Europe and America.*[37] Their ethnographic investigation of minute facets of family life among the Polish immigrants in 1918-1920 revealed a pattern of disorganization in older rural values and the reorganization of social and cultural values in urban American settings. Thomas and Znaniecki noted the inevitable breakdown of communal village

Mr. and Mrs. Manuel Escalante with their children at their homestead on East Irvington Street, Tucson, ca. 1940. Courtesy Arizona Historical Society Library, neg. no. 64966.

A Hispano father teaching his children how to irrigate, ca. 1940. Note adobe home in background. Courtesy Museum of New Mexico, neg. no. 58868.

Jacinto and Carmen Orozco with their family in Tucson about 1940. Courtesy Arizona Historical Society Library, neg. no. 64444.

School yard of a Mexican school in the San Antonio barrio, November 30, 1947. Courtesy The Benson Library, University of Texas, Austin.

social controls in family life and the substitution of hedonistic individualism induced by the American environment. They concluded that the psychological and moral structures of the traditional Polish peasant family inevitably gave way before modern influences.[38]

During the period 1900-1945 Polish families underwent processes of adaptation to the American environment very similar in some respects to those experienced by Mexican immigrants and their offspring. More than one and a half million Polish immigrants came to America between 1880 and 1914. The majority came as landless peasants and settled in eastern industrial cities where they congregated in working-class ethnic enclaves. Polish Americans of the second generation experienced only modest upward social mobility because of the tendency of sons to follow their father's occupations. Women were discouraged from getting a formal education and were expected to limit their involvements to home and family, but economic necessity drove them to seek employment outside the home in low-status domestic and unskilled jobs. Conflicts and tensions between the patriarchal norms of the older peasant traditions and American society continued especially with regard to the family's control of wives, mothers, and daughters.

During the years prior to World War II Polonia, or the community of Polish Americans, developed gradations of ethnic identification depending on socioeconomic status, neighborhood residence, and language usage. In 1942 Louis Adamic in *What's Your Name?* found that Polish Americans of the second and third generations were losing their identification with their ethnic roots by Americanizing their names. A significant number of the descendants of Polish immigrants were thus no longer identifiable to social researchers. At the same time, however, Polonia as scattered urban ethnic enclaves continued to thrive.[39]

Previous discussion of the Italian-immigrant family's experience in relation to the Mexican American's has pointed to the striking parallels between the two groups in the late nineteenth century. These similarities continued into the twentieth century, with the difference that as a group Italian-American families experienced relatively more upward socioeconomic mobility related to generational status. Like the Mexican Americans the Italian immigrants and their children sustained a strong ideal of family solidarity, valued extended kinship relations, socialized children to be *ben educato*, or well educated, in showing respect for their elders and family, maintained their native language in the home, lived in ethnic enclaves, and had a low rate of intermarriage with non-Italian-heritage populations. Immigration from Italy and return migration to the mother country continued to be important forces in maintaining ethnic values. Like many Mexican immigrants, many Italians hoped to return to Italy and considered their stay in the United States only temporary. There was only a modest degree of upward social mobility for the second generation. Once in America Italian immigrants did not rely on the Catholic Church for support in maintaining the vitality of their family life. Often this was because the church hierarchy usually consisted of Irish Catholics, who were thought to be unsympathetic to Italian culture.

While the first- and second-generation Italian-American families paralleled the Mexican-American experience in important affective and structural ways, significant divergencies appeared by the coming of age of the third generation. There was a significant entry into the white-collar middle class, a dramatic drop in the birth rate, and a general increase in the level of education. Egalitarian attitudes regarding family decisions surfaced with this generation. Nevertheless, despite generational changes in the content of ethnic culture some traditional patterns persisted. Husbands and wives were expected to maintain "distinctly separate roles, duties, and obligations and turned to kin of the same sex for advice and companionship so that the society was essentially sex-segregated."[40]

Thus, despite upward social mobility and the passage of generations Italian-American families seemed to maintain some elements of the older culture. In part this may have been due to the strength of identification with Italy related to the continued exchange of immigrants and emigrants between the mother country and the United States.[41]

While the dynamics of the immigrant experience for many European and Mexican immigrants were superficially similar in that both were uprooted from rural, preindustrial ways of life, there were some major differences. The most important was that the mother country, Mexico, was easily accessible to hundreds of thousands of Mexican urban immigrants. This made it possible for families to maintain more frequent contacts with their home villages and towns than was true for the Catholic European immigrants. Psychologically it meant that they could always retain the option of relatively easy return. They were less cut off emotionally as well as physically from their motherland. Frequently they returned to visit friends and family or, as often was the case, sponsored a serial migration of relatives. As in the nineteenth century, many Mexican immigrants considered their residence in the United States only as a temporary episode. While European immigration after World War I declined, Mexican immigration, with the exception of the few years during the repatriation movement in the early 1930s, never really stopped. Even during the years of the Great Depression thousands of immigrants continued to cross the border and seek jobs in the cities and countryside.

Researchers who have studied the Mexican-immigrant families in the period 1900-1945 believe they were not as disrupted by urban pressures as those of the European immigrants. Alex Saragosa has argued that in the United States the Mexican-immigrant family maintained a "Mexican ethos." This was because of the continuing large flow of immigrants as well as the "presence of culturally reinforcing institutions," largely the existence of segregated barrios, the continued use of Spanish as a spoken language, and an autonomous social and cultural life.[42] Added to this was the fact that many urban immigrant families frequently lived and worked part of the year in rural areas where they were less subject to industrial urban influences.

Mario García's study of Mexican-immigrant families in El Paso, Texas, in the 1920s indicates that there was a "continuity and persistence of family patterns common in Mexico; but in an adaptive rather than a static form." Even while adopting their lives to the American environment, Mexican immigrants retained their ethnic and national identity. García identified four areas of continuity: first, a reliance on family and kinship networks; second, the persistence of male responsibility for being wage earners in occupations not radically different from those they had had in Mexico, third, the persistence of Mexican cultural forms, language, foods, and folk customs; and fourth, a continued belief in woman's subordinate position within the family.[43]

From the limited historical research which has been done thus far it appears that there was considerable stability in the cultural contexts of family life for Mexican immigrants. All this would not be to ignore or de-emphasize the evidence of chronic family disorganization noted by the social science studies previously discussed. Most certainly there was diversity within the immigrant experience corresponding to a great number of social and economic factors. Nevertheless, the continuities in the immigrant family's experience may have been the single most significant feature of the social life in the southwestern barrios.

Thus it would appear that prior to World War II, aspects of Mexican-American family history had strong links to that of the previous century. Mexican immigration, the experience of poverty, transiency, the persistence of traditional values, and low rates of intermarriage were commonalities with the past. The magnitude of the social and economic changes which transpired during the first half of the twentieth century intensified already existing patterns of family life. By far the most important changes in family life were those experienced by the sons and daughters of Mexican immigrants who came of age after World War II. After 1945 a new dynamic was added to Chicano social history, that of a enormous growth of consumerism, of multinational corporate expansion, of the powerful effect of modern media, and of a postwar prosperity unparalleled in American history. The subject of the next chapter will be a review of the effects of these postwar phenomena on the contemporary Chicano family.

CHAPTER 8

The Contemporary Chicano Family

> *It is no accident that social science depictions of the Chicano, whether they involve the family or some other area, are almost inevitably pejorative and/or pathological, for they reinforce and legitimate the lowly status of Chicanos. . . . The myth of the Mexican-American family, then, is a useful myth in blaming the problems and oppression of Chicanos on themselves.*
> –Alfredo Mirandé and Evangelina Enríquez, *La Chicana: The Mexican-American Woman*, pp. 115–116.

THE STUDY OF THE present-day Chicano or Mexican-American family is a subject complicated by a lack of satisfactory theories, methodologies, and data. One indication of this is the inevitable academic debate that arises when deciding what terminology to use in describing the group. In this chapter I have used the term "Chicano" interchangeably with "Mexican American." Of the two words, "Chicano" probably has the widest usage as a self-referent (see Appendix B). Just as those working in the general field of family studies, those working on Chicano subjects have not evolved an acceptable framework to describe, much less explain, the psychological subtleties and changing realities of family life.

Contemporary researchers are attempting to move beyond the stereotypical and simplistic approaches which characterize much of the early literature. As yet, however, there has been no attempt to integrate historical approaches into a general description of family life. Most sociological and psychological models of family life have been differentiated into normal vs. pathogenic types rather than being focused on the adaptive processes that characterize all human cultures.

112

THE SOCIAL SCIENTIFIC LITERATURE: 1945-1960

After World War II social scientists turned their attention more and more to Spanish-speaking families in the United States. Prior to the 1960s researchers like Clyde Kluckholn, William Madsen, Arthur Rubel, Cecila Heller, and Margaret Clark published influential studies that probed Mexican-American social life. A number of other investigators summarized what were thought to be the main characteristics of Mexican-American families. A covert and sometimes not so hidden assumption of many of these early postwar studies was that the ethnic family was somehow responsible for preventing the full assimilation of Mexicans into American society. They implicitly considered the acculturation of middle-class Anglo-American values as an inevitable process. Consequently they evaluated the ethnic familistic behaviors and attitudes among Mexican Americans as being less desirable and possibly even pathological when contrasted with those of other Americans.

This new interest in Mexican-American families coincided with the rapid urbanization of Spanish-speaking minorities in eastern and western cities and a massive postwar surge in Mexican immigration, two demographic events which were to have long-term effects on American society. The first movement, that of urbanization, transformed the ambiance of inner-city life and eventually had political consequences as Mexicanos came to displace some older populations in metropolitan regions. In the postwar years Mexican Americans became a national urban minority. They were the fastest urbanizing group in the United States. Three-fourths of the increase of the Mexican-American urban population took place in large metropolitan areas. Los Angeles and San Antonio, in particular, reached critical masses in their Spanish-speaking populations by the 1970s. This in turn created a demographic basis for a political and social revitalization movement, the birth of "Chicanismo," a new pride in the history and culture of Mexicanos in the United States.[1]

The second demographic trend that promised to change American society and have international consequences as well was a new surge of Mexican immigration. Between 1945 and 1960 Mexican immigration reached unprecedented proportions. More than five million new immigrants entered the United States as legal immigrants, braceros, and undocumented workers (see Table 23). To put this movement into perspective, it is necessary only to note that during the twenty years after World War II more Mexican immigrants entered the United States than had come during the previous one hundred years. Due to changes in United States immigration laws much of this immigration, perhaps a majority of it, was illegal. This meant that increasing numbers of Mexican Americans in the cities lived in constant fear of apprehension, subject to extortion and to unbelievable exploitation. It also meant that due to this proliferating source of cheap labor the Sun-Belt states took the lead in national economic growth.

Unfortunately most of the research that was conducted on the Mexican-American family during these years ignored or tended to de-emphasize the important demographic changes which were taking place in the urban Southwest. Most studies were of Mexican Americans in rural or small towns or in cities with relatively static Mexican-American populations (see Table 24). The approach taken in these works tended to bias the portrait of the Chicano family in the direction of static and traditional cultures. Often they viewed the Mexican-American family in terms of exotic varieties or anachronistic survivals. Patriarchy, archaic child-rearing practices, *curanderismo* (faith and herb healing), Catholic folk customs, and a host of other rural cultural practices were seen as root causes responsible for the lack of the Mexican American's social and economic progress.

Actually, few of these postwar investigations focused specifically on the Mexican-American family. Rather, they treated the family as part of a

TABLE 23

Mexican Immigration, 1945-1960

Year	Legal Entrants	Aliens Apprehended or Deported
1945	6,455	80,760
1946	6,805	116,320
1947	7,775	214,543
1948	8,730	193,543
1949	7,977	289,400
1950	6,841	469,581
1951	6,372	510,355
1952	9,600	531,719
1953	18,454	839,149
1954	37,456	1,035,282
1955	50,772	165,186
1956	65,047	58,792
1957	49,154	45,640
1958	26,712	45,164
1959	23,061	42,732
1960	32,084	39,750

Note: These figures are not to be taken as an accurate count of the total immigrant flow, since apprehensions and deportations represent only a fraction, perhaps one-sixth of the total undocumented entrants. Also the apprehensions reflect the changing enforcement policies of the Border Patrol.

Source: Stanley R. Ross, *Views Across the Border: The United States and Mexico* (Albuquerque: University of New Mexico Press, 1978), pp. 166-167.

complex social problem. Margaret Clark and Ari Kiev studied community health; Cecila Heller, gangs and juvenile delinquency; and William Madsen and Arther Rubel, rural poverty in the border region. Those researchers who

TABLE 24

Social Science Literature Dealing with the Mexican-American Family, 1945-1960

1. Cecila Heller, *Mexican American Youth: Forgotten Youth at the Crossroads* (New York: Random House, 1966).

Area and Focus of Research:
Mexican-American youth in Los Angeles

2. Margaret Clark, *Health in the Mexican American Culture* (Berkeley, Los Angeles, and London: University of California Press, 1959).

Area and Focus of Research:
Sal Si Puedes barrio in San Jose, California

3. Ari Kiev, *Curanderismo: Mexican American Folk Psychiatry* (New York: Free Press, 1968).

Area and Focus of Research:
Curandero clients in San Antonio

4. William Madsen, *Mexican Americans of South Texas* (New York: Holt Rinehart and Winston, 1963).

Area and Focus of Research:
McAllen, Texas (Hidalgo County)

5. Arthur Rubel, *Across the Tracks: Mexican Americans in a Texas City* (Austin and London: University of Texas Press, 1966).

Area and Focus of Research:
New Lots (Mission, Texas), the Mexiquito barrio

6. Julian Samora and Richard Lamanna, *Mexican Americans in a Midwest Metropolis: A Study of East Chicago* (Mexican American Study Project, Division of Research, Graduate School of Business Administration, U.C.L.A., 1967).

Area and Focus of Research:
East Chicago, Illinois

7. Norman Humphrey, "The Changing Structure of the Detroit Mexican Family: An Index of Acculturation," *American Sociological Review* 9, no. 6 (1944), pp. 622-626.

Area and Focus of Research:
Detroit, Michigan

8. Roland Tharp et al., "Changes in Marriage Roles Accompanying the Acculturation of the Mexican American Wife," *Journal of Marriage and the Family* 30 (August 1968), pp. 404-412.

Area and Focus of Research:
Tucson Mexican-American Women

Note: The above is not intended to be an exhaustive listing of the social science literature bearing on the Mexican-American family published in this period.

studied the urban Mexican-American populations did not deal with the full range of personal and familial experience but only with selected segments of the Spanish-speaking community (barrio youth for Heller, the Sal Si Puedes barrio in San Jose for Clark, *curandero* clients in San Antonio for Kiev, and Tucson women for Tharp et al.). There was no systematic attempt to analyze the diversity in family life-styles in metropolitan areas of the Southwest. A few investigators studied urban barrios in the Midwest. They were mainly interested in the process of familial acculturation (Samora and Lamana), but they gave little attention to the ways in which the Mexican Americans of this region differed from those of the urban Southwest. In general, regional and economic class variations were not issues of concern. The tendency was for the researchers to de-emphasize the heterogeneous nature of urban Mexican-American society.

During the 1970s an emerging group of Chicano social scientists began to question the methodologies and assumptions of this postwar literature. The critics pointed out that many of the previous studies had been biased by an uncritical acceptance of a unidirectional acculturation model. As Lea Ybarra pointed out:

> Social scientists were aided in perpetuating negative stereotypes and in furthering ethnocentric, value laden attitudes by utilizing a model of acculturation which readily allowed them to make assumptions and conclusions of other cultures based on their own societal norms and values.[2]

Others attacked the exaggerated importance that had been ascribed to *machismo*. The researchers of the 1960s had, almost unanimously, accepted the cult of male superiority as an explanation for the dynamics and pathologies of family life. Similarly the postwar researchers accepted the patriarchal family as being solely responsible for the underachievement of Chicano children. Many critics of the 70s felt that the older literature had exaggerated and distorted certain aspects of Chicano family life. Alfredo Mirandé summarized the "tangle of pathology" that the old research assumed to arise due to family dynamics:

> It [the Mexican-American family] propagates the subordination of women, impedes individual achievement, engenders passivity and dependence, stifles normal personality development and, on occasion, even gives rise to incestuous feelings among siblings.[3]

Basically the Chicano social scientists argued that more empirical research needed to be done, that Chicano family studies should be more cautious about stereotypes and generalizations, and that future research should take into account the diversity of family experience.

In 1970, at the very time that these calls for more objective research were being raised, a major research project, conducted by U.C.L.A.'s Graduate School of Business, resulted in the publication of *The Mexican-American People* by Leo Grebler, Joan W. Moore, and Ralph Guzmán. This massive study while reflecting some of the methodologies and assumptions that had been criticized by Chicano social scientists, promised to break new ground in the study of the family. It was based on large representative samples of urban populations. The research team formed their conclusions after conducting in-depth interviews and gathering survey data in Los Angeles and San Antonio.

The major conclusions reached by Grebler et al. with respect to the Mexican-American urban families were as follows:

(1) Only 3 to 4 percent of the urban families lived in extended-family households, "disproving the notion that Mexican Americans are familistic enough to establish joint households in an urban setting."

(2) *Compadrazgo* was no longer a major familial reality among urban families: "although still viable, [*compadrazgo*] appears to be a minor feature of kinship and community social organization in the major urban centers."

(3) There was little difference between Mexican-American and other families with respect to the degree of familial help given to its members. Kinship support was greatest among high-income Mexican Americans living outside the barrio.

(4) A high proportion of broken homes existed. Almost one-third of the sample respondants stated that they had been reared by one parent.

(5) There was a wide divergence between the ideal of patriarchal authority in decision-making and the actual practice of joint decision-making within urban families. Deviations from the ideal of patriarchy were greatest among the younger second- and third-generation Mexican Americans. *Machismo* was not a salient characteristic of ethnic family life but was related more to geographic segregation and socioeconomic class status.

(6) A close study of parents' attitudes toward the ideal child revealed that there was no significant difference in the educational goals desired. Parents expected that, for both boys and girls, a good education would be one of strict discipline.[5]

Many of the hypotheses raised by Grebler et al. in *The Mexican-American People* have yet to be tested by other social scientists. The finding of a high proportion of broken homes and family instability, for example, has not been pursued by subsequent research. Consequently, we do not know the exact social meaning of this finding. Our analysis of household composition from the previous century suggests this phenomenon may well be a long-term phenomenon, most likely the result of endemic poverty and job insecurity. A close study of the class and generational variations in broken homes may reveal other factors that have had historical precedents. Grebler's view that patriarchal values and the ideal of family stability were myths that existed because of "weaknesses in both the family structure and the male role" has not been clarified or challenged by the most recent research. Indeed, the whole area of family ideology is fertile ground for further investigations.

Our findings for the nineteenth century suggest that the gap between familial expectations and day-to-day reality may always have been an important characteristic of family life. Certainly the idealization of sex roles and paternal authority stems from the historical culture, just as the forces that create family instability are the result of long-term urban and industrial processes. The gap between what is believed to exist and what in fact is encountered in everyday life may provide psychologically oriented researchers with a clue to understanding mental health problems in a family context. But explaining the consequences of this conflict will also have to take into consideration that it has existed at least since the nineteenth century.

Recent research tends to confirm rather than challenge the conclusions reached in *The Mexican-American People*. Jaime Sena-Rivera's study of extended kinship among a sample of midwestern urban Chicanos found that residential extended-family households were almost nonexistent. He emphasized, however, that the *casa* (household) expression of familism was less important in Mexican-American culture than the kinship networks outside the home (*familia*). *La familia* was an all-emcompassing term describing a variety of relatives and *compadres*, most of whom lived close by and rendered mutual aid. Rivera concluded that *compadrazgo* was a dying institution. It was "insignificant for viable *familia* structure." A much more important feature of contemporary family life was volunteerism. "In no instance . . . did authority appear among adults where it did not seem to rest upon voluntary asking and receiving guidance for behavior, even for children in regard to promoting family interaction norms."[6]

The hypothesis that Mexican-American families are not strictly speaking patriarchal in decision-making has found support in a number of other studies. A 1975 survey of seventy-six farm-labor families in California, many of which consisted of urban migrants, concluded that egalitarian decision-making and action-taking was the predominant norm.[7] A 1977 study found that marital satisfaction was highest among those families where there were egalitarian power relationships. Generally class rather than ethnicity was important in explaining a couple's satisfaction in marriage, with lower-class couples being less satisfied when the wife was working than in the case of middle- and upper-class couples.[8]

Maxine Baca Zinn has undertaken perhaps the most sophisticated analysis of the complex interaction of culture, the economy, and changing women's roles. She found that Mexican-American families were mixed with regard to "traditional" and "modern" values. The ideals of patriarchy mediated how much power women exercised within marriage, but these ideals were not the sole determinates of their status. Where women worked outside the home, they had more power in their relationship to their husbands. In these households "their families were less male dominant but not less male authoritarian."[9] Baca Zinn concluded that cultural norms of male authority were important but not overriding in influencing decision-making within families. While retaining patriarchal values and ideals, these families of working women also demonstrated egalitarian decision-making and shared conjugal power. Thus ethnicity, more specifically ethnic culture, was important but not singularly so in understanding the texture of daily life.[10]

Since the Grebler study in 1970 several researchers have produced findings demonstrating that family solidarity among Mexican Americans is more than just an ideal or a myth. There has been a growing sophistication in defining familism and family solidarity. In comparison to other groups Mexican Americans have been found to have greater behavioral familism. One study of 666 Mexican Americans and 340 Anglo-Americans in Southern California cities found that Mexican Americans of the second and third generations tended to score higher on measures of familism. This difference was most related to ethnicity.[11] A similar finding has been reported for Chicano families in San Jose, California, where kinship networks among Chicanos were significantly larger than those of other ethnic groups. And in Kansas City, Missouri, Mexican Americans were found to exhibit a greater degree of familistic behavior than others, including blacks.[12]

The familistic behavior and the pervasiveness of family solidarity as an ideology seem to be greater among the native-born Mexican Americans than among Mexican immigrants. Emerging research, which is using the rich data gathered by the National Chicano Research Network, suggests that familism among Mexican Americans is a complex multidimensional phenomenon with many intervening variables. Preliminary findings indicate that native-born Chicanos demonstrate more behavioral familism than do the Mexican-born, even when controlling for the numbers of kin residing in the area.[13] The same preliminary finding using the NCRN data was reported by Oscar Ramírez with regard to the prevalence of extended-family support and mental health.[14] These findings have historic parallels with what has been found in the nineteenth century. Residential extended-family households were more common among the native-born than among other Americans and Mexican immigrants. The historical continuity of patterns of familistic behavior, although expressed differently today, suggests the persistant effects of cultural values and socioeconomic pressures. They also indicate a need to examine in more detail the concepts of family solidarity held in Mexico as well as the reasons why the native-born Mexican Americans historically tend to have more cohesive family-support systems.

INTERMARRIAGE

Intermarriage among Mexican Americans since 1945 seems to have increased, at least in those few metropolitan areas that have been studied thus far. For Los Angeles in the middle 1960s Moore and Middelbach reported that "40 percent of the marriages involving Mexican Americans were exogamous, and that 25 percent of the Mexican-American individuals married outside their ethnic group."[15] As was true in the nineteenth century, women were more exogamous than men, and the second and third generations were more likely to intermarry with non-Chicanos than the first. Those of higher socioeconomic standing also were more likely to intermarry than those from the lower classes. A major change from the past was that the third-generation men and women were "more likely to marry 'Anglos' than to marry immigrants from Mexico."[16] In 1960 Bean and Bradshaw observed considerably lower rates of exogamy in San Antonio. Twenty percent of all marriages with at least one partner of Spanish surname were of a mixed type. Ten years earlier, in 1950, this proportion had been 16.6 percent. Both these rates of intermarriage in San Antonio were much higher than those measured in the nineteenth century. Bean and Bradshaw hypothesized that the reason for the increase in intermarriage was lessening of ethnic barriers. Another explanation, one linked to the changing demography of San Antonio, would be that Mexican Americans felt more secure in their social and political status.[17]

While the rates of intermarriage in both Los Angeles and San Antonio were higher in the postwar period than previously, they still showed a surprising continuity with the patterns from the previous century. One hundred years earlier Los Angeles had had a consistently higher rate of intermarriage than San Antonio. That this difference persists to this day points to the reality of regional, economic, and cultural differences in relations between the groups in the Southwest.

Edward Murguía has recently studied intermarriage in both its historical and contemporary aspects. He found that historical rates of intermarriage varied considerably according to geographical region. The climate of prejudice against exogamy has varied according to locale. Overall he concluded that there was "a clear trend of increasing outmarriage over time" but that high rates had stabilized in such places as Bernalillo County (New Mexico) and Southen California.[18] Intermarriage rates have always been lowest, although increasing over time, in Texas and highest in California.

One of the contributions Murguía has made to our understanding of intermarriage is his development of the concept of "breaking of ties." This is an attempt to conceive of intermarriage from the perspective of both the minority and majority individual's point of view and move beyond an assimilationist model. From his theoretical perspective both majority and minority individuals are conceived as being tied to their respective groups by bonds of family and community relationships. His concern is to study those factors that are related to "breaking the ties" from both groups. He found that many of the same forces that operated to break the ties of majority individuals to their group were also important for Chicanos. Among thsese were the influence of the American school system, the church, military service, and geographical mobility.[19] Murguía hypothesized that intermarriage could result in at least four kinds of familial outcomes: (1) marriages where ethnicity was not emphasized; (2) the involvement of the majority partner in the culture of the minority partner; (3) the independence of each partner, with each continuing to be responsive to his/her culture; and (4) "blended intermarriage," where both partners attempted to participate equally in each culture.[20] Murguía's conclusion regarding intermarriage and its effect on the cohesion of Chicano culture is this: given the absence of increased prejudice resulting from international events or economic depressions, intermarriage will probably continue to slowly increase. His closing statement is worth restating:

> Increased acceptance by the majority and upward social mobility of Chicanos lead to cultural and structural assimilation and to intermarriage. This results in a loss of ethnic cohesion and a loss of ethnic language and culture, not a desirable state of affairs for many Chicanos. Cultural maintenance in an open society will be one of the major issues to be faced by Chicanos in the future.[21]

In 1980 the United States Bureau of the Census' *Current Population Survey* reported that the rate of Mexican-American exogamy in the five southwestern states, over a five-year period 1976-1980, had declined for females but had increased for males. In the five states male exogamy rose from 12.3 percent in 1970 to 13.5 percent, while female exogamy declined from 13.4 percent to 11.9 percent. The data were not available for metropolitan or nonmetropolitan regions, but in the Midwest and Northeast, where Mexican Americans are predominantly urban, the rates of intermarriage were almost triple those in the Southwest. Midwestern Mexican Americans had a five-year average of 36.9 for males and 39.4 for females (see Table 25).[22]

As refined data on exogamy among urban Mexican Americans is made available from the 1980 census, we will be able better to interpret various factors that explain these trends. At this juncture it appears that there no longer is a large differential between male and female exogamy and that marriage barriers between the two groups have become less, at least in urban areas. The demographic factors tending to promote exogamy have intensified since 1945, namely, the coming of age of a large Spanish-surnamed population of the third generation. This group is more affluent, better educated, and more acculturated than the Mexican-immigrant and second-generation population. Further research will probably show that it is this group which is intermarrying most.

As the European-immigrant population has become increasingly assimilated and as larger numbers of Mexican immigrants have flooded the barrio, it seems that more and more Mexican Americans of the second and third generation have come to marry non-Chicanos rather than Mexican immigrants. In the nineteenth century a third-generation Mexican-heritage population hardly existed, except among the Hispanos of New Mexico, a group which did not consider itself of Mexican nationality or culture. The continued flow of Mexican immigrants into the southwestern cities after 1880 has assured a constant growth of second- and third-generation families. If these families continue to live and work in metropolitan areas, and if political and economic conditions are favorable, intermarriage rates will probably continue to increase.

TABLE 25

Rates of Exogamy, 1976-1980
(expressed as a percentage)

	1976	1977	1978	1979	1980	Five-Year Average
United States						
Males	14.6	15.0	14.4	17.5	17.6	15.9
Females	17.3	16.4	14.1	18.1	16.8	16.5
Five Southwestern States						
Males	12.3	11.6	11.0	13.0	13.5	12.3
Females	13.4	11.9	11.3	13.8	11.9	12.5
Non-Southwest						
Males	28.7	39.3	36.0	43.5	37.1	36.9
Females	37.1	45.3	32.9	43.2	38.5	39.4

Source: From U.S. Department of Commerce, Bureau of the Census, *Persons of Spanish Origin in the United States 1976-1980*, P-20, nos. 310, 329, 339, 354; in *La Red*, no. 52 (March 1982), p. 3.

PROSPECTS FOR THE FUTURE

In reading over the sociological literature, both empirical and nonempirical, that has been produced since the 1970s it is evident that a more sophisticated understanding of Chicano families is emerging. At the same time the complexities involved in analyzing the family life of a population, which is experiencing rapid change, make it difficult to be confident that we will ever approach certitude regarding the exact nature of the processes of family life. The qualitative dimensions of the family experience continue to elude social investigators, despite a massive, and somewhat cumbersome, methodological tradition and rapidly proliferating sources of empirical data. The sociological imagination, with its propensity to think in terms of multivariate designs, cross-sectional research, models, and ideal types, has yet to account for multifaceted day-to-day reality.

It appears that a satisfactory understanding of the Mexican-American family will be impossible unless we are able to explain the psychological and social processes of immigration and acculturation. These two processes continue to be at the heart of the Mexican-American family experience. Yet the exponentially growing literature on Mexican immigration remains keyed to economic and political considerations. It will contribute little toward our understanding of familial and personal dynamics.

At any given point in time a large segment of the urban Spanish-speaking families in the nation is composed of recent, temporary, and long-term, immigrants from Mexico. This group increasingly is from large- and middle-size Mexican cities, and thus they have had a prior experience with urban life-styles and cultures. These immigrants are Mexican in their familial orientations. The social meaning of this statement is made ambiguous by the increased economic development of Mexico as well as the spread of American influence south of the border. Compared to the pre-1945 experience, it seems probable that most immigrant families have less of a jump to make between Mexican and American cultures than did their ancestors. The Mexican dimension to Chicano family experience will probably always be important: quantitatively in terms of the numbers of people who are transitional and thus psychologically marginal in terms of the intermarriage, contacts, visiting, and "doubling up" which occurs between Mexican Americans and Mexicans.

Perhaps the most promising approach to understanding the multifaceted dimensions of family life-style of the Mexican immigrant and the native-born is a developmental perspective. This approach allows researchers to account for the influence of individual life events and long-term historical and cultural changes. This methodology has been advocated by a number of public-health researchers. From their perspective it is crucial to know more about how the family mediates the life crises of individual members, in particular the Mexican immigrant, since poverty and immigration are seen as being responsible fro a good deal of family instability, which is in turn related to poor mental and physical health.[23] What is so far missing from their approach is an appreciation of how Mexican Americans have historically coped with health problems in a changing sociocultural environment.

THE CHICANO FAMILY—MODERN OR POSTMODERN?

It is easier to call for the use of history in contemporary family research than to carry out such a project. One contribution social historians can make to such a task is to indicate those features of family life that have had a long history as opposed to those being of recent origin. History can place contemporary family life within a perspective of centuries of gradual change as well as documenting the long-term conflict between cultural ideals and economic realities.

Laurence Stone, an English historian of the family, has identified the major structural and affective features of the modern type of family as arising over three centuries ago. He has argued that the main features of the contemporary middle-class family arose concomitantly with the growth of capitalism between 1500 and 1800. This new bourgeois family was characterized by increased individualism. Relations between the husband, wife, and children were invested with more egalitarian and emotional meaning. Simultaneously families expressed their need for privacy and increasingly withdrew from the controls of a communal society. A hedonistic individualism in the selection of marriage partners, along with the erosion of patriarchal controls and values, emerged first within the families of the bourgeois. Stability, at least in outward appearance, was a hallmark of this new middle-class family. By folk custom the poorer classes were able to divorce and remarry with relative ease. In the late seventeenth century the very rich were able to obtain legal divorces by special governmental action. But this avenue was too expensive for the middle classes. In Stone's words, marital divorce was "impossible for the great majority of the middle class who could not afford the cost." Stone's key point was that the familial transition between the preindustrial and the modern era was a stratified one. Changes in the family occured at different rates within the various social and economic classes.[24]

In recent years some historians and sociologists have prophesied the decline of the nuclear middle-class family and the rise of new configurations in family life. Edward Shorter, for example, has argued that since World War II, most particularly since 1960, there has emerged a postmodern family type. This family is a product of a new social consciousness emerging during the 1960s: increased emphasis on woman's rights within and outside the family, a new interest in urban community, and a "systematic devaluation of the 'nest notion' of nuclear family life."[25] Symptoms of these changes have been the startling increase in teenage pregnancies, an unprecedented rise in the divorce rate, an open discussion of the availability and desirability of birth control and abortion, a revolution in sexual values promoted by the media, and delayed marriages and child birth with couples establishing nontraditional families in the interim.

Where do Chicano families fit within the variegated panorama of Western family history? Mexican Americans are one of many historic ethnic groups in a world society. An ethnic group can be defined as "a group with shared feelings of people-hood" or attachments to others formed out of perceived commonalities of religion, race, or national origin. Ethnic groups are further supported as a result of cultural, psychological, and historical "ties" binding individuals to each other. Ethnic group identity has often been strengthened because of socioeconomic, regional, religious, linguistic, or racial prejudices within the larger society.[26]

The persistence of ethnic identity despite considerable pressures for conformity testifies to its continued importance in human affairs. The persistence of ethnic groups may be a functional response as well. Ethnicity has provided more meaningful relationships in an increasingly depersonalized urban industrial society. Ethnicity has fostered new avenues for achievement and success within samll groups, created a basis for political and interest-group organization, and explained the meaning of the larger society to those of a particular cultural heritage. In all this the family has been central to the transmission and perpetuation of ethnic culture, mediating how individuals are socialized into the group. The ethnic family has interpreted the group's' history and life experience for the individual. It has provided the definition of the world, the aspirations, values, and life-styles that have made up the core of ethnic culture.

In American society Mexican Americans, blacks, and American Indians are more than cultural groups. They are also historically oppressed "ethclasses." An ethclass may be defined as a subsociety "created by the intersection of the vertical stratification of ethnicity with the horizontal stratification of social class."[27] An ethclass is defined by a coincidence of ethnic and socioeconomic status.

It has been a characteristic of American society that the ethclass structure of Mexican Americans, along with that of other groups, has been skewed in the direction of low social and economic status, so that a preponderance of families have been more heavily concentrated in the low socioeconomic strata than has been true for other ethnic groups.

For all American ethnics of European origin the overall historical pattern has been a generational movement into the middle classes and out of the ethnic enclaves. For structural and racial reasons, however, nonwhite groups have not participated in this movement as a group. From the vantage point of the centuries, America has had a permanent ethclass of black, American Indian, and Hispanic origin families.

Since the vast majority of Chicano families have not been middle class, they have not been part of the broad social world of the modern or post-modern family. Most Mexican-American families have been isolated culturally as well as economically from the sweeping changes that have been at work among the middle class. This has been less true, however, since World War II, when mass media and consumerism brought about a superficial integration of the general population. While the middle-class Mexican-American family is subject to increasing assimilative pressures, it is still linked to older ethnic traditions.[28]

It is stating the obvious to say that Mexican-American families are subject to influences emanating from many areas. Their families seem to have always been characterized by a mixture of attitudes, styles, and practices. In the nineteenth century Mexican frontier families adapted Iberian and central Mexican culture to unique circumstances. With the influx of Americans into the Southwest new influences, largely negative in terms of social stability, were introduced. In the twentieth century, with a constant renewal by Mexican immigration, Mexican-American families have continued to combine "traditional" values with more modern ones. Thus, present-day Chicano families are a bridge between the social and cultural heritages of Anglo and Latin America. The contemporary Mexican-American family's experience touches on some of the most fundamental issues of American society: immigration and urban acculturation, marginalization, discrimination and self-determination, and the importance of class and race in the individual experience. Finally, the contemporary Chicano family embodies the past as well as the future of American society.

CHAPTER 9

Continuities and Changes Since 1848

> *The Chicano family exists within a complex urban-industrial society and is subject to many of the same pressures and sources of influence as the Anglo-American family. Nonetheless, it has certain distinguishing characteristics, some of which have remained in tact since pre-Columbian days.*
> —Alfredo Mirandé and Evangelina Enríquez, *La Chicana: The Mexican-American Woman*, p. 107.

THIS BOOK HAS ATTEMPTED to present a historical view of a limited number of subjects that may be relevant to understanding the private lives of individuals. There are, of course, a larger number of topics that remain for future research. Others may want to go beyond what has been presented here and explore the ways in which the historical evolution of legal and political systems has affected family life; the influence of language and changing community identities; the changing popular culture as it has influenced tides of sentiment and ideology; the evolution of family life as expressed in art forms, literature, and music; the influence of labor and community organizations on the ethnic family and vice versa; educational changes affecting children and socialization processes; the influence of cataclysmic events such as wars and depressions; the long-term effects of racial prejudice and poverty on family life. Each of these topics is a subject for study.

The story of the evolution of the Chicano family seems to take place against a backdrop of progressive and increasingly successful attempts on the part of the majority American society to force Mexicans into a dynamic and ever-changing vision of urban America. Mexicans would have to have been stones not to have been affected by over 150 years of contact, conflict, and coresidence in industrial America. As the twentieth century draws to a close, the assimilation process looms as more and more an issue for the Chicano family.

A general trend, during the past century and a half, seems to have been that of continuity and persistence of ideals regarding family roles and functions. A popular mythology about the Mexican-American family has historic origins in previous centuries. What explains the amazing resilience of ideas about family unity, patriarchy, kinship bonds, and role models, ideas that have been realized only imperfectly in real life? In part these cultural ideals have endured because they have been strongly linked to a spoken language, Spanish. The degree to which Spanish and a variety of Spanish dialects have been spoken in the private recesses of the home has in large part determined the continuance of the Mexican-American family as an ethnically identifiable entity. This family has a worldview conditioned by a language system.

Another factor that has perpetuated an idealized view of family life has been the continued flow of immigrants from Mexico to the United States. While Mexican society is in a state of rapid social and economic change, the beliefs and attitudes brought as part of the baggage by Mexican immigrants are very hard to realize, even after a long residence in the United States. There is no community or national support for Mexican value systems in the United States. In some cases ideals about the "Mexican family" held by long-term residents may in fact be romanticized memories of how it was in the old country.

Briefly let us summarize the main arguments presented in previous chapters. This study has been a historical overview of urban Mexican-American families in the Southwest since 1848. An attempt has been made to assess the interplay of culture and the economy in family life. Mark Poster's theoretical formulations and those of Barbara Laslett have provided the framework for analysis. The basic argument has been that the Mexican-American family has been characterized by a long-term conflict between culturally conditioned beliefs and economic pressures, both of which are seen as historically evolving systems. Diversity in the family lives of Mexican Americans has been the result of many historical forces: Mexican immigration, economic class, intermarriage, urbanization, industrialization, regional differences, and discrimination.

In the nineteenth century the towns of San Antonio and Los Angeles experienced more rapid economic change than did Tucson or Santa Fe. Mexican immigration was relatively more important in the population growth of Tucson and San Antonio. The latter city emerged as the largest Mexican-American barrio by 1880. Los Angeles' and Santa Fe's Mexican-heritage populations were relatively stagnant. All four regional centers experienced varieties of colonialism as defined by Mario Barrera and Joan Moore. The proletarianization of the Mexican-American work force varied according to regional patterns of economic development, historically conditioned attitudes toward race, and the socioeconomic class system. The transition to the modern era differed for the four towns.

Culture as well as economics influenced family life. Patriarchal ideologies modified by Spanish colonial laws, the realities of frontier living, and economic class differences were challenged before 1848. Parental authority eroded as a result of increased economic opportunity but was supported by egalitarian views arising from Spanish Catholic doctrine. At the same time the church supported both the authority of parents and the subjugation of women within the family. In reality Mexican women prior to 1848 were probably freer than women elsewhere in the world, but this varied according to class level. Patriarchy was further eroded due to economic dislocations during the American era. As men had to leave to find jobs and as Mexicans became a subjugated ethclass within American society, poverty, unemployment, and racial conflict led to disruptions in the rhythm of family life. There was an increase in the proportion of families headed by women, increased female employment outside the home, and a general breakdown in family-support networks. Similar developments occurred among blacks and other immigrant groups during the late nineteenth century.

Values and beliefs regarding kinship, family roles, and obligations stemmed from both pre-Columbian and Spanish colonial society. The importance of *limpieza de sangre* in the Spanish mind gave supreme importance to family solidarity, particularly in sexual matters. Solidarity took on new dimensions in the frontier regions. It was necessary for survival and mutual protection. *Compadrazgo* was important in bonding individuals within the community to each other within an extended-family unit. *Mutualistas* reinforced family ties as well, providing a focus for cooperation and self-help, particularly among Mexican immigrants.

A closeness of affection was highly valued by Mexican Americans in the late nineteenth century. But an analysis of household composition shows that the extended-family household declined throughout the urban Southwest, while the proportion of single, unattached individuals grew. There was a probable decline in family cohesion brought on by geographic mobility and economic pressures. Most extended households were established by native-born working-class families, not by Mexican immigrants. Compared to Anglo Americans nationwide and regionally, Mexican Americans had a larger proportion of their households with extended family members. But most Mexican Americans lived seperately from their kin. The extended-family household was a temporary adjustment to life's difficulties. Most of the members of these extended families were younger relatives who were not wage earners. Most were probably the product of broken homes or a result of abandonment, economic dislocation, or death. Mexican-American extended households became havens for homeless children.

Diversity in the forms and functions of Mexican-American families arose due to patterns of Mexican immigration and intermarriage with other groups. Mexican immigration after 1848 was relatively large-scale and affected the urban populations of California, Arizona, and Texas, especially after the completion of the railroad networks in the Southwest in the 1880s. Few Mexican immigrants, however, found their way into New Mexico. The proportion of Mexican-born in the urban areas increased throughout the nineteenth century. Most of the immigrants were probably temporary residents, but those who stayed probably were those who had either brought their families with them or married and established kinship ties in the United States. Mexican-immigrant families were essentially similar in structure to those of the native-born, but the natives had more broken households headed by females, and Mexican-immigrant men were more likely to head families without a spouse than were the natives.

Assimilation through intermarriage with Anglo-Americans was problematic since the "Anglos" were not an undifferentiated group. Most Mexican Americans intermarried with European and Latin American immigrants, not with native-born Americans. Barriers to intermarriage with the majority population were formidable despite disparities in the sex ratio. Racial discrimination and social-class differences blocked intermarriage well into the twentieth century. On the other hand, cross-generational intermarriage promoted a kind of assimilation as Mexican immigrants married the more acculturated Mexican Americans. In the cities increased Mexican immigration was related to declining rates of intermarriage because it created wider gaps between the Mexican-heritage and non-Mexican populations.

Catholic Mediterranean traditions surrounding child rearing and sexual control differed from Anglo-Protestant ones. The emphasis in Hispanic society was on communal control through public shame and on authoritarian external policing rather than on individual guilt. Spanish-Mexican families expected to socialize their children to be well mannered and respectful, upholding the family's honor and dignity. Catholic Mexican families in the nineteenth century became more child centered as the traditional authorities of church and state declined. Styles of child rearing differed according to socioeconomic class, generational distance from Mexico, and the degree of assimilation into American society. Middle-class families seem to have had a more protective, sheltering, and permissive approach to child rearing than the lower classes. Children were regarded as innocents susceptible to sin and temptation who needed a strict religious discipline to be properly brought up. Generally Mexican-American children tended to remain under parental guidance longer than was true in Anglo families, especially in the upper and middle classes.

For some Mexican Americans the movement for women's suffrage and secular public education threatened older notions of sexual roles. Distance between young adults of the opposite sex was seen as essential for insuring the innocence of childhood. Romantic views of love and women were expressed in plays, newspaper articles, poems, and songs; and notions of individualistic love were prevalent by the late nineteenth century. Despite strict norms regulating single women, Mexican-American behavior in sexual matters was more liberated. Notions of sexual equality had surfaced before 1848, but late in the century Victorian notions informed the views of the Mexican-American middle and upper classes. The ideals of women expressed in "The Cult of True Womanhood" made few inroads among the lower classes. For them there was a tradition of acceptance of common-law, free-union liaisons. In some respects Mexican Americans were more modern in their attitudes toward relations between the sexes than Anglos, and this modernization had occurred before 1848. But in all this there remained a contradiction between beliefs of strict control of sexual behaviors and the actual toleration of the double standard and free unions.

In the first half of the twentieth century Mexican-American families were profoundly affected by urbanization and industrialization. Differences in regional economic development and in generational distance from Mexico continued to be important, but urban industrial poverty was a great equalizer in family life. Four types of Mexican-American families can be identified for this period. The middle- and upper-class native-born and immigrant Mexican Americans were secure, bicultural, more assimilated, economically stable, and moved in different cultural orbits than did the lower classes. Mexicano working-class families lived in poverty with chronic unemployment, high rates of geographic mobility, infant mortality, malnutrition, and overcrowding. Their lives were full of economic and social insecurity. The native-born working-class families were similar to the Mexicano working class in terms of living conditions and economic instability. A large proportion of this native-born group were the Hispanos, the families of New Mexico who were being forced to abandon their rural villages to move to urban centers. Despite a long residence in the United States they were still subject to economic and racial discrimination. Intermarriage rates between the Hispanos and the majority population, however, were higher than for Mexican immigrants or the other native-born Mexican Americans. During the 1920s and 1930s Mexican-Americans families seemed to resemble more the Italian Americans in terms of their family values and economic status. The twentieth-century Mexican-American experience shared a continuity with patterns of the previous century. Mexican immigration, widespread poverty, transiency, low rates of intermarriage, and a mixture of older beliefs and customs with newer ones continued to be important features of family life.

Post-World War II patterns of Mexican immigration and urbanization continued to change the context of family life. Social researchers who studied the Mexican-American family, however, did not take these changes into account. They viewed the Mexican-American family as relatively static, tradition bound, and dysfunctional in the American environment. In the 1970s Chicano social scientists challenged these stereotypes and misconceptions. The book *The Mexican-American People* (1970) concluded that the contemporary urban Chicano family was no longer familistic in the traditional ways, i.e., through *compadrazgo*, shared dwellings, or extensive kinship support systems. Large proportions of broken, one-parent, homes existed. Subsequent research has investigated the variety of ways in which Chicanos have deviated from traditional ideals thought to be "typically Mexican." Ideals of patriarchy are no longer the controlling feature of family life. Family solidarity is greatest among middle-class native-born Mexican Americans. Exogamy is now greater for males than females, and rising rates of intermarriage are related to the aging of a third-generation Mexican-heritage population. Mexican-American families, like all American families, are affected by the images propagated by the American consumer-media culture. Nevertheless, Mexican-American families are ethnically identifiable and maintain important links with the past.

Reality is, of course, always more complicated than our conceptualization of it. Mexican Americans live in "iron cages" which have been fashioned by various makers: the Spanish authorities, Mexican liberals, Americanizers, and lately the organizers of the postindustrial state. In the broadest terms private lives have been influenced by the cultures of both English-speaking and Spanish-speaking America. The tension between these two worldviews is what gives the Chicano family its particular uniqueness. But duality is nothing new to Mexicans or Chicanos. It has been an integral part of their history since pre-Columbian times owing to the successions of conquests and mixtures of peoples. In the American era since 1848 another series of economic and cultural changes has added to the complex mosaic which is the Mexican-American family.

Perhaps this is why one is left with the impression that, despite profound changes in the material and cultural enviroment, an essential aspect of the Mexican-American familial experience has remained relatively unchanged. Mexican-American families in the United States have always been characterized by a mixture of older traditions with newer ones and by a conflict between ideals of family life and day-to-day reality arising out of the exigencies of a capitalist economic system. The Mexican-American family has had to be flexible, pluralistic, and adaptive to survive. Its identity has been continually renewed by new currents of Mexican immigration. This ethnic family has always had to cope with assimilative pressures, persistent poverty, discrimination, instability, and racial conflict. Just as many of the social and economic conditions that are changing the lives of Mexican-American families today are a heritage from the past, so too is the promise of love, self-respect, personal dignity, hope, and caring within *la familia*.

Sampling and Statistical Methodology

THE STATISTICAL INFORMATION used for the analysis of family composition and structure was taken from samples of the manuscript census returns for the towns and cities of Los Angeles, Tucson, Santa Fe, and San Antonio. The years sampled were 1850 through 1880. The 1890 manuscript returns were destroyed by fire, and the 1900 returns were made available too late in this study for their economical incorporation. The earliest census for Arizona territory was taken in 1864 and was not amenable to family analysis because it was taken without listing separate households.

The census samples were taken systematically, i.e., every "Nth" listing for the towns in each census year. Every fifth household was selected for those census years where the town or city's population was under 10,000, and every tenth household when the population exceeded this number. For Los Angeles only were all Spanish-surnamed households selected in each census year, and an additional systematic sample of non-Mexican-heritage households was taken for this city in 1860, 1870, and 1880. A listing of the subsets of individual and household data used in the analysis for the nineteenth century are summarized in Tables 26 and 27.

TABLE 26

Sample Size for Individuals in Four Southwestern Cities, 1850-1880

City	1850	1860	1870	1880
Los Angeles				
Mexican American	1,214	2,070	2,160	2,166
Anglo-American/Other	115	512	659	456
Tucson				
Mexican American	–	–	646	1,236
Anglo-American/Other	–	–	99	292
Santa Fe				
Mexican American	396	459	479	418
Anglo-American/Other	35	18	321	81
San Antonio				
Mexican American	422	476	503	335
Anglo-American/Other	292	624	793	651
Subtotals	2,474	4,163	5,560	5,645

133

In order to proceed with an acceptable level of confidence it was necessary to analyze the subtotal of data sets for Anglo- and Mexican Americans
by census year rather than by individual town or city. The adequacy of the
sample, in terms of the confidence level and error range, is a function of the
type of variable being measured. With the exception of the Anglo households
in 1850, all the data subtotals prove to be at least within 5 percentage points
of the true mean of the population with a 90 percent confidence level. Some
of the samples have a higher confidence level (in particular the Mexican-
American samples for 1860, 1870, and 1880), again depending on the variable being measured.

The information gathered from the manuscript listings for each individual in the household was as follows: last name, age, sex, occupation, value
of real and personal property (excluding the 1880 census, which did not list
this statistic), place of birth, literacy, school attendance during the year,
ethnicity or race, and place of the census. Family relationships prior to the
1880 census were not given. This presents a major difficulty for social historians who are dealing with the family.

Two general methodologies have been devised by social researchers for
getting around this problem. Sociologists Rudy Ray Seward and Barbara
Laslett have "recounted" families by using research assistants who have coded
the probable household relationships of individuals through a set of rules
which take into consideration certain regularities occuring in the census: (1)
the surname of the person listed, (2) the order of listing, (3) the sex of
primary adults, (4) the birth place (for siblings), and (5) the past experience
of researchers in coding relationships.[1] Seward checked the accuracy of this

TABLE 27

Sample Size for Households in Four Southwestern Cities, 1850-1880

City	1850	1860	1870	1880
Los Angeles				
Mexican Americans	193	405	276	486
Anglo-Americans	25	98	183	119
Tucson				
Mexican Americans	n.d.	n.d.	148	251
Anglo-Americans	n.d.	n.d.	34	67
Santa Fe				
Mexican Americans	81	88	104	89
Anglo-Americans	14	5	13	42
San Antonio				
Mexican Americans	98	108	118	80
Anglo-Americans	72	233	120	113
Subtotals				
Mexican Americans	372	601	564	906
Anglo-Americans	111	336	350	341

method by comparing the relationships thus generated with the actual relationships listed in the 1880 census. Laslett checked this methodology by comparing the results of two independent coders. Both researchers found that the research coding scheme resulted in acceptable levels of confidence.

Another procedure for generating family relationships has been developed by Buffington Clay Miller and Theodore Hershberg. It is currently in use by the Philadelphia Social History Project. It employs essentially the same rules specified by Laslett and Seward but substitutes computer instructions for coding assistants.[2] Miller's work is largely a mathematical demonstration of the degree of accuracy which can be expected by using his methodology. She has shown that computer-generated relationships are at least as accurate as the more expensive and laborious hand-coding scheme. The plotting of the actual (in the 1880 census) versus the computer-generated family relationships showed that the degree of error varied with the type of relationship. Unmarried children were the most accurately coded (94 to 96 percent accuracy), and children with names different from the head of the household were the most difficult to identify (60 to 70 percent accuracy). The most important limitation of using either the Laslett-Seward method or the computerized one is that it is not possible to code the full range of family relationships. Godparents, uncles, aunts, cousins, and in-laws of all kinds are missed by the family-recounting and computer methodologies.

My approach to the problem has paralleled that of Miller and Hershberg. A computer program, incorporting the rules she developed with modifications being made to determine siblings and common-law marriages, was run on the machine-coded manuscript data. I also checked the accuracy of this program against the 1880 census specified data. A percentage of error was determined for each kind of relationship, along with an estimation of the overall error. Table 28 shows the percentage of over- and underestimation which can be expected by relying on my program-generated relationships.

The effect of unavoidable methodological errors on discussions of household structure and composition presented in this work are, first, to

TABLE 28

*A Comparison of Computer-Generated Family Relationships with
Those Specified in the 1880 Federal Census in Four Southwestern Towns*

Relationship	a. Computer N	b. Actual N	a/b	Percent of Underestimation
Head of Household	247	250	94.0	6.0
Spouse	149	162	91.9	8.1
Child of HH	443	490	90.4	9.6
Related to HH	22	25	88.0	12.0

Average Underestimation for All Types − 8.9 percent

underestimate by about 9 percent the numbers of individuals living in primary households. The undercount of children related to the head of the household will depress the actual average size of families as well as the average number of children in conjugal families. Second, a systematic undercount of related individuals, by about 12 percent, has the effect of reducing the numbers of extended families existing in the actual census. Thus the program-generated relationships err on the conservative side, at least in discussions of family and household structure. The overall error is acceptably low, at least for analyses depending on descriptive statistics. Moreover, it is likely that the degree of error will be reduced as larger samples are processed. There will always be some degree of error associated with using statistical evidence, if only because of the errors made by the original enumerators. What is important for discussions in this book are general trends, not specific statistical relationships. Like literary evidence, quantitative materials must be interpreted with care.

A Note on Terminology

THE TERMS "MEXICAN AMERICAN" and "Anglo-American" are used in this book as convenient and widely accepted nomenclatures to describe two heterogeneous populations. Neither term was used during the nineteenth century. Regional and ethnic differences within each population are obviously blurred by these blanket terms. It has been emphasized in various chapters that the "Mexican-American" and "Anglo-American" populations were not monolithic in culture, condition, or attitude. Consequently these terms should be understood to be merely conveniences and not descriptions of a complex social reality. It may strike some as ahistorical to use these terms in writing about the history of the nineteenth and much of the twentieth century, but it would be confusing and unnecessarily cumbersome to use the scores of historically accurate referents and self-referents used by various sectors of the population.

The complexity involved in the terminology issue can be illustrated by the following list of nineteenth and twentieth-century terms which have been used by both English and Spanish speakers to describe themselves and members of the "other" group:

General Term	Self-Referent	Referred to by Other Groups
Anglo-American	American	bolillos
	White	gringos
	Respectable Element	Americanos
	Anglo-Saxon	Anglo-sajones
	Texan	gavacho
	Californian	Norteamericanos
	Christian	estranjeros
	(Any number of European nationalities such as Irish, German, French, etc.)	

Mexican American	Hispano Americano	greaser
	La raza	Natives
	La gente	Mex
	Hispano	Mexicans
	Españoles	Spanish American
	Mexicanos	Latin
	Cholo	Latin American
	Chicano (after 1900)	Cholo
	Tejano	Californian
	Sonorenses	Mexican American
	(Any number of terms	New Mexican
	referring to regions,	Latino
	state, and home	
	villages of Mexican	
	immigrants)	
	Angelenos	
	Bejareños	
	Tucsonenses	
	Nuevo Mexicanos	
	Mestizos	
	Indios	
	Hispano Hablantes	

Carey McWilliams has probably best summarized the problem of terminology when in 1949 he wrote: "The Spanish-Mexican Americans of the Southwest defy categorical classification as a group and no term or phrase can adequately describe them." The same statement is true for "Anglo-Americans" as well. For a further discussion of the labyrinth of terminological problems past and present see Fernando Peñalosa, "Toward an Operational Definition of the Mexican," *Aztlan* 1, no. 1 (Spring 1970), pp. 1-12, and Richard L. Nostrand, " 'Mexican American' and 'Chicano': Emerging Terms for a People Coming of Age," in *The Chicano*, ed. Norris Hundley, Jr. (Santa Barbara: Clio Books, 1975), pp. 143, 205.

Supplemental Tables

TABLE 29

*The Distribution of Extended-Family Households by Socioeconomic
and Demographic Characteristics of the Head of the Household, 1850-1880
(expressed as a percentage)*

	1850	1860	1870	1880
	N = 48	N = 94	N = 104	N = 98
1. Socioeconomic Status of HH				
Upper/middle	27.1	31.9	25.0	32.7
Lower	72.9	68.1	75.0	67.3
2. Nativity of HH				
Native-born	66.7	63.8	62.5	56.1
Mexican-born	33.3	36.2	37.5	43.6
3. Age of HH				
Under 25	47.9	48.9	61.5	38.8
26-40	35.4	40.4	25.0	35.7
41-over	16.7	10.7	13.5	25.5
4. Sex of HH				
Male	60.4	68.1	67.3	64.3
Female	39.6	30.9	30.8	35.7
5. Marital Status of HH				
Married	43.8	55.3	56.7	46.9
Single parent	43.8	29.8	26.9	37.7
Single adult	12.5	14.9	16.3	15.3

TABLE 30

The Occupational Status of Mexican-American (MA) and Anglo-American (AA)
Relatives Living in Extended Households in Four Urban Areas, 1850-1880
(expressed as a percentage)

	1850		1860		1870		1880	
	MA	AA	MA	AA	MA	AA	MA	AA
Farmer/Rancher	0	0	2.2	4.2	0	2.7	0	0
Professional	0	0	0	4.2	0	0	0	7.1
Mercantile	1.4	0	2.2	4.2	1.2	8.1	.8	2.4
Skilled Laborer	5.8	12.5	3.0	12.5	1.1	2.7	8.7	2.4
Unskilled Laborer	11.1	12.5	20.0	8.3	15.5	18.9	14.2	4.8
Unemployed	82.6	75.0	72.6	66.7	82.2	67.6	76.4	83.3
Percentage Unemployed under Age 19	64.9	33.7	72.4	66.7	66.2	27.8	64.9	66.7

TABLE 31

*The Comparative Demographic and Socioeconomic Characteristics of
Native-Born (NB) and Mexican-Born (MB) Spanish Surnamed
in Los Angeles and San Antonio, 1850-1880*
(expressed as a percentage)

	1850		1860		1870		1880	
	NB	MB	NB	MB	NB	MB	NB	MB
1. Sex								
Male	44.5	59.6	47.1	60.0	45.6	52.7	45.1	50.4
Female	55.5	40.4	52.9	40.0	54.4	47.3	54.9	49.6
2. Age								
1-19	62.6	29.7	65.1	23.6	67.6	25.0	63.7	13.5
20-49	34.1	62.5	31.7	67.6	28.9	64.3	32.5	73.1
50-over	3.4	7.8	3.2	8.8	3.4	10.7	3.8	13.3
3. Occupational Status								
Upper	3.1	4.6	6.9	1.7	4.1	1.5	5.3	.4
Middle	11.3	27.8	16.0	36.9	6.9	12.8	18.6	27.3
Lower	43.1	42.4	58.2	48.6	61.8	69.1	49.2	56.9
Unemployed	42.6	25.2	18.9	12.8	27.2	16.6	26.9	15.4
4. Percent of Women Working (over age 19)	2.1	2.1	6.4	6.4	1.9	4.8	12.7	8.1
5. Family Size N of children								
None	26.2	35.8	44.2	43.2	35.2	36.4	42.6	35.5
1-2	23.6	29.4	22.3	30.3	31.0	33.6	27.8	29.8
3-5	33.0	22.9	24.3	21.3	26.9	22.9	24.9	24.6
7-over	17.3	11.9	9.2	5.2	6.9	7.0	4.6	8.1
Households with un-related adults living with married couple	49.8	46.7	52.5	48.2	44.6	43.7	36.7	33.8

TABLE 32

The Percentage of Exogamy and Endogamy by Sex and Generation, 1850-1880

	1850	1860	1870	1880
1. Native-born men married to				
N of cases	147	200	249	325
Native-born	96.4	86.5	67.4	80.5
Mexican-born	2.2	8.5	25.2	13.8
Anglo native-born	1.4	1.0	.8	1.2
European/Latin American immigrant	0	4.0	4.4	4.5
2. Native-born women married to				
N of cases	155	193	167	270
Native-born	74.4	66.9	40.0	68.6
Mexican-born	21.9	29.0	34.5	26.9
Anglo native	0	1.5	1.5	.8
European/Latin American immigrant	2.5	2.6	4.0	3.7
3. Mexican-born men married to				
N of cases	155	193	197	270
Native-born	41.7	34.2	18.0	19.0
Mexican-born	56.7	65.1	81.4	78.8
Anglo native	0	0	.6	2.2
European/Latin American immigrant	1.6	.7	0	0
4. Mexican-born women married to				
N of cases	38	100	139	207
Native-born	9.5	3.0	5.1	8.0
Mexican-born	89.5	95.0	94.2	87.5
Anglo native	0	1.0	0	0
European/Latin American immigrant	0	1.0	.7	4.5

Notes

1. Myth, History, and Theory

1. Thomas A. Baily, "The Mythmakers of American History," *Journal of American History* 55 (June 1966), pp. 5-21.

2. Hal Bridges, "The Robber Baron Concept in American History," *Business History* 33, no. 1 (Spring 1958), pp. 1-13.

3. Alfredo Mirandé and Evangelina Enríquez, *La Chicana: The Mexican American Women* (Chicago and London: University of Chicago Press, 1979).

4. See Jane Dysart, "Mexican Women in San Antonio, 1830-1860: The Assimilation Process," *Western Historical Quarterly* 7, no. 4 (October 1976), pp. 365-377; Barbara Laslett, "Household Structure on an American Frontier: Los Angeles, California in 1850," *American Journal of Sociology* 81, no. 1 (January 1975), pp. 109-128; and "Social Change and the Family: Los Angeles, California 1850-1870," *American Sociological Review* 42, no. 2 (April 1977), pp. 269-290; Mario T. García, "La Familia: The Mexican Immigrant Family, 1900-1930," in *Work, Family, Sex Roles, Language,* edited by Mario Barrera, Alberto Camarillo, and Francisco Hernández (Berkeley: Tonatiuh-Quinto Sol International, 1980), pp. 117-140. Mario T. García, "The Chicana in American History: The Mexican Women of El Paso, 1880-1920: A Case Study," *Pacific Historical Review* 49, no. 2 (May 1 1980), pp. 315-338; James M. McReynolds, "Family Life in a Borderland Community: Nacodoches, Texas," (Ph.D. diss., Texas Tech University, 1978); Gloria Miranda, "Gente de Razón Marriage Patterns in Spanish and Mexican California: A Case Study of Santa Barbara and Los Angeles."*Southern California Quarterly* 63, no. 1 (Spring 1981), pp. 1-21.

5. See Thomas B. Holman and Wesley R. Burr, "Beyond the Beyond: The Growth of Family Theories in the 1970s," *Journal of Marriage and the Family* 42 (November 1980), pp. 729-741; American social historians have developed but not clearly articulated historical theories on the family. For a discussion of this problem see Lise Vogel, "Rummaging Through the Primitive Past: A Note on Family Industrialization and Capitalism," *The Newberry Papers in Family and Community History*, paper 76-2 (November 1966), pp. 2-6.

6. See Richard Jensen's discussion of the characteristics of these idealized stages in "Modernization and Community History," *The Newberry Papers in Family and Community History*, paper 78-6 (January 1978), pp. 6-20; for a summary of modernization theory see James T. Fawcett and Marc H. Borstein, "Modernization, Individual Modernity and Family," in *Psychological Perspectives on Population*, edited by James T. Fawcett (New York: Basic Books, 1973), p. 106.

7. Tamara K. Hareven, "Modernization and Family History: Perspectives on Social Change," *Signs: Journal of Women, Culture and Society* 2, no. 1 (Autumn 1976), pp. 190-206.

8. Maxine Baca Zinn, "Employment and Education of Mexican-American Women: The Interplay of Modernity and Ethnicity in Eight Families," *Harvard Educational Review* 50, no. 1 (February 1980), p. 48; and "Chicano Family Research: Conceptual Distortions and Alternative Directions," *Journal of Ethnic Studies* 7, no. 3 (Fall 1979), pp. 59-71.

9. For a representative sample of criticism of stereotypes regarding the "traditional" family see Miguel Montiel, "The Social Scientific Myth of the Mexican American Family," *El Grito* (Summer 1970), pp. 56-62.

10. For a discussion of the adaptive role played by Mexican-immigrant families see Mario T. García, "La Familia: The Mexican Immigrant Family, 1900-1930," pp. 17-140. Alberto Camarillo in *Chicanos in a Changing Society: From Mexican Pueblos to American Barrios in Santa Barbara and Southern California, 1848-1930* (Cambridge and London: Harvard University Press., 1979) argues that the social patterns established in the nineteenth century were formative for later Chicano history.

11. Barbara Laslett, "Production, Reproduction and Social Change: The Family in Historical Perspective,"*The State of Sociology: Problems and Prospects*, ed. James F. Short (Beverly Hills, California: Sage Publications, 1981), pp. 239-258.

12. Ibid., p. 14.

13. Ibid., pp. 27-28.

14. See Mario Barrera, *Race and Class in the Southwest: A Theory of Racial Inequality* (Notre Dame, Indiana: University of Notre Dame Press, 1979), pp. 212-219.

15. Mark Poster, *A Critical Theory of the Family* (New York: Seabury Press, 1978).

16. Ibid., p. 155.

17. See Poster's discussion in chapter 6, "Elements of a Critical Theory of the Family."

18. Ibid., pp. 166-205.

2. Urban Cultural and Economic Transformations

1. Mario T. García, *Desert Immigrants: The Mexicans of El Paso, 1800-1920* (New Haven and London: Yale University Press, 1981); Mario Barrera, *Race and Class in the Southwest: A Theory of Racial Inequality* (Notre Dame and London: University of Notre Dame Press, 1979); Rudolfo Acuña, *Occupied America: A History of Chicanos*, 2nd. ed. (New York: Harper and Row, 1981); Richard Griswold del Castillo, *The Los Angeles Barrio, 1850-1890: A Social History* (Berkeley, Los Angeles, and London: University of California Press, 1980); Roxanne Dunbar Ortiz, *Roots of Resistance: Land Tenure in New Mexico, 1680-1980* (Los Angeles: Chicano Studies Research Center Publications and American Indian Studies Center, 1980); Albert Camarillo, *Chicanos in a Changing Society: From Mexican Pueblos to American Barrios in Santa Barbara and Southern California, 1848-1930* (Cambridge, Massachusetts, and London: Harvard University Press, 1979); Robert J. Rosenbaum,

Mexicano Resistance in the Southwest: "The Sacred Right of Self Preservation" (Austin and London: University of Texas Press, 1981).

2. Ray Broussard, *San Antonio During the Texas Republic: A City in Transition*, Southwestern Studies Monograph No. 18 (El Paso: Texas Western Press, 1967), pp. 5-7.

3. Ibid., p. 29.

4. U.S. Department of the Interior, Census Office, "Statistics of the United States, Including Mortality, Property, etc." (Washington, D.C.: G.P.O., 1865), p. 487.

5. Caroline Remy, "Hispanic-Mexican San Antonio: 1836-1861," *Southwestern Historical Quarterly*, 71 (Spring 1968), p. 567.

6. Robert Sturmberg, *History of San Antonio and the Early Days in Texas* (San Antonio: Press of the Standard Printing Co., 1920), p. 116.

7. Vinton Lee James, *Frontier and Pioneer: Recollections of Early Days in San Antonio and West Texas* (San Antonio: Artes Graficas, 1938), p. 22.

8. Kenneth W. Wheeler, *To Wear a City's Crown: The Beginnings of Urban Growth in Texas: 1836-1865* (Cambridge, Massachusetts: Harvard University Press, 1968), p. 119.

9. Lynn I. Perrigo, *The American Southwest: Its People and Cultures* (Albuquerque: University of New Mexico Press, 1971), pp. 151-152.

10. Howard Lamar, *The Far Southwest 1846-1912* (New York: W.W. Norton, 1966), pp. 67-71.

11. Rudolfo Acuña, *Occupied America: A History of Chicanos*, 2nd ed. (New York: Harper and Row, 1981), pp. 65-68.

12. Marta Weigle, *The Penitentes of the Southwest* (Santa Fe: Ancient City Press, 1970).

13. Dunbar Ortiz, *Roots of Resistance*, pp. 102-103.

14. Ibid., p. 98, 103.

15. Lamar, *The Far Southwest*, p. 176.

16. Henry F. Dobyns, *Spanish Colonial Tucson: A Demographic History* (Tucson: University of Arizona Press, 1976), pp. 55-59; James Officer, "Historical Factors in Interethnic Relations in the Community of Tucson," *Arizoniana* 3, no. 1 (1962), p. 12.

17. Acuña, *Occupied America*, p. 73.

18. D. W. Meining, *Southwest: Three Peoples in Geographical Changes, 1600-1900* (New York: Oxford University Press, 1971), p. 23.

19. Acuña, *Occupied America*, pp. 75-81; Lamar, *The Far Southwest*, pp. 422-425.

20. Acuña, *Occupied America*, p. 81; Marcy Gail Goldstein, "Americanization and Mexicanization: The Mexican Elite and Anglo-Americans Within the Gadsden Purchase Lands, 1853-1880" (Ph.D. diss., History, Case Western Reserve University, 1977), pp. 104-136.

21. John G. Bourke, *On the Border with Crook* (1892; reprint ed., Glorietta, New Mexico: The Rio Grande Press, 1971).

22. Bernice Coslish, *Tucson* (Tucson: Arizona Silhouettes, 1953), p. 266.

23. Officer, "Historical Factors," p. 14.
24. Griswold del Castillo, *The Los Angeles Barrio*, pp. 141-143.
25. Ibid., pp. 32-33.
26. Joan W. Moore, "Colonialism: The Case of the Mexican Americans," *Social Problems* 17, no. 4 (Spring 1970), pp. 463-472.
27. Barrera, *Race and Class*, p. 56.
28. Ibid., p. 57.

3. Patriarchy under Attack

1. See, for example, Ramón A. Gutiérrez, "Marriage, Sex, and the Family: Social Change in Colonial New Mexico, 1660-1846" (Ph. D. diss., History, University of Wisconsin, Madison, 1980); Barbara Laslett, "Social Change and the Family: Los Angeles, California, 1850-1870," *American Sociological Review* 42, no. 2 (April 1977), pp. 269-290; Richard Griswold del Castillo, "La Familia Chicana: Social Changes in the Chicano Family of Los Angeles, 1850-1880," *The Journal of Ethnic Studies* 3, no. 1 (Spring 1975), pp. 41-58.
2. See Virginia Yans McLaughlin, "Patterns of Work and Family Organization: Buffalo's Italians," in *The Family in History: Interdisciplinary Perspectives*, ed. Theodore Robb and Robert I. Rotberg (New York, London, and San Francisco: Harper and Row, 1971), pp. 111-126; Sidney M. Greenfield, "Industrialization and the Family in Sociological Theory," *American Journal of Sociology* 58, no. 3 (November 1961), pp. 312-322.
3. Carl Degler, *At Odds: Women and the Family from the Revolution to the Present* (Oxford and New York: Oxford University Press, 1980), p. 50.
4. Sylvia Marina Arrom, "Women and the Family in Mexico City, 1800-1867," (Ph.D. diss., History, Stanford University, 1978).
5. Gutiérrez, "Marriage, Sex, and the Family," p. 33.
6. Verena Martínez-Alier, *Marriage, Class and Colour in Nineteenth Century Cuba: A Study of Racial Attitudes and Sexual Values in a Slave Society* (London and New York: Cambridge University Press, 1974), p. 124.
7. Frances Leon Swadesh, *Los Primeros Pobladores: Hispanic Americans of the Ute Frontier* (Notre Dame and London: University of Notre Dame Press, 1974), pp. 178-179.
8. Gutiérrez, "Marriage, Sex, and the Family," pp. 446-447.
9. Colin M. MacLachlan and Jaime E. Rodríguez, *The Forging of the Cosmic Race: A Reinterpretation of Colonial Mexico* (Berkeley, Los Angeles, and London: University of California Press, 1980), pp. 238-239.
10. The Abeyta Family Collection, Ms, The Museum of New Mexico, Santa Fe, New Mexico, photocopy.
11. Carmen Lucero, "Reminiscences of Carmen Lucero," TS, Arizona Historical Society, Tucson, Arizona.
12. Francisca Solano Leon, "Reminiscences of Francisca Solano Leon," TS, Arizona Historical Society, Tucson, Arizona.
13. José Arnaz, *Recuerdos*, 1877, Ms, The Bancroft Library, Berkeley, California.

14. Antonio Coronel, "Cosas de California," Ms, The Bancroft Library, Berkeley, California, p. 229.

15. *La familia regulada* (n.d.), no author or place of publication, a fragmentary ms in the Coronel Collection, Los Angeles County Museum of Natural History.

16. Ibid., pp. 90, 107.

17. Arrom, "Women and the Family in Mexico City," p. 162.

18. Ibid., p. 172; Arrom believes that the cult of *marianismo*, or the idealization of the long-suffering, self-abnegating, and morally superior mother, did not emerge in Mexico until the late 1850s and then mainly due to influences emanating from Victorian Europe. See p. 191 passim.

19. Gutiérrez, "Marriage, Sex, and the Family," p. 46.

20. Antonio Coronel, *La Mujer*, 1877, Ms, The Coronel Collection, Los Angeles County Museum of Natural History.

21. Kathleen M. Gonzales, "The Mexican Family in San Antonio, Texas" (Master's thesis, Sociology, University of Texas, Austin, 1928), p. 9.

22. Ibid., p. 15.

23. MacLachlan and Rodríguez, *The Forging of the Cosmic Race: A Reinterpretation of Colonial Mexico*, p. 248.

24. Ibid., p. 236.

25. Lesley Byrd Simpson, *Many Mexicos*, 4th rev. ed. (Berkeley and Los Angeles: University of California Press, 1969), pp. 167-168.

26. For a review of the Mexican literature on *las heroinas* see Arrom, "Women and the Family in Mexico City," pp. 4-11.

27. Alfredo Mirandé and Evangelina Enríquez, *La Chicana: The Mexican-American Woman* (Chicago and London: University of Chicago Press, 1979), pp. 64-67; Jane Dysart, "Mexican Women in San Antonio, 1830-1860: The Assimilation Process," *Western Historical Quarterly* 7, no. 4 (October 1976), p. 366. Chicana history after 1900 has continued, in the Mexican tradition, to chronicle the lives of important women in the Southwest and elsewhere. See, for example, the film *La Chicana* by Silvia Morales (1978) which dramatizes the historical importance of such figures as Lucy Gonzales Parsons, Teresa Urrea, La Santa de Cabora, Emma Tenayacu, Dolores Huerta, and others. See also Mirandé and Enríquez, *La Chicana*, pp. 65–68 and pp. 221-241, for an overview of Chicanas who escaped the cage of custom.

28. Arrom found as much in her study of women in Mexico City. She concluded: "Home life varied considerably for women of different socioeconomic classes, but irrespective of status, it did not revolve exclusively around the nuclear family" (p. 295). The main thesis of her work is that women's lives in Mexico before 1857 can best be understood by enlarging the study beyond the family to the larger society.

29. For a view of the crises engendered by the Wars of Independence and the years of the Mexican Republic see Jaime Rodríguez O., "Down from Colonialism: Mexico's Nineteenth Century Crises," Distinguished Faculty Lecture, May 28, 1980, published by the University of California, Irvine.

30. Gutiérrez, "Marriage, Sex, and the Family," pp. 368-405, 435, 445-447; Rebecca McDowell Craver, *The Impact of Intimacy: Mexican Anglo Intermarriage in New Mexico, 1821-1846* (El Paso: Texas Western Press, 1982), p. 6.

31. Manuel Torres, *Peripécias de la vida Californiana*, April 27, 1876, Ms,

the Bancroft Collection, University of California, Berkeley. Torres also complained that the number of servants had declined, making life difficult for the Californio aristocracy.

32. Gilberto Hinojosa has also found an increasing rate of female-headed households in Laredo, Texas, between 1850 and 1860, with a decline in 1870. His analysis of the demographic history of the town suggests that the disruption in traditional family life occurred much earlier in the Spanish era. In 1870 the proportion of female-headed households was about the same as it had been in 1819. See Gilberto Hinojosa, *A Borderlands Town in Transition: Laredo, 1775-1870* (College Station: Texas A and M University Press, 1983), pp. 110-111.

33. Barbara Laslett, "Household Structure on an American Frontier: Los Angeles, California, in 1850," *American Journal of Sociology* 81, no. 1 (January 1975), p. 125; Laslett, "Social Change and the Family," p. 286.

34. Degler, *At Odds*, p. 129.

35. Herbert Gutman, *The Black Family in Slavery and Freedom, 1750-1925* (New York: Pantheon Books, 1976); Elizabeth Pleck, "The Two-Parent Household: Black Family Structure in Late Nineteenth-Century Boston," in *The American Family in Social-Historical Perspective*, 1st ed., edited by Michael Gordon (New York: St. Martin's Press, 1973), pp. 152-178.

36. Gutman, *The Black Family*, pp. 444-445 and p. 489.

37. Laurence A. Glasco, "The Life Cycle and Household Structure of American Ethnic Groups: Irish, German and Native Born Whites in Buffalo, New York, 1855," in *Family and Kin in Urban Communities, 1700-1930*, ed. Tamara K. Hareven (London and New York: New Viewpoints, 1977), p. 138.

38. Degler, *At Odds*, pp. 129-131.

39. The Pearson Correlation of the percentage of female-headed households with the percentage of the male work force unemployed was 0.172 with p = .0278.

40. Joseph F. Park, "The History of Mexican Labor in Arizona During the Territorial Period" (Ph.D. diss., History, University of Arizona, 1961), p. 149.

41. Richard Griswold del Castillo, "Health and the Mexican Americans in Los Angeles, 1850-1887," *Journal of Mexican American History* 4 (1974), p. 67.

42. María Josefa Bandini de Carrillo to Cave Couts, November 20, 1864, Ms, The Huntington Library, San Marino, California.

43. Mariano Vallejo to Platon Vallejo, March 17, 1869, Ms, The Bancroft Library, Berkeley, California.

44. James Tafolla, Sr., "Nearing the End of the Trail: The Autobiography of Rev. James Tafolla Sr. – A Texas Pioneer, 1837-1911," translated by Fidel C. Tafolla, TS, The Tafolla Family Papers, The Benson Library, Mexican American Collection, University of Texas, Austin, p. 71.

45. Albert Camarillo, *Chicanos in a Changing Society: From Mexican Pueblos to American Barrios in Santa Barbara and Southern California, 1848-1930* (Cambridge, Massachusetts, and London: Harvard University Press, 1979), p. 135.

46. McLaughlin, "Patterns of Work and Family Organization," p. 88.

47. John Briggs found a similar low rate of Italian female-headed households in New York and Kansas City in 1905. He concluded that cultural cohesiveness was important in preventing the disorganization of family life among working-class Italian

immigrants. See John W. Briggs, *An Italian Passage: Immigrants to Three American Cities, 1890-1930* (New Haven, Connecticut, and London: Yale University Press, 1978), p. 107.

48. Camarillo, *Chicanos in a Changing Society*, p. 221.

49. Arnoldo De Leon, *The Tejano Community, 1836-1900* (Albuquerque: University of New Mexico Press, 1982), p. 95.

50. Degler, *At Odds*, pp. 139-140.

51. Mario García, *Desert Immigrants: The Mexicans of El Paso, 1880-1920* (New Haven and London: Yale University Press, 1981) p. 200.

52. Barbara Welter, "The Cult of True Womanhood: 1820-1860," in *The American Family in Social-Historical Perspective*, ed. Michael Gordon (New York: St. Martin's Press, 1978), p. 313.

53. For a detailed study of the ways in which the Victorian expectations regarding women led to the creation of the modern companionate family see Robert L. Griswold's *Family and Divorce in California, 1850-1890: Victorian Illusions and Everyday Realities* (Albany: State University of New York Press, 1982). Griswold argues that the Victorian's cult of true womanhood gave women an elevated status in society and a new self-confidence that led to more egalitarian expectations in marriage. His study was based on a sample of divorce records for San Mateo and Santa Clara counties during the period 1850-1890 and did not include any significant number of Mexican Americans. His findings are probably most applicable to the upper- and middle-class assimilated or assimilating Mexican Americans.

4. Varieties of Family Cohesion

1. Jaime Sena-Rivera, "Extended Kinship in the United States: Competing Models and the Case of La Familia Chicana," *Journal of Marriage and the Family* 41, no. 1 (February 1979), pp. 121-129; Oscar Ramírez and Carlos H. Acre, "The Contemporary Chicano Family: An Empirically Based Review," in *Explorations in Chicano Psychology*, ed. Augustine Barron, Jr. (New York: Praeger, 1981), pp. 3-28.

2. Nathan Murillo, "The Mexican American Family, " in *Chicanos: Social and Psychological Perspectives*, 1st ed., ed. Nathaniel N. Wagner and Marsha Haug (St. Louis: C.V. Mosby, 1971), p. 102; Alfredo Mirandé, "The Chicano Family: A Reanalysis of Conflicting Views," *Journal of Marriage and the Family* 39, no. 4 (November 1977), pp. 751-752.

3. See, for example, Ramírez and Arce, "The Contemporary Chicano Family," pp. 9-11, for a review of the literature on the extended family and its importance.

4. For a full discussion of the Nahuatl attitudes and practices regarding family matters see Colin M. MacLachlan and Jaime E. Rodríguez, *The Forging of the Cosmic Race: A Reinterpretation of Colonial Mexico* (Berkeley, Los Angeles, and London: University of California Press, 1980), pp. 45-50.

5. Ramírez and Arce, "The Contemporary Chicano Family," p. 10; Alfredo Mirandé and Evangelina Enríquez, *La Chicana: The Mexican-American Woman* (Chicago and London: University of Chicago Press, 1979), pp. 17-23.

6. MacLachlan and Rodríguez, *The Forging of the Cosmic Race*, p. 206.

7. Ramón Gutiérrez, "Marriage, Sex and the Family: Social Change in Colonial New Mexico, 1680-1848" (Ph.D. diss., History, University of Wisconsin-Madison, 1980), pp. 93-95 and 108.

8. The importance of family ties on the frontier is documented in the histories of Frances Leon Swadesh, *Los Primeros Pobladores: Hispanic Americans of the Ute Frontier* (Notre Dame and London: University of Notre Dame Press, 1974), and David J. Weber, ed., *Foreigners in Their Native Land: Historical Roots of the Mexican Americans* (Albuquerque: University of New Mexico Press, 1973), and Father Angélico Chávez, *Origin of New Mexico Families in the Spanish Colonial Period* (Santa Fe: William Gannon, 1975).

9. Margaret Clark, *Health in the Mexican American Culture: A Community Study* (Berkeley, Los Angeles, and London: University of California Press, 1959), pp. 157-158.

10. Antonio Coronel, "Cosas de California," Ms, The Bancroft Library, Berkeley, California, p. 231.

11. See, for example, Josefa del Valle to her father, Ms, May 29, 1876, The Coronel Collection, Los Angeles County Museum of Natural History.

12. "Diary of a Young Child," 1889, Ms, The Adina de Zavala Collection, Benson Library, University of Texas, Austin.

13. Douglas Foley, Clarice Mota, Donald E. Post, and Ignacio Lozano, *From Peones to Politicos: Ethnic Relations in a South Texas Town, 1900-1977*, University of Texas Monograph No. 3 (Center for Mexican American Studies, 1979), p. 52, 59.

14. James Tafolla, "Nearing the End of the Trail," TS, p. 65.

15. Juan Bandini, *Diary*, typescript, H.E. Huntington Library, San Marino, California.

16. Adina de Zavala, *Journal*, January 15, 1882, Ms, The Benson Library, University of Texas, Austin.

17. See David Maciel, *La clase obrera en la historia de Mexico. Al norte del Rio Bravo (pasado inmediato) (1930-1980)*, Vol. 17 (Mexico D.F.: Siglo Veintiuno, 1982) for a detailed discussion of *mutualista* activity in relation to the labor movement. See also José Amaro Hernández, *Mutual Aid for Survival: The Case of the Mexican American* (Malabar, Flordia: Robert E. Krieger Publishing Co., 1983).

18. Sociedad de la Unión, *Membership Books*, Ms, Catholic Archives of San Antonio, Books 1-4 (1886-1935).

19. Kay Lynn Briegal, "La Alianza Hispano Americana, 1894-1965: A Mexican American Fraternal Insurance Society" (Ph.D. diss., History, University of Southern California, 1974).

20. Arnoldo De Leon, *The Tejano Community, 1830-1900* (Albuquerque: University of New Mexico Press, 1982), pp. 127-130.

21. See Appendix A for a discussion of these family types and their relation to the census data.

22. Frederick Law Olmstead, *A Journey Through Texas: Or, A Saddle-Trip on the Southwestern Frontier* (1857; reprint edition, Austin and London: University of Texas Press, 1978), p. 164; Acūna, *Occupied America* pp. 46-50; Weber, *Foreigners in Their Native Land*, pp. 152-153.

23. Griswold del Castillo, *The Los Angeles Barrio*, pp. 41-50.

24. Barbara Laslett, "Social Change and the Family: Los Angeles, California, 1850-1870," *American Sociological Review* 42, no. 2 (April 1977), p. 227.

25. Francisco Solano, "Historical Address," Ms, Arizona Historical Society.

26. Carl Degler, *At Odds: Women and the Family in America from the Revolution to the Present* (New York and Oxford: Oxford University Press, 1980), p. 105.

27. Rudy Ray Seward, *The American Family: A Demographic History* (Beverly Hills and London: Sage Publications, 1978), pp. 130-131; this explanation of the increases in urban industrial extended families also has been advanced by Michael Anderson, who has studied the industrial towns of Lancashire, England. See Michael Anderson, "Family, Household and the Industrial Revolution" in *The American Family in Sociohistorical Perspective*, 2nd ed., Michael Gordon, (New York: St. Martin's Press, 1978), pp. 67, 82.

28. The statistical association of ethnicity with extended-family households (Anglos = 1, Mexican Americans = 0) was a Lambda of -.639 with family-type dependent. For all household types the association was a Tau C score of .051 at a significance level of .0001 (x^2 = 101.8, sig. .0001).

29. Stephen Thernstrom, *The Other Bostonians: Poverty and Progress in an American Metropolis* (Cambridge, Massachusetts: Harvard University Press, 1973), pp. 222-223.

30. Alwyn Barr, "Occupational and Geographic Mobility in San Antonio, 1870-1900," *Social Science Quarterly* 5, no. 2 (September 1970), p. 401.

31. Griswold del Castillo, *The Los Angeles Barrio,* pp. 36-38.

32. Ibid., p. 65.

33. Dolores P. de Bennet to Dolores Aguirre, Ms (1910), Samaniego Collection, Arizona Historical Society, Tucson, Arizona.

34. Mrs. Juana Armizo, "Reminiscences of Juana Armizo," TS, Arizona Historical Society, Tucson, Arizona.

35. Judge Benjamin Hayes, *Pioneer Notes from the Diaries of Judge Benjamin Hayes, 1849-1878* (Los Angeles: Privately Printed, 1929), p. 153.

36. Howard P. Chudacoff and Tamara K. Hareven, "Family Transitions into Old Age" in *Transitions: The Family and Life Course in Historical Perspective*, ed. Tamara K. Hareven (New York, San Francisco, and London: Academic Press, 1976), pp. 217-243.

37. Howard P. Chudacoff, "Newlyweds and Family Extension: The First Stage of the Family Cycle in Providence, Rhode Island: 1864-1865 and 1879-1880," ibid., pp. 179-205.

38. Michael Anderson, "Family, Household and the Industrial Revolution," p. 69.

39. Herbert Gutman, *The Black Family in Slavery and Freedom, 1750-1925* (New York: Pantheon Books, 1976), pp. 448-449.

5. Mexican Immigration and Intermarriage

1. Richard Griswold del Castillo, *The Los Angeles Barrio 1850-1890: A Social History* (Berkeley, Los Angeles, and London: University of California Press, 1980), p. 38.

2. Mark Reisler, *By the Sweat of Their Brow: Mexican Immigrant Labor in the United States, 1900-1940* (Westport, Connecticut: Greenwood Press, 1976), pp. 4-5.

3. Joseph F. Park, "The History of Mexican Labor in Arizona During the Territorial Period" (Ph.D. diss., History, University of Arizona, 1961), pp. 53, 104, 136.

4. Ibid., November 1, 1879, p. 148.

5. Ibid., pp. 222-229.

6. For a recent study of the comparative economic development of Anglo-American and Mexican-immigrant societies in South Texas during this period see Arnoldo de Leon and Kenneth Stewart, "Lost Dreams and Found Failures: Mexican and Anglo Immigrants in South Texas, 1850-1900," *Western Historical Quarterly* 14, no. 3 (July 1983): pp. 291-310.

7. *Comisión pesquisidora de la frontera del norte, Reports of the Committee of Investigation Sent in 1873 by the Mexican Government to the Frontier of Texas*, translated from the official edition (New York: Baker and Goodwin, 1875), pp. 401-402.

8. Oscar Martínez, *Border Boom Town: Ciudad Juárez Since 1848* (Austin and London: University of Texas Press, 1975), pp. 33-36, 158, 160.

9. Moïses González Navarro, *La colonización en México, 1877-1910* (Mexico, 1960), p. 123.

10. Ibid., p. 134.

11. Ibid., *El Pais*, September 22, 1904, p. 124.

12. Richard Lee Nostrand, "The Hispanic American Borderlands: A Regional Historical Geography" (Ph. D. diss., Geography, UCLA, 1968); Elizabeth Broadbent, "The Distribution of the Mexican Population in the United States" (Master's thesis, Geography, University of Chicago, 1941), p. 4; Oscar Martínez, "On the Size of the Chicano Population: New Estimates 1850-1900," *Aztlán* 6, no. 1 (Spring 1975), pp. 50-61.

13. A similar argument that Mexican immigration was significant during the late nineteenth century appears in Juan Gómez Quiñones and David Maciel, *Al norte del rio bravo (Pasado lejano) (1600-1930)* (Mexico: Siglo Veintiuno, 1981), pp. 27-33.

14. See Niles Hansen, *The Border Economy: Regional Development in the Southwest* (Austin and London: University of Texas Press, 1981), pp. 112-113.

15. See, for example, the autobiographies collected by Manuel Gamio in *The Life Story of the Mexican Immigrant*, 2nd ed. (New York: Dover Publications, 1971); also the autobiography of Ernesto Galarza, *Barrio Boy* (Notre Dame, Indiana: University of Notre Dame Press, 1971) and the autobiographical novel by José Villarreal, *Pocho* (Garden City, New York: Doubleday, 1970).

16. Richard Griswold del Castillo, "Health and the Mexican American in Los Angeles, 1850-1887," *Journal of Mexican American History* 4 (1974), pp. 19-27; Degler, *At Odds*, p. 60.

17. Milton Gordon, *The Blending American: Patterns of Intermarriage* (Chicago: Quadrangle Books, 1972), p. 14.

18. Ibid., p. 169.

19. Taken from the United States manuscript census returns for Tucson, 1870, household number 153.

20. Household number 252, federal census manuscript returns for Los Angeles, 1880.

21. Jane Dysart, "Mexican Women in San Antonio, 1830-1860: the Assimilation Process," *Western Historical Quarterly* 7, no. 4 (October 1976), p. 371.

22. Ibid., p. 375.

23. Rebecca McDowell Craver, *The Impact of Intimacy: Mexican-Anglo Intermarriage in New Mexico, 1821-1846*, Southwestern Studies Monograph No. 66 (El Paso: Texas Western Press, 1982), pp. 4, 47-48.

24. Leonard Pitt, *Decline of the Californios: A Social History of the Spanish Speaking Californians, 1846-1890* (Los Angeles, Berkeley, and London: University of California Press, 1966), pp. 72-73. See also the genealogies prepared by Irene Soberanes for the Californio families of Berreyesa, Pacheco, Higuera, and Soberanes, TS, The Bancroft Library, n.d.

25. Beverly Trullio, "Anglo-American Attitudes Towards New Mexican Women," *Journal of the West* 12, no. 2 (April 1977), p. 239.

26. Arnoldo de Leon, "White Racial Attitudes Towards Mexicanos in Texas, 1821-1900" (Ph.D. diss., History, Texas Christian University, 1974), pp. 125-128.

27. Ibid, pp. 115-116.

28. Carl Degler, *At Odds*, p. 47; Julie Roy Jeffrey, *Frontier Women: The Trans-Mississippi West, 1840-1880* (New York: Hill and Wang, 1979), p. 50.

29. See Constantine Panunzio, "Intermarriage in Los Angeles, 1924-1933," *American Journal of Sociology* 48, no. 5 (March 1942), p. 700.

30. Virginia Yans McLaughlin, *Family and Community: Italian Immigrants in Buffalo, 1880-1930* (Ithaca: Cornell, 1977), p. 257.

31. Ruby Jo Kennedy, "Single or Triple Melting Pot? Intermarriage in New Haven, Connecticut, 1870-1950,"*American Journal of Sociology* 58, no. 1 (July 1952), p. 56.

32. One example was the marriage of 14-year old Altracia Salazar in Tucson. In 1871 her family arranged for her to marry Mariano Ochoa, a well-known prosperous Chihuahua-born merchant. See Mrs. Juana Armizo, "Reminiscences of Mrs. Juana Armizo," Ms, typescript, Arizona Historical Society, Tucson, Arizona.

6. Child Rearing, Discipline, and Sex

1. Ronald L. Takaki, *Iron Cages: Race and Culture in Nineteenth-Century America* (New York: Alfred A. Knopf, 1979).

2. Ibid., p. 10.

3. See Edward Shorter, *The Making of the Modern Family* (New York: Basic Books, 1975); also Ramón Gutiérrez, "Marriage, Sex, and the Family: Social Change in Colonial New Mexico, 1690-1846" (Ph.D. diss., History, University of Wisconsin, Madison, 1980).

4. David Rothman reviewing Robert H. Bremmer, ed., *Children and Youth in America: A Documentary History*, in *The Family and History: Interdisciplinary Essays*, ed. Theodore I. Robb and Robert I. Rotberg (New York: Harper and Row, 1971), p. 181.

5. "Diary of a Young Child," Ms, 1889, Adina de Zavala Collection, University of Texas, Austin, Box 2J148.

6. Ibid., pp. 237-238.

7. The Coronel Collection, Los Angeles County Museum of Natural History, Item No. 696.

8. Ibid., p. 25.

9. Ibid., p. 39.

10. John E. Baur, *Growing Up With California: A History of California's Children* (Los Angeles: Will Kroner, 1978), p. 77.

11. See J.R. Spell, "Mexican Society As Seen by José Joaquin Fernandez de Lizardi," *Hispania* 8, no. 3 (May 1925), pp. 145-165.

12. Baur, *Growing Up With California*, p. 80.

13. Ethel Shorb, "Home and Home Life of an Early Spaniard in California," TS, The Shorb Collection, Box 16, The Huntington Library, San Marino, California.

14. Hubert Howe Bancroft, *California Pastorale 1769-1848* (San Francisco: History Company, 1888).

15. Baur, *Growing Up With California*, p. 100.

16. See Robert McGlone, "Suffer the Children: The Emergence of Modern Middle-Class Family Life in America: 1820-1870" (Ph.D. diss., History, U.C.L.A., 1971), p. ix.

17. See Jane Atkins, "Who Will Educate: The Schooling Question in Territorial New Mexico, 1846-1911" (Ph.D. diss., History, University of New Mexico, 1982), pp. 367-373; The editors of *El espejo* (Taos), *La revista evangélica* (Santa Fe), and *El abogado cristiano* (Albuquerque) followed Gasparri's position on secular education and suffrage, opposing both.

18. *La revista católica*, March 24, 1877, p. 141.

19. *El fronterizo*, June 9, 1882.

20. Ibid., August 4, 1882.

21. Ibid., April 20, 1883; this article was a reprint of an article appearing in *El correo de las señoras*, a newspaper published in Mexico City.

22. *Las dos repúblicas*, September 16, 1877; August 5, 1877.

23. *El clamor público*, February 2, 1855.

24. Ibid., April 19, 1856.

25. *La revista católica*, June 10, 1876, p. 284.

26. Ibid., June 17, 1876.

27. The Ritch Collection, Ms, Notebook, vol. 2, p. 373, The Huntingon Library, San Marino, California.

28. *El clamor público*, July 17, 1858.

29. *El ranchero*, July 19, 1856.

30. Ibid., August 1, 1856.

31. *El clamor público*, December 22, 1855.

32. The archival holdings of the plays and prompt books of the Villalongín Company are in the Mexican American Collection of the Benson Library at the University of Texas, Austin. There are 247 playscripts by Mexican and Chicano authors along with photographs and other materials. See plays number 122, 135, and 146, which are discussed in this chapter.

33. *Las dos repúblicas*, September 16, 1877.

34. *El fronterizo*, July 29, 1883.

35. Harrison Clifford Dale, ed., *The Ashley-Smith Explorations and Discovery of the Central Route to the Pacific, 1822-1829* (Cleveland: The Arthur H. Clark Co., 1918), pp. 220-221, quoted in Arnoldo de Leon, *The Mexican Image in Nineteenth-Century Texas* (Boston, Massachusetts: American Press, 1982), p. 9.

36. Janet Lecompte, "The Independent Women of Hispanic New Mexico, 1821-1846," *Western Historical Quarterly* 12, no. 1 (January 1981), pp. 17-36.

37. Ibid., p. 24.

38. Ibid.

39. *Las sietas partidas*, Partida IV, Titulo XIV, in Woodrow Borah and Shelburne Cook, "Marriage and Legitimacy in Mexican Culture: Mexico and California," *California Law Review* 54 (May 1966), p. 950.

40. Ibid., pp. 997, 1001.

41. Ramón Gutiérrez, "Marriage, Sex, and the Family," pp. 115-120, 127.

42. José Arnaz, *Recuerdos*, p. 15, in Griswold del Castillo, *The Los Angeles Barrio*, p. 68.

43. Madame Calderón de la Barca, *Life in Mexico During a Residence of Two Years in That City* (London: Chapman and Hall, 1843), p. 182.

44. Odin to Blanc, August 24, 1840, in Fane Downs, "The History of Mexicans in Texas, 1820-1845" (Ph.D. diss., History, Texas Technical University, 1970). For a good discussion of the reasons for the breakdown in clerical morality on the Mexican American frontier prior to 1848 see David J. Weber, "Failure of a Frontier Institution: The Secular Church in the Borderlands under Independent Mexico, 1821-1846," *Western Historical Quarterly* 12, no. 2 (April 1981), pp. 125-143.

45. The Ritch Collection, Ms, Notebook, vol. 1, p. 65, The Huntington Library, San Marino, California.

46. Rudolfo Acuña, *Occupied America*, p. 68; Robert J. Rosenbaum, *Mexicano Resistance in the Southwest: "The Sacred Right of Self-Preservation"* (Austin and London: University of Texas Press, 1981), pp. 68-82.

47. Edward Shorter, "Illegitimacy, Sexual Revolution and Social Change in Modern Europe," in *The Family in History: Interdisciplinary Essays*, ed. Theodore Rabb and Robert I. Rotberg (New York: Harper and Row, 1971), pp. 67-69.

48. Christopher Lasch, *Haven in a Heartless World: The Family Besieged* (New York: Basic Books, 1975).

7. Mexican-American Families, 1910–1945

1. See, for example, the social histories of Albert Camarillo, *Chicanos in a Changing Society: From Mexican Pueblo to American Barrios in Santa Barbara and Southern California, 1848-1930* (Cambridge, Massachusetts, and London: Harvard University Press, 1979); Mario García, *Desert Immigrants: The Mexicans of El Paso, 1880-1920* (New Haven, Connecticut, and London: Yale University Press, 1981).

2. John W. Caughey, *California*, 2nd. ed. (Englewood Cliffs, New Jersey: Prentice-Hall, 1953), pp. 496-498; Lynn I. Perrigo, *The American Southwest: Its Peoples and Cultures* (Albuquerque: University of New Mexico Press, 1971), pp. 331-344.

3. Ricardo Romo, "The Urbanization of Southwestern Chicanos in the Early Twentieth Century," *New Directions in Chicano Scholarship*, ed. Ricardo Romo and Raymond Paredes, Chicano Studies Monograph Series (San Diego: Chicano Studies Program, University of California, San Diego, 1978), pp. 188-189.

4. *Fifteenth Census of the United States: 1930, Population: Special Report on Foreign-Born White Families by Country of Birth of Head with an Appendix Giving Statistics for Mexican, Indian, Chinese and Japenese Families* (Washington, D.C.: G.P.O., 1933).

5. Alex Saragoza has proposed four kinds of families related to the degree of acculturation and/or generational distance from Mexico. See Alex Saragoza, "Conceptualization of the History of the Chicano Family," paper presented at Stanford University's Chicano Research Center, Symposium on Work, Migration and the Family, March 3-6, 1982.

6. Richard A. García, "The Making of the Mexican-American Mind, San Antonio, Texas, 1929-1941: A Social and Intellectual History of an Ethnic Community" (Ph.D. diss., History, University of California, Irvine, 1980), p. 303.

7. Selden C. Menefee and Orin C. Corsmore, *The Pecan Shellers of San Antonio* (Federal Works Agency, W.P.A., Division of Research, G.P.O., 1940), pp. i-x.

8. Ibid., p. xviii.

9. Ibid., p. 24.

10. Manuel Gamio, *The Life Story of the Mexican Immigrant: Autobiographic Documents* (New York: Dover, 1971), reprint of 1931 University of Chicago edition. Paul Taylor, *Mexican Labor in the United States*, 2 vols. (Berkeley and London: University of California Press, 1932).

11. California, *The Report of Governor C.C. Young's Mexican Fact-Finding Committee* (1930; reprint, San Francisco: R and E Associates, 1980).

12. *Fifteenth Census of the United States: Population*, vol. II, p. 250.

13. *Report of Governor C.C. Young's Mexican Fact-Finding Committee*, pp. 180, 183.

14. In 1930 the Department of Social Welfare reported that 16.4 percent of the orphan population in public and private institutions were of Mexican descent. Ibid., p. 190, 317.

15. Ibid., p. 178.

16. Ibid., p. 210.

17. Richard Romo, "Mexican Workers in the City: Los Angeles 1915-1930" (Ph.D. diss., History, U.C.L.A., 1975), pp. 152-154.

18. Manuel Gamio, *Mexican Immigration to the United States: A Study of Human Migration and Adjustment* (1930; reprint ed., New York: Dover Publishers, 1971), p. 209.

19. See, for example, Olen Leonard and C. P. Loomis, *Culture of a Contemporary Rural Community: El Cerrito, New Mexico*, Rural Life Studies No. 1 (Washington, D.C.: U.S. Bureau of Agricultural Economics, 1941). During the 1930s the U.S. Department of Agriculture sponsored numerous studies of the threatened village life of New Mexico. A complete listing of these appear in Nancie González' bibliography in *Spanish Americans of New Mexico*, pp. 232-234 (see note 25 below).

20. Alfredo Jiménez Nuñez, *Los Hispanos de Nuevo Mexico: contribución a una antropología de la cultura hispana en el USA* (Seville: Publicaciones de la Universidad de Sevilla, 1974), pp. 47-49.

21. Charles Loomis, "War Time Migration from the Rural Spanish Speaking Villages of New Mexico," *Rural Sociology* 7, no. 2 (June 1942), pp. 394-395.

22. *Sixteenth Census of the United States: Population*, vol.2, p. 993.

23. For a firsthand account of how these changes affected one New Mexican family see Bruce Johansen and Roberto Maestas, *El Pueblo: The Gallegos Family's American Journey, 1503-1980* (New York and London: Monthly Review Press, 1983), pp. 134-146.

24. Cleofas M. Jaramillo, *Shadows of the Past (Sombras del Pasado)* (1941; reprint ed., New York: Arno Press, 1974), p. 97.

25. Nancie González, *Spanish-Americans of New Mexico* (Albuquerque: University of New Mexico Press, 1969), p. 129.

26. Laura Waggoner, "San Jose, A Study in Urbanization" (Master's thesis, Sociology, University of New Mexico, 1941).

27. Sigurd Johansen, "Family Organization in a Spanish-American Cultural Area," *Sociology and Social Research* 28, no. 2 (November-December 1943), p. 131.

28. González, *Spanish-Americans of New Mexico*, pp. 136-137, 167, 176.

29. Donovan Senter, "Acculturation Among New Mexican Villages in Comparison to Adjustment Patterns of Other Spanish-Speaking Americans," *Rural Sociology* 10, no. 1 (March 1945), p. 47.

30. González, *Spanish-Americans of New Mexico*, pp. 157, 162.

31. Frank G. Mittelbach, Joan Moore, and Ronald McDaniel, *Intermarriage of Mexican Americans*, Mexican-American Study Project, Advance Report 6 (Los Angeles: Division of Research, Graduate School of Business Administration, U.C.L.A., 1966), p. 12.

32. Gamio, *Mexican Immigration to the United States*, pp. 55, 172, 213.

33. Constantine Panunzio, "Intermarriage in Los Angeles, 1924-1933," *American Journal of Sociology* 48, no. 5 (March 1942), pp. 693, 701; Irma Y. Johnson, "A Study of Certain Changes in the Spanish-American Family in Bernalillo County, 1915-1946" (Master's thesis, Sociology, University of New Mexico, 1946), pp. 45-47.

34. See Frank D. Bean and Benjamin S. Bradshaw, "Intermarriage Between Persons of Spanish and Non-Spanish Surname: Changes from the Mid-Nineteenth to the Mid-Twentieth Century," *Social Science Quarterly* 50, no. 2 (September 1970), pp. 390-395; Leo Grebler, Joan W. Moore, and Ralph C. Guzman, *The Mexican-American People: The Nation's Second Largest Minority* (New York: Free Press, 1970), pp. 405-407.

35. Ellen Horgan Biddle, "The American Catholic Irish Family," in *Ethnic Families in America: Patterns and Variations*, ed. Charles H. Mindel and Robert W. Habenstein (New York and Oxford: Elsevier Science Publishers, 1981), pp. 97-98.

36. Horgan Biddle, "The American Catholic Irish Family," pp. 86-106.

37. William I. Thomas and Florian Znaniecki, *The Polish Peasant in Europe and America*, 2 vols. (1918-1920; reprint, New York: Dover Publications, 1958).

38. Ibid., p. 1168.

39. See Helena Znaniecka Lopata, "Polish-American Families," in Mindel and Habenstein, *Ethnic Families in America*, pp. 17-37.

40. Herbert Gans, *The Urban Villagers* (Glencoe, Illinois: Free Press, 1962), p. 52; in Mindel and Habenstein, *Ethnic Families in America*, p. 78.

41. Jill S. Quadagno, "The Italian-American Family," in Mindel and Habenstein, *Ethnic Families in America*, pp. 61-85.

42. Saragoza, "Conceptualization of the History of the Chicano Family," pp. 9-10.

43. Mario García, "La Familia: The Mexican Immigrant Family, 1900-1930," in *Work, Family, Sex Roles, Language: Selected Papers of the National Association of Chicano Studies*, ed. Mario Barrera, Albert Camarillo, and Francisco Hernández (Berkeley: Tonatiuh Quinto Sol International, 1980), pp. 117-139.

8. The Contemporary Chicano Family

1. Leo Grebler, Joan Moore, and Ralph Guzman, *The Mexican-American People: The Nation's Second Largest Minority* (New York: Free Press, 1970), pp. 105-141.

2. Lea Ybarra, "Empirical and Theoretical Developments in the Study of Chicano Families," paper presented at the Stanford Symposium on Chicano Research and Public Policy, March 4, 1982, p. 8. For detailed criticism of the shortcomings of the postwar social science analysis of the Chicano family see Miguel Montiel, "The Chicano Family: A Review of the Research," *Social Work* 8, no. 2 (March 1973), pp. 22-31; idem, "The Social Scientific Myth of the Mexican American Family," *El Grito* (Summer 1970), pp. 56-62; Alfredo Mirandé, "The Chicano Family: A Reanalysis of Conflicting Views," *Journal of Marriage and the Family* 39, no. 4 (November 1977), pp. 747-758; Maxine Baca Zinn, "Chicano Family Research: Conceptual Distortions and Alternative Directions," *Journal of Ethnic Studies* 7, no. 3 (Fall 1979), pp. 57-71.

3. Alfredo Mirandé, "The Chicano Family: A Reanalysis of Conflicting Views," p. 479.

4. Grebler, Moore, and Guzman, *The Mexican-American People*, Appendix H, pp. 631-665.

5. Ibid., pp. 353-367.

6. Jaime Sena Rivera, "Extended Kinship in the United States: Competing Models and the Case of La Familia Chicana," *Journal of Marriage and the Family* 41, no. 1 (February 1979), pp. 126-128.

7. Glenn Hawkes and Ninna Taylor, "Power Structure in Mexican and Mexican American Farm Labor Families," *Journal of Marriage and the Family* 37, no. 4 (November 1975), pp. 807-811.

8. Frank D. Bean, Russell L. Curtis, Jr., and John P. Marcum, "Familism and Marital Satisfaction Among Mexican Americans: The Effect of Family Size, Wife's Labor Force Participation and Conjugal Power," *Journal of Marriage and the Family* 39, no. 4 (November 1977), pp. 759-770.

9. Maxine Baca Zinn, "Marital Roles, Marital Power and Ethnicity: A Study of Changing Chicano Families" (Ph.D. diss., Sociology, University of Oregon, 1978), p. 150.

10. See Maxine Baca Zinn, "Employment and Education of Mexican American Women: The Interplay of Modernity and Ethnicity in Eight Families," *Harvard Educational Review* 50, no. 1 (February 1980), pp. 47-61, for a restatement of this thesis. Other recent studies have found egalitarianism as a norm within Chicano urban families. See V. Cromwell and R. Cromwell, "Perceived Dominance in Decision-Making and Conflict Resolution Among Black and Chicano Families," *Journal of Marriage and the Family* 40, (November 1978), pp. 749-759; Lea Ybarra, "Conjugal Role Relationships in the Chicano Family" (Ph.D. diss., Sociology, University of California, Berkeley, 1977).

11. Oscar Ramírez and Carlos Arce, "The Contemporary Chicano Family: An Empirically Based Review," in *Explorations in Chicano Psychology*, ed. Augustine Barrion, Jr. (New York: Praeger, 1981), p. 13. This review by Ramírez and Arce is by far the most complete summary of contemporary research on the Chicano family.

12. Ibid., p. 14.

13. Carlos Arce, "Dimensions of Familism," paper presented before the Pacific Sociological Association, San Diego, California, April 22, 1982.

14. Oscar Ramírez, "Extended Family Support and Mental Health Status Among Mexicans in Detroit," *La Red*, no. 28 (May 1980), p. 2.

15. Frank G. Mittelbach, Joan W. Moore, and Ronald McDaniel, *Intermarriage of Mexican Americans*, Mexican-American Study Project, Advance Report 6, (Los Angeles: Graduate School of Business, U.C.L.A., 1966) pp. 7-16. Other social scientists like Edward Murguía in *Chicano Intermarriage: A Theoretical and Empirical Study* (San Antonio: Trinity University Press, 1982) believe that Mittelbach et al. slightly underestimated the percentage of Mexican Americans outmarrying (see Murguía, p. 51, n. 10).

16. Ibid., p. 9.

17. Frank Bean and Benjamin S. Bradshaw, "Intermarriage Between Persons of Spanish and Non-Spanish Surname: Changes from the Mid-Nineteenth to the Mid-Twentieth Century," *Social Science Quarterly* 50, no. 2 (September 1970), p. 304.

18. Edward Murguía, *Chicano Intermarriage: A Theoretical and Empirical Study* (San Antonio: Trinity University Press, 1982), p. 47.

19. Ibid., pp. 60, 109.

20. Ibid., p. 112.

21. Ibid., p. 114.

22. For an analysis of these statistics see Carlos Arce and Armando Álvarez, "Regional Differences in Chicano Intermarriage," *La Red*, no. 52 (March 1982), pp. 2-3.

23. See a discussion of a proposed developmental model in William Vega, Richard Hough, and Annelisa Romero, "Family Life Patterns of Mexican Americans," in *Psychosocial Development of Minority Group Children*, ed. Gloria Powell, Joe Yamamoto, Armando Morales, and Annelisa Romero (New York: Bruner-Mazel, 1982).

24. Laurence Stone, *The Family, Sex and Marriage in England 1500-1800* (New York: Harper Colophon, 1977), pp. 23, 35.

25. Edward Shorter, *The Making of the Modern Family* (New York: Basic Books, 1975), pp. 269-280.

26. This definition derives from Charles H. Mindel and Robert W. Habenstein's discussion in "Family Lifestyles of America's Ethnic Minorities: An Introduction," in *Ethnic Families in America: Patterns and Variations*, ed. Charles H. Mindel and Robert W. Habenstein, 2nd ed. (New York and Oxford: Elsevier Science Publishers, 1981), pp. 4-5, and Milton Gordon, *Assimilation in American Life: The Role of Race, Religion, and National Origin* (New York: Oxford University Press, 1964), p. 24. For a discussion of current sociological theory regarding ethnic group formation see Richard Griswold del Castillo, *The Los Angeles Barrio 1850-1890: A Social History* (Berkeley and Los Angeles: University of California Press, 1980), chapter 4.

27. Gordon, *Assimilation in American Life*, p. 51.

28. Ibid., p. 269.

Appendix A

1. See Ray Seward, *The American Family: A Demographic History* (Beverly Hills and London: Sage Publications, 1978), pp. 216-220, and Barbara Laslett, "Household Structure on an American Frontier: Los Angeles, California in 1850," *American Journal of Sociology* 81, no. 1 (January 1975), pp. 108-128.

2. See Buffington Clay Miller, "A Computerized Method of Determining Family Structure from Mid-Nineteenth Century Census Data" (Master's Thesis, Moore School of Electrical Engineering, Philadelphia, 1972), and Theodore Hershberg, "A Method for the Computerized Study of Family and Household Structures Using the Manuscript Schedules of Population, 1850-1880," *The Family in Historical Perspective* 1, no. 3 (Spring 1973), pp. 6-30.

Bibliography

Manuscripts

Austin, Texas, University of Texas, The Barker Library. The Adina de Zavala Collection. "Diary of a Young Child, 1889."

Austin, Texas. University of Texas. The Barker Library. Journal of Adina de Zavala.

Austin, Texas. University of Texas. The Benson Library. Villalongín Collection. Manuel Farmayo y Daies. *Hija y madre.* 1872.

Austin, Texas. University of Texas. The Benson Library. Villalongín Collection. Enríque Zumel. *Me inconviene esta mujer.* Mexico City: n.p., 1888.

Austin, Texas. University of Texas. The Benson Library. Villalongín Collection. n.a. *La mujer adultera.*

Austin, Texas. University of Texas. The Benson Library. Tafolla Family Papers. James Tafolla, Sr. "Nearing the End of the Trail: the Autobiography of Rev. James Tafolla Sr.—A Texas Pioneer, 1837-1911." TS. Trans. Fidel C. Tafolla.

Berkeley, California. The Bancroft Library. José Arnaz. *Recuerdos.* 1887.

Berkeley, California. The Bancroft Library. Antonio Coronel. "Cosas de California."

Berkeley, California. The Bancroft Library. Manuel Torres. *Peripécias de la vida Californiana.* April 1876.

Berkeley, California. The Bancroft Library. Mariano Vallejo to Platon Vallejo, 17 March 1869.

Los Angeles, California. County Museum of Natural History. Antonio Coronel. *La mujer.* 1877.

Los Angeles, California. County Museum of Natural History. Coronel Collection. *La familia regulada.* n.d.

Los Angeles, California. County Museum of Natural History. The Coronel Collection. Josefa del Valle to Ygnacio del Valle, 29 May 1876.

San Antonio, Texas. Catholic Archives of San Antonio. Sociedad de la Union. *Membership Books*, 1-4 (1886-1935).

San Marino, California. The Huntington Library. María Josefa Bandini de Carrillo to Cave Couts, 20 November 1864.

San Marino, California. The Huntington Library. Diary of Juan Bandini. TS.

San Marino, California. The Huntington Library. The Ritch Collection. Notebooks, 1-2.

San Marino, California. The Huntington Library. The Shorb Collection. Ethel Shorb. "Home and Home Life of an Early Spaniard in California."

Santa Fe, New Mexico. Museum of New Mexico. The Abeyta Family Collection.

Tucson, Arizona. The Arizona Historical Society. Reminiscences of Juana Armizo.
Tucson, Arizona. The Arizona Historical Society. Samaniego Collection. Dolores P.
    de Bennet to Dolores Aguirre, 1910.
Tucson, Arizona. The Arizona Historical Society. Reminiscences of Carmen Lucero.
Tucson, Arizona. The Arizona Historical Society. Reminiscences of Francisca Solano
    Leon.
Tucson, Arizona. The Arizona Historical Society. Francisco Solano. "Historical
    Address."

Newspapers

El clamor público (Los Angeles), 2 February 1855; 22 December 1855; 17 July 1858.
Las dos repúblicas (Los Angeles), 16 September 1877; 5 August 1877.
El fronterizo (Tucson), 9 June 1882; 29 July 1883.
El pais (Mexico City), 22 September 1904.
El ranchero (San Antonio), 19 July 1856.
La revista católica (Las Vegas, New Mexico), 10 July 1876; 24 March 1877.

Government Publications

San Francisco, California. *The Report of Governor C.C. Young's Mexican Fact-
    Finding Committee.* 1930. Reprint. San Francisco: R and E Associates, 1980.
U.S. Department of Interior. Census Office. *Statistics of the United States, Including
    Mortality, Property . . . 1865.* Washington, D.C.: G.P.O., 1865.
U.S. Department of Commerce. Bureau of the Census. *Fifteenth Census of the United
    States, 1930.* Washington, D.C.: G.P.O., 1933.
U.S. Department of Commerce. Bureau of the Census. *Fifteenth Census of the United
    States, 1930. Special Report on Foreign-Born White Families by Country of
    Birth of Head with an Appendix Giving Statistics for Mexican, Indian, Chinese
    and Japanese Families.* Washington, D.C.: G.P.O., 1933.
U.S. Department of Commerce. Bureau of the Census. *Sixteenth Census of the United
    States, 1940.* Washington, D.C.: G.P.O., 1943.
Works Projects Administration. Federal Works Agency. Division of Research. Selden
    C. Menefee and Orin C. Corsmore. *The Pecan Shellers of San Antonio.* Wash-
    ington, D.C.: G.P.O., 1940.

Secondary Works

Acuña, Rudolfo. *Occupied America: A History of Chicanos.* 2nd. ed. New York:
    Harper and Row, 1981.
Anderson, Michael. "Family Household and the Industrial Revolution." In his *The
    American Family in Social-Historical Perspective.* New York: St. Martin's
    Press, 1973.
Balderrama, Francisco. *In Defense of La Raza: The Los Angeles Mexican Consulate
    and the Mexican Community 1929 to 1936.* Tucson: University of Arizona
    Press, 1982.

Bancroft, Hubert Howe. *California Pastorale 1769-1848*. San Francisco: The History Company, 1888.

Barrera, Mario. *Race and Class in the Southwest: A Theory of Racial Inequality*. Notre Dame and London: University of Notre Dame Press, 1979.

Baur, John E. *Growing Up With California: A History of California's Children*. Los Angeles: Will Kroner, 1978.

Biddle, Ellen Horgan. "The American Catholic Irish Family." In *Ethnic Families in America: Patterns and Variations*. Ed. Charles H. Mindel and Robert W. Haberstein. New York and Oxford: Elsevier Science Publishers, 1981.

Bourke, John G. *On the Border with Crook*. 1922. Reprint. Glorietta, New Mexico: The Rio Grande Press, 1971.

Briggs, John W. *An Italian Passage: Immigrants to Three American Cities, 1890-1930*. New Haven and London: Yale University Press, 1978.

Broussard, Ray. *San Antonio During the Texas Republic: A City in Transition*. Southwestern Studies Monograph No. 18. El Paso: Texas Western Press, 1967.

Calderón de la Barca, Madame. *Life in Mexico During a Residence of Two Years in That City*. London: Chapman and Hall, 1843.

Camarillo, Albert. *Chicanos in a Changing Society: From Mexican Pueblos to American Barrios in Santa Barbara and Southern California, 1848-1930*. Cambridge and London: Harvard University Press, 1979.

Caughey, John W. *California*. 2nd ed. Englewood Cliffs, New Jersey: Prentice Hall, 1953.

Chávez, Angelico. *Origin of New Mexico Families in the Spanish Colonial Period*. Santa Fe: William Gannon, 1975.

Chudacoff, Howard P. "Newlyweds and Family Extension: The First Stage of the Family Cycle in Providence, Rhode Island: 1864-1865 and 1879-1880." In *Transitions: The Family and Life Course in Historical Perspective*. Ed. Tamara K. Hareven. New York, San Francisco, and London: Academic Press, 1976.

_____ and Tamara K. Hareven. "Family Transitions into Old Age." In *Transitions: The Family and Life Course in Historical Perspective*. Ed. Tamara K. Hareven. New York, San Francisco, and London: Academic Press, 1976.

Clark, Margaret. *Health in the Mexican-American Culture: A Community Study*. Berkeley, Los Angeles, and London: University of California Press, 1959.

Comisión pesquisidora de la frontera del norte: Reports of the Committee of Investigation Sent in 1873 by the Mexican Government to the Frontier of Texas. New York: Baker and Goodwin, 1875.

Coslich, Bernice. *Tucson*. Tucson: Arizona Silhouettes, 1953.

Craver, Rebecca McDowell. *The Impact of Intimacy: Mexican-Anglo Intermarriage in New Mexico, 1821-1846*. Southwestern Studies Monograph No. 66. El Paso: Texas Western Press, 1982.

Degler, Carl. *At Odds: Women and the Family in America from the Revolution to the Present*. New York and Oxford: Oxford University Press, 1980.

De Leon, Arnoldo. *The Tejano Community, 1836-1900*. Albuquerque: University of New Mexico Press, 1982.

Dobyns, Henry F. *Spanish Colonial Tucson: A Demographic History*. Tucson: University of Arizona Press, 1976.

Fawcett, James T. "Modernization, Individual Modernity and Family." In his *Psychological Perspectives on Population*. New York: Basic Books, 1973.

Foley, Douglas; Mota, Clarice; Post, Donald E.; and Lozano, Ignacio. *From Peones to Politicos: Ethnic Relations in a South Texas Town, 1900-1977*. Center for Mexican-American Studies Monograph No. 3. Austin: University of Texas, 1979.

Galarza, Ernesto. *Barrio Boy*. Notre Dame, Indiana: University of Notre Dame Press, 1971.

Gamio, Manuel. *The Life Story of the Mexican Immigrant: Autobiographical Documents*. 1931. Reprint. New York: Dover, 1971.

_____. *Mexican Immigration to the United States: A Study of Human Migration*. 1930. Reprint. New York: Dover Publishers, 1971.

Gans, Herbert. *The Urban Villagers*. Glencoe, Illinois: Free Press, 1962.

García, Mario. *Desert Immigrants: The Mexicans of El Paso, 1880-1920*. New Haven and London: Yale University Press, 1981.

_____. "La Familia: The Mexican Immigrant Family 1900-1930." In *Work, Family, Sex Roles, Language*. Selected Papers of the National Association of Chicano Studies. Ed. Mario Barrera, Alberto Camarillo, and Francisco Hernandez. Berkeley: Tonatiuh-Quinto Sol International, 1980.

Glasco, Laurence A. "The Life Cycle and Household Structure of American Ethnic Groups: Irish, German and Native-Born Whites in Buffalo, New York, 1855." In *Family and Kin in Urban Communities 1700-1930*. Ed. Tamara K. Hareven. New York and London: New Viewpoints, 1977.

Goldstein, Marcy Gail. "Americanization and Mexicanization: The Mexican Elite and Anglo-Americans Within the Gadsden Purchase Lands, 1853-1880." Ph.D. dissertation, Case Western Reserve University, 1977.

González, Nancie. *Spanish-Americans of New Mexico: A Heritage of Pride*. Albuquerque: University of New Mexico Press, 1969.

González Navarro, Moises. *La colonización en Mexico, 1877-1900*. Mexico: n.p., 1960.

Gordon, Milton. *Assimilation in American Life: The Role of Race, Religion and National Origin*. New York: Oxford University Press, 1964.

_____. *The Blending American: Patterns of Intermarriage*. Chicago: Quadrangle Books, 1972.

Grebler, Leo; Moore, Joan W.; and Guzman, Ralph C. *The Mexican American People: The Nation's Second Largest Minority*. New York: Free Press, 1970.

Griswold del Castillo, Richard. *The Los Angeles Barrio, 1850-1890: A Social History*. Berkeley, Los Angeles, and London: University of California Press, 1980.

Gutman, Herbert. *The Black Family in Slavery and Freedom, 1750-1925*. New York: Pantheon Books, 1976.

Hansen, Niles. *The Border Economy: Regional Development in the Southwest*. Austin and London: University of Texas Press, 1981.

Hayes, Benjamin. *Pioneer Notes from the Diaries of Judge Benjamin Hayes, 1848-1878*. Los Angeles: Privately Printed, 1929.

Hinojosa, Gilberto Miguel. *A Borderlands Town in Transition: Laredo, 1755-1870*. College Station: Texas A and M University Press, 1983.

James, Vinton Lee. *Frontier and Pioneer: Recollections of Early Days in San Antonio and West Texas.* San Antonio: Artes Graficas, 1938.

Jaramillo, Cleofas M. *Shadows of the Past (Sombras del Pasado).* Santa Fe: Seton Village Press, 1941. Reprinted in Carlos E. Cortes, ed. *The New Mexican Hispano.* New York: Arno Press, 1974.

Jeffrey, Julie Roy. *Frontier Women: The Trans-Mississippi West 1840-1880.* New York: Hill and Wang, 1979.

Jiménez Nuñez, Alfredo. *Los Hispanos de Nuevo Mexico: contribución a una antropología de la cultura hispana en el USA.* Seville: Publicaciones de la Universidad de Sevilla, 1974. De Leon, Arnoldo. *The Tejano Community, 1830-1900.* Albuquerque: University of New Mexico Press, 1982.

_____. *The Mexican Image in Nineteenth-Century Texas.* Boston: American Press, 1982.

Lamar, Howard. *The Far Southwest 1848-1912.* New York: W.W. Norton, 1966.

Lasch, Christopher. *Haven in a Heartless World: The Family Besieged.* New York: Basic Books, 1975.

Laslett, Barbara. "Production, Reproduction and Social Change: The Family in Historical Perspective." In *The State of Sociology: Problems and Prospects.* Ed. James F. Short, Jr. Beverly Hills: Sage Publications, 1981.

Leonard, Olen, and Loomis, C. P. *Culture of a Contemporary Rural Community: El Cerrito, New Mexico.* U.S. Bureau of Agricultural Economics. Rural Life Studies No. 1. Washington, D.C.: G.P.O., 1941.

Lopata, Helena Znaniecka. "Polish American Families." In *Ethnic Families in America: Patterns and Variations.* Ed. Charles H. Mindel and Robert W. Habenstein. New York and Oxford: Elsevier Science Publishers, 1981.

McLachlan, Colin M., and Rodríguez, Jaime E. *The Forging of the Cosmic Race: A Reinterpretation of Colonial Mexico.* Berkeley, Los Angeles, and London: University of California Press, 1980.

McLaughlin, Virginia Yans. *Family and Community: Italian Immigrants in Buffalo, 1880-1930.* Ithaca, New York: Cornell University Press, 1977.

María Claret, D. Antonio. *Avisos saludables para los niños que para su bien espiritual* (Barcelona: n.p., 1859).

Maciel, David. *La clase obrera en la historia de México al norte del Rio Bravo (pasado inmediato) (1930-1980).* Vol. XVII of *La clase obrera en la historia de México.* Mexico, D.F.: Siglo Veintiuno, 1982.

Martínez, Oscar. *Border Boom Town: Ciudad Juarez Since 1848.* Austin and London: University of Texas Press, 1975.

Martínez-Alier, Verena. *Marriage, Class and Colour in Nineteenth-Century Cuba: A Study of Racial Attitudes and Sexual Values in a Slave Society.* London and New York: Cambridge University Press, 1974.

_____. "Patterns of Work and Family Organization: Buffalo's Italians." In *The Family in History: Interdisciplinary Essays.* Ed. Theodore Rabb and Robert I. Rotberg. New York, London, and San Francisco: Harper and Row, 1971.

Meining, D.W. *Southwest: Three Peoples in Geographical Change, 1600-1900.* New York: Oxford University Press, 1971.

Mindel, Charles H., and Habenstein, Robert W. "Family Lifestyles of America's

Ethnic Minorities: An Introduction." In their *Ethnic Families in America: Patterns and Variations.* New York and Oxford: Elsevier Science Publishers, 1981.

Mirandé, Alfredo, and Enríquez, Evangelina. *La Chicana: The Mexican-American Woman.* Chicago and London: University of Chicago Press, 1979.

Mittelbach, Frank G.; Moore, Joan W.; and McDaniel, Ronald. *Intermarriage of Mexican Americans.* Mexican-American Study Project, Advance Report 6. Los Angeles: U.C.L.A., Graduate School of Business Administration, 1966.

Murguía, Edward. *Chicano Intermarriage: A Theoretical and Empirical Study.* San Antonio: Trinity University Press, 1982.

Murrillo, Nathan. "The Mexican American Family." In *Chicanos: Social and Psychological Perspectives.* St. Louis: C.V. Mosby, 1971.

Olmstead, Fredrick Law. *A Journey Through Texas: Or A Saddle-Trip on the Southwestern Frontier.* 1857. Reprint. Austin and London: University of Texas Press, 1978.

Ortíz, Roxanne Dunbar. *Roots of Resistance: Land Tenure in New Mexico 1620-1980.* Los Angeles: Chicano Studies Research Center and American Indian Studies Center, 1980.

Perrigo, Lynn I. *The American Southwest: Its People and Cultures.* Albuquerque: University of New Mexico Press, 1971.

Pitt, Leonard. *Decline of the Californios: A Social History of the Spanish-Speaking Californians 1846-1890.* Los Angeles, Berkeley, and London: University of California Press, 1966.

Pleck, Elizabeth. "The Two-Parent Household: Black Family Structure in Late Nineteenth-Century Boston." In *The American Family in Social-Historical Perspective.* Ed. Michael Gordon. New York: St. Martin's Press, 1973.

Poster, Mark. *A Critical Theory of the Family.* New York: Seabury Press, 1978.

Quadragno, Jill S. "The Italian American Family." In *Ethnic Families in America: Patterns and Variations.* Ed. Charles H. Mindel and Robert W. Habenstein. New York and Oxford: Elsevier Science Publishers, 1981.

Ramírez, Oscar, and Arce, Carlos H. "The Contemporary Chicano Family: An Empirically Based Review." In *Explorations in Chicano Psychology.* Ed. Augustine Barron, Jr. New York: Praeger, 1981.

Reisler, Mark. *By the Sweat of Their Brow: Mexican Immigrant Labor in the United States, 1900-1940.* Westport, Connecticut: Greenwood Press, 1976.

Romo, Richard. "The Urbanization of Southwestern Chicanos in the Early Twentieth Century." In *New Directions in Chicano Scholarship.* Ed. Richard Romo and Raymond Paredes. Chicano Studies Monograph Series. San Diego: Chicano Studies Program, University of California, San Diego, 1978.

Rosenbaum, Robert. *Mexicano Resistance in the Southwest: "The Sacred Right of Self-Preservation."* Austin and London: University of Texas Press, 1981.

Seward, Rudy Ray. *The American Family: A Demographic History.* Beverly Hills and London: Sage Publications, 1978.

Shorter, Edward. "Illegitimacy, Sexual Revolution and Social Change in Modern Europe." In *The Family in History: Interdisciplinary Essays.* Ed. Theodore Rabb and Robert I. Rotberg, New York: Harper and Row, 1971.

———. *The Making of the Modern Family.* New York: Basic Books, 1975.

Simpson, Lesley Byrd. *Many Mexicos.* 4th rev. ed. Berkeley and Los Angeles: University of California Press, 1969.

Stone, Laurence. *The Family, Sex and Marriage in England 1500-1800.* New York: Harper Colophon, 1977.

Sturmberg, Robert. *A History of San Antonio and the Early Days in Texas.* San Antonio: Standard Printing Co., 1920.

Swadesh, Frances Leon. *Los Primeros Pobladores: Hispanic Americans of the Ute Frontier.* Notre Dame and London: University of Notre Dame Press, 1974.

Takaki, Ronald L. *Iron Cages: Race and Culture in Nineteenth-Century America.* New York: Alfred A. Knopf, 1979.

Taylor, Paul. *Mexican Labor in the United States.* 2 vols. Berkeley and London: University of California Press, 1932.

Thernstrom, Stephen. *The Other Bostonians: Poverty and Progress in an American Metropolis.* Cambridge: Harvard University Press, 1973.

Thomas, William I., and Znaniecki, Florian. *The Polish Peasant in Europe and America.* 2 vols. 1918-1920. Reprint. New York: Dover, 1958.

Vega, William; Hough, Richard; and Romero, Annelisa. "Family Life Patterns of Mexican Americans." In *Psychosocial Development of Minority Group Children.* Ed. Gloria Powell, Joe Yamamoto, Armando Morales, and Annelisa Romero. New York: Bruner-Mazel, 1983.

Villarreal, José. *Pocho.* Garden City, New York: Doubleday, 1970.

Weber, David J., ed. *Foreigners in Their Native Land: Historical Roots of the Mexican Americans.* Albuquerque: University of New Mexico Press, 1973.

Weigle, Marta. *The Penitentes of the Southwest.* Santa Fe: Ancient City Press, 1970.

Wheeler, Kenneth W. *To Wear a City's Crown: The Beginnings of Urban Growth in Texas: 1836-1855.* Cambridge: Harvard University Press, 1968.

Unpublished Theses, Dissertations, and Papers

Arce, Carlos. "Dimensions of Familism." Paper delivered at the Pacific Sociological Association, San Diego, California, 22 April 1982.

Arrom, Sylvia Marina. "Women and the Family in Mexico City, 1800-1867." Ph.D. dissertation, Stanford University, 1978.

Atkins, Jane. "Who Will Educate: The Schooling Question in Territorial New Mexico, 1846-1911," Ph.D. dissertation, University of New Mexico, 1982.

Baca Zinn, Maxine. "Marital Roles, Marital Power, and Ethnicity: A Study of Changing Chicano Families." Ph.D. dissertation, University of Oregon, 1978.

Briegel, Kay Lynn. "La Alianza Hispano Americana, 1894-1965: A Mexican-American Fraternal Insurance Society." Ph.D. dissertation, University of Southern California, 1974.

Broadbent, Elizabeth. "The Distribution of the Mexican Population in the United States." Master's thesis, University of Chicago, 1941.

Downs, Fane. "The History of Mexicans in Texas, 1820-1845." Ph.D. dissertation, Texas Technical University, 1970.

García, Richard A. "The Making of the Mexican-American Mind, San Antonio,

Texas, 1929-1941: A Social and Intellectual History of an Ethnic Community." Ph.D. dissertation, University of California, Irvine, 1980.

Gonzales, Kathleen M. "The Mexican Family in San Antonio, Texas." Master's thesis, University of Texas, Austin, 1928.

Gutiérrez, Ramón A. "Marriage, Sex, and the Family: Social Change in Colonial New Mexico, 1660-1846." Ph.D. dissertation, University of Wisconsin, Madison, 1980.

Johnson, Irma Y. "A Study of Certain Changes in the Spanish American Family in Bernalillo County, 1915-1946." Master's thesis, University of New Mexico, 1946.

De Leon, Arnold. "White Racial Attitudes Towards Mexicanos in Texas, 1821-1900." Ph.D. dissertation, Texas Christian University, 1974.

Miller, Buffington Clay. "A Computerized Method of Determining Family Structure from Mid-Nineteenth Century Census Data." Master's thesis, Moore School of Electrical Engineering, Philadelphia, 1972.

McGlone, Robert. "Suffer the Children: The Emergence of Modern Middle-Class Family Life in America: 1820-1870." Ph.D. dissertation, U.C.L.A., 1971.

Nostrand, Richard Lee. "The Hispanic American Borderlands: A Regional Historical Geography." Ph.D. dissertation, U.C.L.A., 1968.

Park, Joseph F. "The History of Mexican Labor in Arizona During the Territorial Period." Ph.D. dissertation, University of Arizona, 1961.

Romo, Richard. "Mexican Workers in the City: Los Angeles, 1915-1930." Ph.D. dissertation, U.C.L.A., 1975.

Saragoza, Alex. "Conceptualization of the History of the Chicano Family." Paper delivered at the Symposium on Work, Migration, and the Family, Stanford University, Palo Alto, California, 3 March 1982.

Waggoner, Laura. "San Jose, A Study in Urbanization." Master's thesis, University of New Mexico, 1941.

Ybarra, Lea. "Conjugal Role Relationships in the Chicano Family." Ph.D. dissertation, University of California, Berkeley, 1977.

_____. "Empirical and Theoretical Developments in the Study of Chicano Families." Paper delivered at the Symposium on Chicano Research and Public Policy, Stanford University, 4 March 1982.

Periodicals

Arce, Carlos, and Álvarez, Armando. "Regional Differences in Chicano Intermarriage." La Red, no. 52 (March 1982): 2-3.

Baca Zinn, Maxine. "Employment and Education of Mexican-American Women: The Interplay of Modernity and Ethnicity in Eight Families." Harvard Educational Review 50, no. 1 (February 1980): 47-61.

_____. "Chicano Family Research: Conceptual Distortions and Alternative Directions." Journal of Ethnic Studies 7, no. 3 (Fall 1979): 57-71.

Baily, Thomas A. "The Mythmakers of American History." Journal of American History 55 (June 1966): 5-21.

Barr, Alwyn. "Occupational and Geographical Mobility in San Antonio, 1870-1900" 5, no. 2 (September 1970): 396-403.

Bean, Frank D., and Bradshaw, Benjamin S. "Intermarriage Between Persons of Spanish and Non-Spanish Surname: Changes from the Mid-Nineteenth to the Mid-Twentieth Century." *Social Science Quarterly* 50, no. 2 (September 1970): 390-395.

Bean, Frank D.; Curtis, Russell L.; and Marcum, John P. "Familism and Marital Satisfaction Among Mexican Americans: The Effect of Family Size, Wife's Labor Force Participation and Conjugal Power." *Journal of Marriage and the Family* 39, no. 4 (November 1977): 759-770.

Borah, Woodrow, and Cook, Shelburne E. "Marriage and Legitimacy in Mexican Culture: Mexico and California." *California Law Review* 54 (May 1966): 946-1008.

Bridges, Hal. "The Robber Baron Concept in American History." *Business History* 33, no. 1 (Spring 1958): 1-13.

Cromwell, V., and Cromwell, R. "Perceived Dominance in Decision-Making and Conflict Resolution Among Black and Chicano Families." *Journal of Marriage and the Family* 40 (November 1978): 749-759.

Dysart, Jane. "Mexican Women in San Antonio, 1830-1860." *Western Historical Quarterly* 7, no. 4 (October 1976): 365-377.

Greenfield, Sidney M. "Industrialization and the Family in Sociological Theory." *American Journal of Sociology* 58, no. 3 (November 1961): 312-322.

Griswold del Castillo, Richard. "Health and the Mexican Americans in Los Angeles, 1850-1887." *Journal of Mexican American History* 4 (1974): 19-27.

_____. "La Familia Chicana: Social Changes in the Chicano Family of Los Angeles, 1850-1880." *The Journal of Ethnic Studies* 3, no. 1 (Spring 1975): 41-58.

Hareven, Tamara K. "Modernization and Family History: Perspectives on Social Change." *Signs: Journal of Women, Culture and Society* 2 (Autumn 1976): 190-206.

Hawkes, Glenn R. and Taylor, Ninna. "Power Structure in Mexican and Mexican-American Farm Labor Families." *Journal of Marriage and the Family* 37, no. 4 (November 1975): 807-811.

Hershberg, Theodore. "A Method for the Computerized Study of Family and Household Structures Using the Manuscript Schedules of Population, 1850-1880." *The Family in Historical Perspective* 1, no. 3 (Spring 1973): 6-30.

Holman, Thomas B. and Burr, Wesley R. "Beyond the Beyond: The Growth of Family Theories in the 1970s." *Journal of Marriage and the Family* 42 (November 1980): 729-741.

Jensen, Richard. "Modernization and Community History." *The Newberry Papers in Family and Community History*, paper 78-6 (January 1978).

Johansen, Sigurd. "Family Organization in a Spanish-American Cultural Area." *Sociology and Social Research* 28, no. 2 (November-December 1943): 123-131.

Kennedy, Ruby Jo. "Single or Triple Melting Pot? Intermarriage in New Haven, Connecticut." *American Journal of Sociology* 58, no. 1 (July 1952): 56-59.

Laslett, Barbara. "Household Structure on an American Frontier: Los Angeles, California in 1850." *American Journal of Sociology* 81, no. 1 (January 1975): 109-128.

_____. "Social Change and the Family: Los Angeles, California, 1850-1870." *American Sociological Review* 42, no. 2 (April 1977): 269-290.

Lecompte, Janet. "The Independent Women of Hispanic New Mexico, 1821-1846." *Western Historical Quarterly* 12, no. 1 (January 1981): 15-36.

Loomis, Charles. "War Time Migration from the Rural Spanish-Speaking Villages of New Mexico." *Rural Sociology* 7, no. 2 (June 1942): 394-399.

Martínez, Oscar. "On the Size of the Chicano Population: New Estimates, 1850-1900." *Aztlan* 6, no. 1 (Spring 1975): 50-61.

Mirandé, Alfredo. "The Chicano Family: A Reanalysis of Conflicting Views." *Journal of Marriage and the Family* 39, no. 4 (November 1977): 747-758.

Moore, Joan W. "Colonialism: The Case of the Mexican Americans." *Social Problems* 17, no. 4 (Spring 1970): 463-472.

Montiel, Miguel. "The Chicano Family: A Review of the Research." *Social Work* 8, no. 2 (March 1973): 22-31.

_____. "The Social Scientific Myth of the Mexican-American Family." *El Grito* (Summer 1970): 56-62.

Officer, James. "Historical Factors in Interethnic Relations in the Community of Tucson." *Arizoniana* 3, no. 1 (1962): 12-16.

Panunzio, Constantine. "Intermarriage in Los Angeles, 1924-33." *American Journal of Sociology* 47, no. 5 (March 1942): 690-701.

Ramírez, Oscar. "Extended Family Support and Mental Health Status Among Mexicans in Detroit." *La Red*, no. 28 (May 1980): 2-3.

Remy, Caroline. "Hispanic-Mexican San Antonio: 1836-1861." *Southwestern Historical Quarterly* 71 (Spring 1968): 564-569.

Sena-Rivera, Jaime. "Extended Kinship in the United States: Competing Models and the Case of La Familia Chicana." *Journal of Marriage and the Family* 41, no. 1 (February 1979): 121-129.

Senter, Donovan. "Acculturation Among New Mexican Villages in Comparison to Adjustment Patterns of Other Spanish-Speaking Americans." *Rural Sociology* 10, no. 1 (March 1945): 45-60.

Spell, J.R. "Mexican Society As Seen by José Joaquin Fernandez de Lizardi." *Hispania* 8, no. 3 (May 1925): 145-165.

Weber, David J. "Failure of a Frontier Institution: The Secular Church in the Borderlands Under Independent Mexico, 1821-1846." *Western Historical Quarterly* 12, no. 2 (April 1981): 125-143.

Index

171